DAILY WALK WITH JESUS

Christian Devotions
for
Each Day of the Year

by

Robert L. Tasler

Published by "Bob's Books" through CreateSpace.
An earlier electronic book (e-book) edition of this
daily devotional is available.

DEDICATION AND GRATITUDE

This devotional book is dedicated to my parents, Ed and Martha Tasler, my sister Marian Niebuhr, and my brothers Edward, Fred and Bill Tasler. Without their love and Christian example, I would not have known the grace and mercy of God in Jesus.

I am forever grateful to my wife Carol for her patient encouragement and assistance in publishing this revised print version of the Electronic Book by the same name. Special thanks go to Paul Maier for writing the Foreword and Phyllis Reece for her valued assistance in proofreading. Thanks also to Mark Alan Hill for his encouragement and for being my Colorado coffee buddy.

Rev. Robert L. Tasler, LCMS Retired
Castle Rock, CO and Casa Grande, AZ
September, 2013

TABLE OF CONTENTS

FOREWORD

My father, *Lutheran Hour* founder Dr. Walter A. Maier, published devotions each year called *Day by Day with Jesus*. They were leaflets for each day of the year with a message, an illustration called "Thought for the Day," a hymn verse and a prayer. Independently but happily, Robert Tasler has done much the same thing in title and content. Maybe, though, Tasler's is better for our hurry-up age since he combines all this material into one daily devotion.

And done so with sparkling success! This gifted pastor knows how to snag your attention effortlessly, and then weld it onto words of wisdom that he offers on a biblical basis. Take any day of the year and read his words for that day. I challenge you to claim that your thoughts wandered or that you breathed an exasperated "Same ole, same ole."

These "devos" (as young people call them) are anything but "same ole." Very much in the style of Max Lucado and others blessed with communicative talents, Tasler resists any serving up of stale pabulum and offers instead material that is fresh, relevant to everyday life, and, above all, shot through with illustrations that will be memorable from year to year. And yes, why not use this book on an annual basis? No harm, and great blessing in that!

Using vivid illustrations - usually a story - is not something that Robert Tasler invented, nor did Lucado or any other current writer. The original master story-teller was none other than Jesus Christ himself. So much of his teaching and preaching was in parables. In fact, one of the Gospels tells us, **"Without a parable He did not teach them." (Matthew 13:34)** Parables, of course, are stories that run parallel to everyday life. Hearers identify with them immediately, as they did in Jesus' day and surely do also today.

Sometimes, of course, stories can become so riveting that they may replace their application. Not so in these pages. Tasler keeps a strong tether on his material, so that it balances out beautifully for the lesson he supplies for each day of the year.

Whether these meditations are used for morning, noon, or evening devotions, they will catch your interest, offer illuminating insights, and instill an even greater appreciation for the great gospel God has given us in word and in His Son, Jesus Christ. As the familiar church prayer goes, "Read, mark, learn, and inwardly digest!"

-- Paul L. Maier

DAILY WALK WITH JESUS in...
JANUARY

+ + +

JANUARY 1

Happy New Year! A pastor friend of mine preached a New Year's Day sermon, and suggested interesting New Year's resolutions. (1) Gain weight because you will anyway, (2) Stop trying to exercise because you won't really do it, (3) Read fewer books and watch more TV, and (4) Procrastinate - Put off any resolutions until next year, since you won't keep them anyway. I briefly toyed with making these resolutions mine because I knew I could keep them!

As we go into the New Year, how much should we look back at the past? Some say we should forget the past and forge ahead. But rearview mirrors can be helpful if we use them to see what God has done in our lives. Look at the people God has brought into your life and how they have blessed you! Look at where you have been and the progress you have seen. Consider the gifts and talents God has given you. Our good times as well as our struggles help make us stronger.

As we reflect on God's blessings in the past year, we can look forward to His help in the days to come. God has blessed us before, and He will do it again. **"You, Lord, have made me glad; I will triumph in the works of Your hands." (Ps. 92:4)**

What happens to us in life is not just a matter of chance. Christians know the Lord has helped us, directing events of our lives and managing their outcome faithfully. Looking in the rearview mirror this time of year can give us a good picture of God's good works and blessings in our lives.

Looking ahead isn't as clear. We're not sure what will come in the next twelve months. The road ahead is unknown and may be filled with danger. As we move into the New Year, look into your rearview mirror and see what He has done.

"I will never leave you nor forsake you." (Heb. 13:5)

What resolutions have you made for the New Year?

1

JANUARY 2

A New Year signals that God has given us a new beginning and a second chance. I love new beginnings and pray the beginning of this New Year will bless you always.

Acts 15 tells us that Paul and Barnabas, prominent early Christians, got into an argument about taking John Mark with them on a trip. Paul didn't want the young man since he'd already left them before the end of an earlier trip.

But John Mark was Barnabas' cousin, so Barnabas left Paul and took John Mark with him. Paul continued with Silas to a different area. God used their argument to bring the Gospel to more people than ever. The four of them in pairs did far more than three of them together could have done.

Later on we hear Paul has been reconciled with John Mark. We don't know the details, but being in prison, Paul was pleased to have John Mark visit him and to realize how his faith had grown. Paul gave a second chance to the man who later became known as St. Mark, the man who wrote to tell early Christians about the life of Jesus in his Gospel account.

Second chances start with forgiveness which you and I always need from God. Our friends and family need our forgiveness, too. Jesus' death on the cross of Calvary is our best hope, because all who believe in Him will have eternal life. His sacrifice on the cross is the best second chance we could ever have.

We rejoice that God gives us second chances. I saw a plaque on someone's office wall that said, *"O God of New Beginnings and Second Chances, Here I Am Again."* I like that saying. It reminds me of God's forgiveness which will be very important in the coming New Year.

"Bear with each other and forgive one another if any of you has a grievance against someone. Forgive as the Lord forgave you." (Colossians 3:13)

God be with you every day in the New Year! May all your second chances be a blessing to you and those around you.

JANUARY 3

Sir Edmund Hillary was the first man known to have conquered Mt. Everest. Though I respect what mountain climbers do, I've never understood what moves people to climb mountains. There are enough mountains (mental, financial, relationship, emotional) to climb each day without adding the physical demands of moving one's body into rarified air many thousands of feet higher than where we normally live.

Yet there are always men and women who tackle mountain peaks. They must take serious precautions as they scale such rugged terrain. Mountain climbers utilize a number of safety measures including one called the "belayer."

A belayer is a cleat, heavy pin or other fixed object, even a person, who controls the amount of rope fed out to a climber. If a climber loses his balance or falls, the belayer holds him securely until the climber can regain footing and continue the ascent or descent. To "belay" is to anchor and hold securely in order to keep someone safe.

Life is the mountain we are climbing, and Jesus is the best belayer we can have. People can help us, but people can also fail us. Jesus never fails. He is always there for us. Friends can be good belayers, but Jesus is our truest Friend. People can be taken from us by illness, age, tragedy or choice. They may not be able to hold us tightly enough to keep us from falling. But Jesus can and will, if we put our trust in Him.

Do you have a belayer, someone you can trust when you stumble or lose your grip during your climb in life? Are you a belayer for someone else, holding their rope in times of spiritual or physical trials? Could you be one? A pastor can be a belayer for some in the church, but not for everyone. Church members can and should try to belay other members as well. But if you are not in a church, or do not have that special friend in your life, who will keep you from falling?

"Now I call you friends, for everything that I learned from my Father I have made known to you." (John 15:15)

Whose rope could you hold for someone else?

JANUARY 4

What is your name? Do you like it? Would you like a different name? Names are important, but how parents choose a name for their child has changed with the times.

Long ago we based our names on descriptive things, like vocation (Miller) or location (Aufdemberg - "On the Mountain") or relationship (Johnson). We named our children after loved parents or friends, or gave them names descriptive of our relationship to God (Timothy - "Honors God"). People who give such names often hoped that person's life would reflect the meaning of the name they were given.

Today names are often based on sound or popularity. Many current names have become cute, trendy or even silly, but fortunately parents have returned to enduring names, such as Emily, Olivia, Jacob or Daniel. Whatever our name is, we hope it will be honored and people will think good of us when they hear it.

A few people dislike their names and have them changed. They hope it will alter how people view them, or perhaps change their destiny. Some have had restored family names to the original spelling, because they feel that name is important.

Those who put their trust in Jesus as their Savior are promised eternal life and given a name that changes their destiny. Believers are baptized, **"In the name of the Father, Son and Holy Spirit,"(Matthew 28:19)** and they are called Christian, a name that carries the identity of Christ. The apostles performed miracles in the name of Jesus. They cast out demons, healed the sick, taught the Gospel, and proclaimed Jesus as Lord and Savior. Christ's name gives life to all.

Through the name of Jesus we have access to the God of the Universe who made the heavens and the earth. When we become Christians at baptism, we share in the meaning and power of Jesus. Christians try to live as Jesus lived, striving to become like Him, reflecting His love and compassion.

"Let your light shine, that people may see your good deeds and praise your Father in heaven." (Matthew 5:16)

Do you know the meaning of your name?

4

Most fairy tales have much in common. There's a villain and a pretty girl, perhaps a princess, who is oppressed and waiting for someone to come and rescue her. Prince Charming delivers her by defeating the villain and taking her away to live with him happily ever after. Fairy tales express hope to struggling people that someone or something good will come along and make their life better.

A few years ago in January, I went to a local motel room to see three young adults and two small children, one about three years old and the other barely a year. Their mother was in her early twenties, hoping to find work. The young man was just out of jail and also looking for work.

The other girl had no identification and was probably a runaway. I asked about their plans, gave them some grocery certificates and information about a temp work agency. I paid for three nights rent at the motel office and took one of them to get some warmer clothes from our church's clothing bank.

Through it all, I kept trying to hold down a nasty cough as well as a nasty feeling about their future. These three young folks weren't related and had little in common except the will to survive another day. All they wanted was a day's rent and some work. I'm not sure they looked beyond each day. The mother said she'd work while the others cared for her children. I had no idea what the future held for them, and today there are many such people with no Prince Charming to rescue them.

But there is cause for hope, not merely the hope of work or money or home, but the kind of hope that lasts, the hope God gives us from trusting His Son Jesus to bring us through our daily troubles. Jesus taught us to pray, **"Give us this day our daily bread," (Matthew 6:11)** and that is a prayer of faith.

You and I will live our lives only one day at a time in this coming New Year, and any day that includes Jesus will be a better one. True, our days will still have struggles and pain, but when Jesus is our **"God With Us," (Matthew 1:23)** we will be okay, no matter what the New Year may bring.

May your New Year be filled with such hope and faith.

JANUARY 6

Today is Epiphany Day, the day when Eastern Orthodox Christians remember and celebrate the birth of the Savior Jesus just as western Christians did on December 25. January 6 also commemorates the visit of the Magi from the east who came to see the baby.

There is an old story about the star in the east, that when it had finished its task of directing the Magi to the baby, it fell from the sky and dropped into the city well in Bethlehem. According to some, that star can still be seen by looking into the well, and the hearts of people who see it will become pure and clean.

Legends about the Magi are plentiful. People once believed there were twelve Wise Men, but now most believe there were three, based on their number of gifts. Legend even has named them: Old Melchior had a full beard and gave the gift of gold; Balthasar was younger and gave the baby myrrh; beardless young Casper gave the gift of frankincense.

Another legend says that after seeing the baby, the Magi continued on to Spain, telling people of the newborn King. Legends often add color to true stories that don't need it. Sometimes legends become so colorful they make the true story seem unbelievable. Today we don't need anything more that makes the Bible seem like a book of legends.

The Bible is God's Word, and it stands on its own. It needs no proof or justification. God offers salvation to the world through His Only Son born in Bethlehem. The baby grew to become the Savior, and all who believe in Him will benefit eternally from His work of salvation.

Years ago on January 6, we made the first contacts to begin a new church in a town which had a forty foot lighted star high on a hill. We named it Epiphany Lutheran Church. In our eight years there, the star guided over 400 wise men, women and children to join our new congregation. I thank God for all who still seek and worship the King of kings.

"We have seen His star in the east and have come to worship Him." (Matthew 2:2)

Wise men and women still come to worship Him!

6

JANUARY 7

"Just Because You Can, Doesn't Mean You Should." That was the title of a sermon I once wrote about the choices we make in our privileged society. This sentiment is still valid, whether it's about things we do or words we speak. In life we will see many open doors before us, but that doesn't mean we should go through them all. We need the wisdom and guidance of God's Word to help us choose which doors to take.

We who live in America have many choices, and the more we have the more apt we are to make bad ones. Our computer can take us many places, but should we go to them all? We have the money, but should we make that purchase? If it's not against the law or it feels good, is it okay to do it? If it tastes good or seems such fun, should we try it?

When you and I have enough time, money, energy or skill, it is tempting to think we can do whatever we wish. But we must still use good judgment and common sense in life. Proverbs 15:21 tells us, **"Folly delights a man who lacks judgment, but a man of understanding keeps a straight course."** We must take care in making our choices, for the consequences may be with us for years.

A young man struggles to grasp his coffee cup because of a motorcycle accident. A young unmarried woman clutches a tissue as she tells a friend of her pregnancy. A young man looks pleadingly at his counselor due to his drug addiction. A middle aged man stares at the floor as he relates his financial woes. A single woman wonders what really led to her divorce.

In our many choices, we must seek the guidance of God's Word. We have forgiveness through Jesus, but He still wants us to pay attention to what He says. Just because the Lord doesn't stop us from doing something doesn't mean He wants us to continue doing it. Just because we can, doesn't mean we should.

"Seek first the Kingdom of God and His righteousness, and all these things shall be added unto you." (Matthew 6:33)

May God lead you to good choices in the New Year!

7

A man went to a barbershop to have his hair cut and beard trimmed. During their conversation, the barber said: *"I don't believe God exists."* *"Why do you say that?"* asked the customer. *"You only have to go out into the street to see it,"* said the barber. *"If God existed, why are there so many sick people? Or poor people? Why are there abandoned children? If God existed, there should be no suffering or pain. I can't imagine a caring God who would allow such bad things."*

The customer paid the barber and left. As he did, he saw a man with long hair and a scraggly beard. The customer went back into the barbershop and said, *"I don't believe that barbers exist."* *"Now what do you mean by that?"* asked the barber. *"I'm here, and I'm a barber, and I just cut your hair."*

"No!" the customer said. *"Barbers do not exist because if they did, there would be no people with long hair and scraggly beards, like that man who just walked past."* *"Barbers do exist!"* the barber said. *"What you saw happens only when people don't come to me."*

"Good point," said the customer. *"We know barbers exist because we can see evidence of what they do. The same is true of God. We know He exists because we see evidence of what He does. Much of the trouble in this world happens because so many do not go to Him or look to Him for help. If more people went to God for help, there would surely not be as much pain and suffering in the world."*

Some might say this is a weak case for proof of God. Others will say they're not sure there would be less tragedy if more people prayed or that suffering is a result of sin and our need for God. But without Christian faith and prayers, our world would surely be a far worse place than it is.

Psalm 50:15 tells us, **"Call upon Me in the day of trouble. I will deliver you and you shall glorify Me."** That's God's promise and I believe it. Many secular people think we'd all be better off if we denied the existence of God and banished Him from our schools, government, and just about all other places, including churches. But would denial of God really make us and our country better?

What do you think of the trend to remove God from society? What are you doing about it?

JANUARY 9

In the Midwest there is a pasture with two horses. From a distance, each one looks like most any other horse, but if you look closely you will notice something quite amazing. You will see that one of the horses is blind. His owner has made a good home for him in the pasture, and if you listen closely you will hear the sound of a bell.

The sound comes from the other smaller horse who is always nearby. Attached to her halter is a small bell. It lets the blind horse know where she is, so he can follow her. If you stand and watch these two horses, you will notice how the seeing horse is always checking on its blind friend. You will also notice that the blind horse listens for the bell and then slowly walks to where the other horse is, trusting that she will show him the way.

Like the owner of those horses, God does not get rid of us just because we are not perfect or because we have problems or challenges. Rather, He watches over us and brings other people into our lives to help us when we are in need. Sometimes we are the blind horse being guided by God's representative which He places in our life. At other times we are the guide horse, helping others to know the way and being their eyes in life.

Psalm 68:6 tells us, **"God sets the solitary into families."** People are meant to live in relationships. Few of us prefer loneliness. Most of us wish to have others as friends, family and associates. Marriage and family are part of this, but so are good friendships. Our extended family can be for us to help, or those from whom we can get help.

The Church is a God's family in Christ. God opens its doors and invites us in where we will find blessings for now and for eternity. The Church is a hospital for the sick and a refuge for the weary. All who enter God's open doors in faith will find His help. The Church is not perfect, but God the Father is. His mercies are new to us every morning.

This is God's way to help us grow in love and maturity.

JANUARY 10

An elderly man wanted to join a church. Upon asking, he discovered this church interviewed all its new members by committee. During his interview, someone asked him what his favorite book of the Bible was. Being a bit flustered, he said, *"The Book of the Parables."* The interviewer said, *"Oh? And what is your favorite parable?"* This was the old man's reply:

"A man was going from Jerusalem to Jericho and fell among thieves, and thorns grew up and choked the man, leaving him half dead. And as he lay there, a priest came by and said, 'Come to the banquet.' But he said, 'I cannot come for I have married a wife and bought me a cow.' But he compelled him to come, and so he came, riding on a donkey, on a colt, the foal of a donkey."

"And as he rode, his hair got caught in some tree branches, and he hung there forty days and forty nights. The ravens brought him food to eat and water to drink. One night his wife Delilah came by and cut off his long hair, and the man fell onto stony ground. But being in fear of the Jews, he ran and hid himself in a cave until a still, small voice said, 'Come, ye blessed of my Father and inherit the kingdom.' So he set his face toward Jerusalem."

"As he approached the holy city he saw Queen Jezebel, high and exalted, seated upon a throne, and she was laughing. He said, 'Throw her down,' and so they threw her down. And he said, 'Throw her down again,' and they threw her down, not once, not twice, but seventy times seven times, and of the fragments they picked up twelve baskets full. Now tell me, sir, in the Kingdom, whose wife will she be?"

The interviewers at the church were so impressed, they asked him to teach a Sunday Bible Class!

Sometimes we get things mixed up in our Bible knowledge, don't we? How many different Bible stories can you identify in the old man's "parable?" Psalm 119:105 says, **"Your word is a lamp for my feet, a light on my path."** Because of that basic truth, we rejoice that we can know exactly who Jesus is, that He is the Son of God who has come to be our Savior.

How would you like that fellow teaching your Bible Class?

10

Some say there are two kinds of people in the world -- Keepers and Tossers. Keepers have a hard time with change, and their closets are full of stuff they don't want to throw away. Tossers like something new, and they're always cleaning the closet and tossing things out. Keepers value stability and accept change reluctantly.

The interesting thing is that Keepers and Tossers often marry each other! But even married, Tossers think Keepers carry around too much baggage. Keepers think Tossers throw away valuable things they should have kept. I once cleaned a cluttered closet in a church, and accidentally threw out the boxes containing new Sunday School booklets for the coming three months. An expensive mistake!

My wife loves it when I clean the basement or garage so long as I don't throw anything away. She even checks our computer to read the messages I've sent. Tossers find it easier to ask forgiveness than ask for permission. I once gave away a flower vase and later on had to replace it. Tossers love Good Will stores that take their "junk." Keepers shop there.

Keepers have empty boxes "for when we'll need them," and they have empty boxes everywhere. A Tosser married to a Keeper had better ask permission first. Tossers like it when a Keeper spouse finds a thing that he or she lost so they don't have to buy it. Clean basements are one of the reasons why Keepers like Tossers.

Remember Zacchaeus, the rich little man from Jericho who climbed a tree to see Jesus? When he became a follower of Jesus, he said, **"Look, Lord! I will give half of my possessions to the poor, and if I have cheated anybody out of anything, I will pay back four times the amount." (Luke 19:8)** Maybe he was a Tosser and needed to get rid of things.

Isn't it great Jesus is a Keeper – of us? It would be so easy for Him to toss out all us sinners who never seem to learn. But He doesn't. He keeps us in His grace, no matter what. I pray your New Year will be filled with new challenges but old memories, new experiences but old blessings.

How is your New Year going so far!

For centuries mankind has used windmills to pump water, grind grain and saw wood. In the past few decades. a new use for windmills has been found, producing electricity.

My old family farm in Minnesota may once again have a windmill, a larger, more technical version of the one we pulled down fifty years ago after getting our new electric well pump. The owner may soon have power turbine windmills on that land to generate electricity.

But there may be a "fly in the ointment." Wind turbines have encountered a problem that causes them to malfunction. While they work fine at lower speeds, at higher wind velocity the blades can get hit by bugs, and enough dead bugs on the blades reduce their efficiency and output. Some operators have found they need to wash off the insects periodically to avoid decreased output. This only makes sense.

In a similar way, the buildup of small sins in a Christian's life can be a serious problem. Unrepented sin can build up in life and drag us down. We need regularly to repent and be forgiven. Lack of repentance can harm our faith and our life. That's why Christ's disciples urged each other to confess their sins often. 1 John 1:9 tells us, **"If we confess our sins, God is faithful and just, and will forgive our sins, and cleanse us from all unrighteousness."**

Repentance means recognizing sin, stopping it, and asking God for forgiveness and the strength not to do it again. Small unrepented sins can lead to big problems. They rob us of joy and make us feel spiritually defeated. When we try to live only by our own strength, we will run out of power. Satan loves sin and he makes us think sin is acceptable, even virtuous. *"It's not wrong. Everyone does it,"* he tells us.

But we know better. Repentance is necessary. We need to be cleansed by God's mercy. When Christ forgives us, life is new again. He helps us see our sin and get focused on what is right and wrong. Best of all, He gives us strength to live a godly life. Repentance keeps the bugs of life from overwhelming us.

Sin drains our power, but forgiveness restores it!

JANUARY 13

It was going to be a bleak Christmas for a sad family. Their home had no tree and little holiday décor because their six year old boy had died only months before. The mother felt empty, wishing that someone understood how she felt. As Christmas approached, she prayed, *"God I know You know how I feel. You lost a son, but it's different, because You're God. I wish I could meet someone who knows the loss I feel."*

Late one evening they decided to go to the Mall so they might be cheered up. As she and her husband carried their baby and their four-year-old, it was crowded, and they thought it was a mistake to have come. She left her family on a bench and went into her deceased son's favorite toy store, tears streaming down her face, wishing he were there with her.

As they left to find Santa, she saw a sign that said, *"Sorry, you just missed Santa."* But her husband saw him walking down the hall. *"Hey Santa,"* he yelled, *"you have one more kid here to see you."* Santa turned and came back.

He opened the gate and kindly sat the boy on his lap. *"Thank you Santa,"* the Mom said. *"Our son is having a hard time this year because he just lost his big brother three months ago."* Santa said, *"I know a little how you feel."* She wanted to say, *"You have no idea how I feel!"* Instead she quietly said, *"Thank you."*

Santa said, *"I lost my son three years ago."* In that instant a bond developed between them. *"How old was he?"* she asked. *"Fourteen." "What did he die of?" "A heart condition."* The mother was intrigued. *"What kind of heart condition?" "Well,"* said Santa, *"his heart kept getting bigger."* She gasped, *"Dilated Cardiomyopathy?" "Why, yes,"* he said in amazement.

Their sons had died of the same rare childhood illness! *"Where did he die?"* she continued. *"Children's Hospital, Room 319."* Both their sons had died of the same disease in the same room of the same hospital! God is a God of details. He does care about all of life. In Jesus, He cares for us completely.

"Bless the Lord, O my soul: and all that is within me, bless His holy name." (Psalm 103:1)

God is the only One who can love our kids more than we do.

Have you ever said, *"Oh my God!"* and considered what those three words mean? Have you ever thought of that phrase as an expression of gratitude? How do we show our gratitude when we are truly grateful?

One night in the desert I saw a marvelous sunset, its vibrant colors on fleecy clouds in a clear and changing sky with deepening reds, yellows and blues. It was a sight only God could create in such grand fashion. I quietly said, *"Oh my God!"* because it was so beautiful and so fleeting.

"Oh my God!" a teenager says. I have often been critical of hearing those words flippantly spoken, yet they can have great meaning. Something worthwhile was seen, a connection made to cause us to cry out to our Creator, *"Oh my God!"*

Sometimes our day starts out grey and chilly, but ends with a warm display of brilliance we could not have imagined. Today is God's gift, and this very moment it is the only thing we can truly own. Today has such great value to our existence that gratitude to Him should be our response.

Today we will experience life, our own and the lives of others. Let's open our eyes and see the sky and the weather. It is wondrous and ever changing. Look at the faces of the people you meet. They are unique, original and perhaps interesting, and you have eyes to see them. Millions cannot see with eyes like yours, for their world is darkness.

Turn on the faucet and see the clean water coming out, hot or cold, and realize many millions do not have this gift you take for granted. Smile at a friend and realize for just a moment the value of that person smiling back at you. Perhaps they like you, maybe even love you.

God loves you forever through Jesus, His Son. If you can count even a few small blessings in your life, then let your gratitude overflow to others around you, and also to your Creator. Then it is most appropriate to say, *"Oh my God!"*

"Give thanks to the Lord for He is good; His love endures forever." (Psalm 107:1)

God loves to hear us call out to Him, no matter when it is.

JANUARY 15

Let us mourn the passing of an old friend. His name is Common Sense. C.S. lived a long life but died from heart failure. He was as old as the ages and devoted his life to schools, hospitals, homes and offices, helping folks live without fanfare and foolishness. For decades, petty rules and frivolous lawsuits held no power over C.S. He was credited with teaching valued lessons like knowing when to come in out of the rain, working hard, and that life isn't always fair.

C.S. lived by sound financial policies ("Don't spend more than you earn") and reliable teaching ("The adult is in charge, not the child"). A veteran of the Industrial Revolution, the Great Depression, and the Technological Revolution, C.S. survived trends of feminism, body piercing, bilingual education and new math. His health declined with the arrival of the *"If-It-Only-Helps-One-Person-It's-Worth-It"* virus.

His waning strength proved no match for the ravages of incomprehensible regulations. He watched in pain as people became ruled by self-serving politicians, government auditors, and college professors who'd formerly been in jail.

His health deteriorated as schools implemented zero-tolerance policies, resulting in six year-old boys charged with sexual harassment for kissing, teens suspended for using mouthwash after lunch, or teachers fired for reprimanding unruly students. C.S. finally lost his will to live as the Ten Commandments were declared contraband, churches became businesses, criminals got better treatment than victims, and judges began to make laws rather than enforce them.

As the end neared, C.S. was overwhelmed by regulations for low-flow toilets and "green" items that cost more to make than they saved. Finally, when told that homeowners groups wouldn't allow flying the flag, he breathed his last.

He was preceded in death by parents, Right and Wrong, his wife Discretion, his daughter Responsibility and his son Reason. His funeral was small, because few knew he'd died.

"God made foolish the wisdom of the world." (1 Corinthians 1:20)

Hopefully common sense is still in your heart and home!

Have you ever considered how fortunate you are to be a citizen of a free nation? What if you had been born into another country that limited your choices or oppressed you or demanded great sacrifices from you at the hands of a dictator?

In 2011 a terrible earthquake hit northern Japan with a resulting tsunami that killed twenty thousand people. We might have been born there instead of in America.

What if you had been born in Japanese? How would life be for you now? If you had lived through that earthquake, how would you have found food, medical help, or found out if friends or family had perished? How would you handle all of the destruction around you?

What if we didn't have a television to hear the news or a cell phone to call family? What if we did not know where our next meal was coming from? How would we sleep wondering if someone would harm us during the night? What if we were trapped under rubble, struggling for our next breath? What if we were starving or injured? How would we handle all this?

These questions are not just musings of an idle mind; they are rational to ask. God has given us so much privilege and so many possessions. Americans are well fed, healthy, wealthy and we are free. We can choose what we do today. The fact that we are reading this book confirms this. We can change our surroundings, our clothes or even our friends.

Jesus Christ is our Lord and Savior. If we died today, God has a place prepared in heaven for us. We were not born into a religion that twists the truth into lies, or worships a god who demands we kill others. We don't make women slaves or sacrifice what little we have to gods who don't exist.

We are citizens of a free nation, and we know Jesus is Lord! We are free to alter things around us, free to read the Bible, and our lives are better than 90% of the rest of the world. But are we grateful for all this, or do we just complain?

"O give thanks unto the Lord; call upon His name: make known His deeds among the people." (Psalm 105:1)

Then why are so many free and privileged people so unhappy?

JANUARY 17

Years ago, Richard DeVos, founder of Amway, was told his heart was failing and his only hope was a heart transplant. Not finding a donor in the United States, he was advised to go to England for the possibility that a heart might become available there if it was not claimed by a British citizen.

In June, 1997, just as his health took a downward turn, a heart did become available, one unsuitable for any Englishman but a perfect match for him. The operation was a success.

DeVos anguished that somebody had to die so that he could live, but his concern was short-lived. Not only did God provide him with a new heart, He also allowed him to meet the donor! A young woman needed a heart-lung transplant, but her old heart was good enough to donate. She now lived with new heart-lungs, and so did he with her heart.

Coincidence? Yes, and it was life-changing. His experience led DeVos to contemplate God's sovereignty in his life and to write about the lessons he'd learned. His book, Hope From My Heart: Ten Lessons for Life, identifies the principles he has found indispensable for a good life, such as:

HOPE: It gives us courage to overcome adversity, because hope is the conviction that *the future is in God's hands.* The problem with this for modern people, is that to place our hope in God, we must relinquish control. Not being in control is an idea that doesn't come naturally to us.

FAITH shapes life. *"Faith,"* he writes, *"is the foundation on which all my life rests."* Without faith in a personal, creator God, the universe is meaningless and moral principles impossible.

GRACE is God's love for us without which hope and faith are meaningless. God's grace makes life worthwhile.

His surgery and the other blessings in his life, taught him that everything he had, his entire life itself, was a gift from God. Richard DeVos' life experience is a powerful confirmation of God's grace, His undeserved love for us all.

"My heart is glad and my tongue rejoices." (Ps. 16:9)

May you experience HOPE, FAITH and GRACE today!

17

JANUARY 18

Here is a fine prayer to start your day. It was written by William Barclay, pastor and professor at the University of Glasgow, who lived in the last century:

"Help me, O God, to meet in the right way and the right spirit everything that occurs today. Help me approach my work cheerfully and perform my tasks diligently. Help me to meet disappointments and frustrations calmly and without irritation. Help me to meet delays with patience, and unreasonable demands with graciousness. Help me to think of the feelings of others as much as I think of my own. Help me to think before I speak so that I do not thoughtlessly or tactlessly hurt or embarrass anyone.

"O God, help me all through this day: to do nothing to upset those who love me; to do nothing to let down those who trust me; to do nothing which would make it easier for someone else to do wrong. Help me not to be too busy to listen to anyone who is in trouble, nor to help anyone in difficulty. Help me not to be too busy to remember the needs of my home and family.

"Give me today, dear Lord, some of the wisdom that was in Your words; some of the love that was in Your heart; some of the help that was in Your hands. Help me to live today that others may know that I begin and end the day with You, and that, however dimly, others may see You in me. Thank You, in the name of Jesus, amen."

You will hear me speak of prayer often in this devotional book. Prayer is the heart reaching out to God, the soul hearing God's response, and the lifeblood of a believer. God's Word tells us, **"The prayer of the righteous person has great effect." (James 5:16)**

Prayer is our heart-to-heart talk with God. It matters not how eloquent our words are, how smoothly we speak them, or whether our thoughts express our exact feelings. God just wants us to pray to Him. When we do, He always hears us and grants our needs, as well as some of our wants.

"I call upon the Lord, who is worthy to be praised, and I am saved from my enemies." (Psalm 18:3)

May the Holy Spirit move you to pray to God often today.

It is nearly three weeks into the New Year, and we should take account of how we're doing with New Year's resolutions, those great "dreams of self-improvement." Two resolutions made most often by Americans are to (1) Lose weight and, (2) Get more exercise. It's estimated fully one half of all Americans make resolutions include those two. We all seem to want to weigh less and be more physically fit, and that makes these resolutions good ones.

The Body of Christ, the Church, needs strengthening, too. 1 Corinthians 12:26 says, **"Now you are the Body of Christ, and each one of you is a part of it."** Hebrews 12:12 says, **"Strengthen your feeble arms and your weak knees."**

For the Body to be strengthened, we, the parts, must first be Committed to Christ. It all begins with our relationship to Christ. But we also must Acknowledge our fellow believers. People who leave a church service feeling ignored are testaments to the neglect of others in the Body.

Strengthening the body also means Regularity in worship and prayer. As we eat food every day, so also we need the nourishment of God's spiritual food every day, or at least every week. Strengthening the Body also means Encouraging each other. A compliment costs nothing and yet can be so needed and very priceless when received. Whom have you complimented recently? You'll see these letters spell **C-A-R-E**. Strengthening the Body of Christ then means:

Commitment to Christ,

Acknowledgement of each other,

Regularity in worship

Encouragement of other people.

A Hallmark Card slogan said, *"When you care enough to send your very be*st!" God cared enough to send us His best gift, His only Son Jesus. Taking our sins upon Himself, Jesus gave us His very best also. Thanks be to God that He did!

C-A-R-E *strengthens the body in many ways.*

Isaiah 42:1 foretold that Jesus of Nazareth would be a servant who dispensed justice in the world, something we sorely need today. But what is this thing we call "justice?" Part of its meaning is the quality of an act to be right or lawful. Justice is also a standard which determines righteous conduct, and it has to do with the outcome of an act being right or wrong. Injustice is something that is not right. A deed may be legal or protected by law, but it's not necessarily just or right.

For example, in 1998, a Los Angeles man was awarded $74,000 when his neighbor ran over his hand with his car. It apparently didn't matter the young man was trying to steal his neighbor's hubcaps at the time.

In May of 2000, a Philadelphia restaurant owner was ordered to pay a young woman $113,000 after she slipped on a soft drink and broke her pelvis. Never mind that she had thrown a soda at her boyfriend and slipped in her own mess.

An Austin, Texas, jury found a furniture store owner negligent after a woman broke her ankle tripping over an unruly toddler in their store. The jury awarded the woman $750,000, despite the fact the misbehaving toddler was her own son. The verdicts were all legal, but they were not justice.

Jesus came as a holy servant of God to bring justice to the world, not by fixing legal problems but by fixing sin problems. We are not always innocent and the other guy is not always guilty, but we are all sinful. Sin levels the playing field. In a western movie, a young man praised an old gunfighter for shooting the bad guy. *"He had it coming,"* he said. The old gunfighter quietly said, *"Son, we all have it coming."*

Because of sin, "we all have it coming," but because of Jesus, we won't get it. Christ rescued us and saved us when He died for us. We all should work to correct injustice, but also to praise God He did not mete out justice to each of us.

"I will put my Spirit on my servant, and he will bring justice to the nations." (Isaiah 42:1)

Because of Jesus we don't get what we deserve.

I enjoyed Paul Harvey, the famous news commentator who was also a Christian. Here's what he wrote years ago:

"We tried so hard to make things better for our kids that we made them worse. For my grandchildren, I'd like something better. I'd really like for them to know about hand-me-down clothes and homemade ice cream and leftover meatloaf sandwiches. I hope you learn humility by being humiliated and honesty by being cheated.

"I hope you learn to make your own bed and mow the lawn and wash the car. And I really hope nobody gives you a brand new car when you are sixteen. It will be good if at least one time you can see puppies born and your old dog put to sleep.

"I hope you get a black eye fighting for something you believe in, and I hope you have to share a bedroom with your little brother. And it's all right if you have to draw a line down the middle of the room, but when he wants to crawl under the covers with you because he's scared, I hope you let him. When you want to see a movie and your little brother wants to come, I hope you'll let him.

"If you want a slingshot, I hope your Dad teaches you how to make one instead of buying one. I hope you learn to dig in the dirt and read books. When you learn to use computers, I hope you also learn to add and subtract in your head. I hope you get teased by your friends when you have your first crush on a girl, and when you talk back to your mother I hope you learn what Ivory Soap tastes like.

"May you skin your knee climbing a mountain, burn your hand on a stove, or even stick your tongue on a frozen flagpole. I don't care if you try beer once, but I hope you don't like it. And if a friend offers you dope or a joint, I hope you realize he is not your friend.

"I hope your mother punishes you when you throw a baseball through your neighbor's window, and that she also hugs you and kisses you at Christmas time when you give her a plaster mold of your hand. These things I wish for you: tough times and disappointment, hard work and happiness. To me, it's the only way to appreciate life."

"A wise son brings joy to his father, but a foolish man despises his mother." (Proverbs 15:20)

That was Paul Harvey... GOOD DAY!

Have you ever wondered if the Lord really knows what you want or even cares? Does He take time from His busy schedule to pay attention to your meager needs? David Smallbone, an Australian business man, learned of this. He felt God was leading him to promote Christian concerts in his homeland where so few people believed in Christ. But in his first concert promotion, David lost $250,000.

Creditors repossessed his home, he spent every penny paying off the debt, and he began looking for work elsewhere. A top artist offered him a promising job in Nashville, so David sold their furniture and most possessions and purchased tickets for his family to come to the United States with only a few suitcases and far too little money.

A few weeks after they arrived, however, David was informed that his position was *"no longer available."* The news hit him so hard he literally could not get out of bed for days. When he and his wife explained to their children what happened, they all got on their knees and asked God to help them. It was all that was left for them to do.

But then interesting things began to happen. Through new American friends, God provided bags of groceries, small paying jobs, a nicer apartment, and even an old minivan to drive. Then came the biggest surprise of all. It was a recording contract for David's oldest daughter, Rebecca, who was only fifteen years old. Someone had heard her sing and encouraged her to audition. She recorded her first album using an old family name, St. James. That was years ago.

Flash forward to today. Rebecca St. James has become one of the hottest Christian artists in America. David Smallbone promotes his daughter's sold-out concerts. *"Christianity Today"* named her one of the top emerging young evangelical leaders. It wasn't what David had planned, but it was what God had in mind. All along, God knew what He was doing. Like him, we need to learn to trust God and follow His leading.

"My times are in Your hands." (Psalm 31:15)

How has God shown His good plan in your life?

The world often looks different through the eyes of a child. There was a father who took his three young children to church faithfully every week. They all sat in the front row so that the children could see and participate in everything. One Sunday the minister was baptizing an infant. The man's little five-year-old girl was taken by this, observing the pastor saying something while pouring water over the infant's head. The little girl turned to her father and asked, *"Daddy, why is he brainwashing that baby?"*

Some people feel the church really does brainwash people. But if we're going to embrace a belief, we need to know what that church teaches. Whether they are beliefs in Baptism, Communion, or the content of the Bible, it's important that we know what we believe. The only way we can know this is by studying the Bible, and the teachings of our church. Perhaps we've not done well with our New Year's Resolutions, but it's never too late to improve. Resolving to read from the *"Good Book"* is a good thing, no matter what date is on the calendar.

Read a chapter or two each day and start with the easier books, such as Psalms or the Gospels. For variety, read it in more than one translation, such as English Standard Version, New King James Version, or the New International Version. Different translations are good comparisons for a better understanding. Start with a short prayer, read a few chapters, then finish with a prayer, asking God to lead you that day.

The whole point of the Bible is to show us Jesus is our Savior. The Old Testament points forward to the coming Savior, and the New Testament points back to show Jesus is the promised Savior. No one is brainwashing us to follow God. God makes no unreasonable demands on us. He opens our hearts to trust His Word, and promises us eternal life.

"Heaven and earth shall pass away, but my words shall not pass away." (Matthew 24:35)

Always remember – God keeps His promises!

My wife and I have visited Germany several times, seeing several significant sites of the Reformation. Since some of these places were in the area formerly called East Germany, we also saw some of the changes that had taken place in the years since Germany has become re-unified.

Old cities are being remodeled, skeptical people are becoming hopeful, and beauty is being restored. Yet churches were not filling up. In fact they seem emptier now than before. A guide said the state churches can't seem to gain the interest of the young, but some of them are responding to the Gospel and the Bible in the independent churches.

It is sad that a country once rich in faith and fervor now displays so little faith in God. But at least that nation is now free again. Without freedom it is hard for faith to grow. But it is possible that freedom can be taken too far.

In 1973, the U. S. Supreme Court made legalized abortion the law of the land. Women now have the freedom to choose this procedure, yet that freedom is certainly a **"stumbling block"** to the lives of "unwanted" unborn children.

There is great disagreement today about this, whether it is necessary or wrong. Many people in our world deserve our empathy because of difficult decisions they've had to make. But I pray that one day the whole world will recognize the value of unborn human life so that abortions will no longer be done.

Jesus was born of the Virgin Mary. She trusted Joseph to tell him what the angel said, and Joseph trusted God enough to believe her. Joseph could have divorced her or even had her stoned, but he believed Mary through the message of the angel.

Because one couple trusted God rather than the laws of the land, the whole world has been blessed. May there come a day when the exercise of our freedom will not be a stumbling block in the terrible business of selectively aborting human life.

"Be careful that the exercise of your freedom does not become a stumbling block." (1 Corinthians 8:9)

May God grant this, for Jesus' sake!

God's Word comforts the afflicted, and sometimes it also afflicts the comfortable. That can be a problem, however, because most people believe they have a right not to be made uncomfortable. *"Don't tell me anything that will make me uncomfortable."* Thus, many won't hear the truth of God's Word, only what makes them feel good. But God's Word often does make us uncomfortable, and well it should.

A story is told about two elderly women who always sat up front for each Sunday service. One Sunday the Pastor's sermon was about the Ten Commandments and these two women were ready for it, for they prided themselves in their obedience to the Ten Commandments.

The Pastor said, *"You shall have no other Gods, and you shall not take God's name in vain."* The two women muttered their approval with an agreeable and quiet, *"Amen."* The Pastor continued, *"You shall honor your parents and elders and you shall not kill."* To this the women spoke a firm, *"Amen!"*

Pastor continued, *"You shall honor the marriage bed and you shall not steal."* The two women fairly shouted out, *"Amen, brother!"* But when their pastor said, *"You shall not gossip or speak unkindly about others,"* one of them blurted out, *"Now you're getting personal!"*

God's Word of Law should afflict the comfortable, but His Word of Gospel should bring comfort to the afflicted. It soothes the sinner and forgives the debtor. The Gospel of our Lord Jesus Christ dying and rising to forgive us and love us is very comforting. Jesus loves us despite our sins.

But first we need to become uncomfortable with the knowledge of our sins. Only then can we understand our need for forgiveness and the depth of His love for us.

"So in everything, do to others what you would have them do to you." (Matthew 7:12, the "Golden Rule")

Does that make sense to you? I hope so.

God never does anything halfway. The Bible says God's ways are always very good. Someone has said it well, *"God made you, and He doesn't make junk."* There are no low quality people, no "losers" in the eyes of God.

We are all worth a fortune to God, no matter what we have or don't have. No matter how much we've sinned, no matter how lowly we may feel, we're all precious to Him and worth the very life of His Son.

When Jesus turned water into wine at Cana's wedding, it showed He always saves the best until last. Just as a fine wine can improve with age, or a good worker can improve his skills, or a good marriage can get better, so also a Christian can become more like Christ through the power of the Holy Spirit.

In Christ, life gets better, or else there's something wrong. True, we will have our setbacks, and the Christian life does not come without troubles. Satan never lets us alone, but he has been defeated, so we can't really use him as an excuse.

In Christ, the best comes last, for the best is life with God forever. It's like the woman who was making funeral preparations and asked her pastor that a fork be placed in her hand in her casket when she died. When he asked why she wanted this, she said it would remind people of when they're told at after potluck lunch is finished, *"Keep your fork, because the best is yet to come. I want them to know that when your life is over and you have faith in Jesus, the best is yet to come."*

When this earthly life is over, believers know the best is yet to come, the best music, best worship, best fellowship, best health, best relationships, even the best heavenly food. In eternity we will have no worries about waistline or weight. Won't that be wonderful? As in Cana's feast the best wine came last, so in heaven with Christ, the best of everything will remain with us always.

"My child, do not forget my teaching, but keep my commands in your heart." (Proverbs 3:1)

May today be your best ever.

Prayer not only brings us answers, it strengthens our faith. God answers prayer which brings us closer to Him and helps us trust Him. Never underestimate the power of prayer!

A pastor had just brought home a kitten for his family when it climbed up a tree in his backyard and wouldn't come down. The pastor coaxed it several ways, but the kitten just stayed there. The tree was small and not sturdy enough to climb, so the pastor decided to throw a rope over the upper branches, tie it to his car bumper and carefully bend the tree down so he could then reach up and grab the kitten.

This was working just fine until he drove a little too far, and the rope broke. The tree catapulted the kitten through the air clear across the street. The pastor felt terrible! He walked all over the neighborhood trying to find the kitten, praying, *"Lord, I commit that cat to your care."*

A few days later at the grocery store he met one of his members. *"Pastor,"* she said, *"the strangest thing happened. My little girl has been begging me for a cat, but I kept saying no. She begged and begged and one day asked me that if God gave her a cat, could she keep it. I finally said 'yes' to that, thinking I was safe. Then I watched her go out in the backyard, get down on her knees to pray, and Pastor, a kitten came flying out of the sky and landed right in front of her! What an unforgettable answer to prayer!"*

Obviously this story is fiction, but it tells us something important. When you ask God for something in prayer, be prepared for His answer. It may not come in the way you think. Jesus prayed in the Garden that He might be spared the suffering that was to come. God's answer was to continue His plan. Despite the pain, good would come for all people. And we know on Easter Sunday it did. However, Jesus first had to go through the pain of Good Friday. The answer to His prayer became the answer to all our prayers as well.

"Ask and it shall be give to you, seek and you will find, knock and the door will be opened to you." (Matthew 7:7)

Never underestimate the power of prayer, or God's humor!

JANUARY 28

Back when I was learning how to drive our old Chevy pickup with a standard transmission, I often stalled the motor. I tried again and again, but when I let our the clutch, I would stall the motor because I had it pointed the wrong direction and also in the wrong gear. There was a small rise in our farmyard, and I always forgot to point the pickup downhill when I parked it. Starting to drive uphill didn't work well. Dad also said if I want to drive up a hill, I must use a lower gear and let the clutch out slowly.

In life also, using a lower and more powerful gear will get us up a hill better than a faster and weaker one. As we live and work in this New Year, it will often be tempting to put life in high gear and gun the motor just to make it through.

Just because we think we can do something doesn't mean we will. Just because we have enough money doesn't mean we should spend it unwisely. Just because the food is there doesn't mean we have to eat it all. Just because our car can go fast doesn't mean we should speed. Our lives depend on God's grace, so we need to make wise decisions in order to follow His leading each day.

God gives each of us human beings the exact same gift: three hundred sixty-five days of twenty-four hours each. He wants us to use them wisely, not going too fast or too slow. He wants us to use the right gears, and also read the map book of His Holy Word. He knows this will help us get up the hills so we can get where we want to go with time enough to spare.

May God move us to trust our Savior who forgives our sins and grants us eternal life. And may we travel safely each day.

"The race is not to the swift or the battle to the strong, nor does food come to the wise or wealth to the brilliant or favor to the learned." (Ecclesiastes 9:11)

Today, remember these three words – "Easy does it!"

Years ago a doctor was making a house call on a very sick man. He gave him medicine and instructions about what to do when he began to feel worse, for his illness was very severe. As he was preparing to leave, the man asked, *"Doctor, I am afraid to die. Tell me what lies on the other side."* Very quietly, the doctor paused and told him, *"I don't know." "You don't know?"* the patient said. *"You, a Christian man, do not know what is on the other side? How can this be?"*

The doctor at that moment was holding the door handle when they both heard scratching and whining from the other side. As he opened the door, a dog leaped into the room, eager to see the doctor.

Turning to the patient, the doctor said, *"Do you see my dog? He's usually at home, and has never been in this room before today. He didn't know what was inside. But he knew I, his master, was here. So when the door opened, he ran in without fear. I know little of what is on the other side of this life, but I do know one thing: my Master is there and I want to go to Him, and for me, that knowledge is enough."*

All of us at some time have considered what it is going to be like when we die. Believers in Christ, however, have the advantage of not fearing passing from this world into the next. We may not want to die, but when we do, we know we have God's promise that life with Him in heaven will be very good, far better than we have it here.

By faith we know our Master is on the other side, and because we have known His divine love, we believe that to be enough. Faith does not require a full explanation. It only needs trust that our Master is there waiting for us.

"The Lord has heard my cry for mercy; the Lord accepts my prayer." (Psalm 6:9)

Till then, we rejoice in the life He's given us!

Early in our marriage my wife and I visited a newly discovered cave in southeastern Minnesota. Nearly forty years later, I can still recall a moment from that visit when our inexperienced young guide took us into a deep and large cavernous room and shut off all the lights. Was it ever dark! The young man then joked about how much money our family could save in burial costs if the place caved in on us. But none of us there laughed.

Though his foolish chatter was unsettling, so was that darkness! Human eyes are not able to see in that kind of complete darkness, for there is no light at all in a deep cave. But then the young man struck a match and the entire room was filled with light. It was just one single match, but it was bright enough to cut through the darkness.

There are not enough matches in the universe to cut through the darkness of our world's Sin. It's not merely a darkness of ignorance or superstition, it's a darkness of the soul. And it's especially evident among so many supposedly wise people, educated people, people who deny the existence of God and make human beings the center of everything. Rather than let the light of God's divine wisdom shine, they prefer people to remain in darkness.

The purpose of light is to oppose darkness, to overcome and dispel it. Jesus came to get rid of the darkness of sin, evil and death. He said, **"I am the light of the world. Whoever follows me will never walk in darkness, but will have the light of life." (John 8:12)**

The Good News today is that no matter how strong or deep the darkness may seem, the Light of Christ will always overcome it. Jesus is the Light of the World, and the prince of darkness can never extinguish His light. God's light always rules over Satan's darkness.

"Let your light shine, so that people can see your good works and give glory to God in heaven." (Matthew 5:16)

Even the blackness of a cave is overcome by a single match.

Life surely can take a sudden turn in life when you least expect it. Moses discovered this when he met the Lord in a burning desert bush, and Jonah did when God told him to take a trip to Nineveh. Paul discovered life's sudden turn as he travelled to Damascus, and Martin Luther discovered it when a fellow traveller died in a raging storm one night.

A few years ago my wife saw her life take a big turn, too. At a friend's house she missed a step and broke her leg. It was a complete break that required surgery and pins. If the surgery was wasn't successful, the doctor said she might even need a hip replacement. We prayed hard this wouldn't be needed, but even after her successful surgery we found life very different around our home as she healed.

Things can take a turn in life when you least expect it. You plan a fun day and wake up to clouds and rain. You train for a life occupation and find that you dislike the life it brings. You plan a good family life and end up in the divorce court, or you plan a winter of activities and break a leg.

Not every unfortunate event carries the same result or requires the same effort to overcome. Legs can heal more easily than marriages, and husbands can actually learn patience as they help around the house. When our plans go awry, we long for the day when we can get back to normal.

When life takes a sudden turn, it helps to look for hidden blessings. If you are in the midst of a sudden turn of life, or if recent events have made your life shaky, trust God to help you see and accept them as a part of God's good plan for you. And whatever happens, always remember this: God loves you, no matter what.

"I praise You, O Lord, because I am fearfully and wonderfully made; Your works are wonderful, and I know this full well." (Psalm 1139:14)

Give thanks for the fine medical personnel, medicines, and procedures we have in our country.

DAILY WALK WITH JESUS in...
FEBRUARY

+ + +

FEBRUARY 1

I once flew to a snowy Colorado mountain retreat for a wedding in the month of February. On the way, I was reading one of Max Lucado's books. In it he wrote that people on a plane and people in a church pew have a lot in common. All are on a journey. Most are well-behaved and presentable. Some doze while others gaze out the window. For many, a good flight and a good worship service are about the same.

A few, however, are not content with "nice." They long for something more, like the little boy who asks the flight attendant, *"Will they really let me meet the pilot?"* His question reaches the cockpit, causing the pilot to say, *"Bring him in!"*

The youngster enters the cockpit with all its controls and gauges and emerges exclaiming, *"Wow! I'm so glad to be on this plane!"* No one else's face showed that kind of wonder, that kind of enthusiasm. Travelers are content just to be on the plane, glad to be going to their destination, glad to be out of the airport, content to sit, doze or read a little.

People on a plane and people on a pew have much in common. The next time you enter a church service, take a look at the faces. They're content to sit there and look straight ahead, maybe dozing, then leaving when the service is over.

Since a nice worship service is what most Christians seek, a nice service is often what they find. A few, however, seek more. They come with the childlike enthusiasm of the boy and leave as he did, wide-eyed with the wonder of having stood in the presence of the Heavenly Pilot Himself.

"Let birds fly above the earth in the open expanse of the heavens." (Genesis 1:20)

Are you glad to be on the Lord's airplane?

33

FEBRUARY 2

After the 2007 Super Bowl, quarterback Eli Manning was awarded Most Valuable Player trophy for his winning performance. The rest of his family was there, too, mother Olivia, former Homecoming Queen at the University of Mississippi, father Archie, former NFL quarterback, and Eli's brother Peyton, MVP quarterback of the 2006 Super Bowl. They all had wildly cheered Eli in a thrilling football game.

Another man was there, too, older brother Cooper Manning, who also graduated from "Ole Miss." Cooper did not play college football. I'm sure he wondered what he might have achieved had his career not been ended by a spinal injury. Yet he, too, cheered his brother's achievement.

Life's successes are fleeting, and professional sports are surrounded by many problems. But to have two sons achieve the highest award of their profession, doing what he was not able to do, must have filled father Archie's heart with joy.

People seek to achieve success, to win the prize, to take home the trophy. Only few will win first prize, and those who do will quickly fade from memory. But the promise of victory gives people hope. Deep down we'd all like to be #1.

The Good News today is that in Jesus Christ, we are #1! His death and resurrection earned us forgiveness so that we can have eternal life. His love and mercy lift us to the heights of heaven, to a glory that will never fade. Jesus excelled in human life perfectly and defeated Satan, so that we could all be winners forever. No one loses who has faith in Jesus.

Before Super Bowl Forty-Two, the papers and newscasts were filled with interesting articles about it. A morning or two later, however, no one talked about it. Other stories had taken its place, and by week's end those had faded too.

Faith in Jesus has no end. Its effects never fade. All who trust in Him for salvation have an eternity of joy awaiting them and an eternal award that will never fade.

"Whoever believes in Jesus shall not perish but have eternal life." (John 3:16)

In Jesus, we're all new Saints!

After World War One, Robert Watson-Watt invented Radio Detection and Ranging, shortened to "Radar." Radar emits electromagnetic waves that are reflected off a target and bounce back to a receiver, showing location, size and speed of the target. Radar can see where people cannot.

Most all of us have traveled by airplane, but do we realize that all airplanes today are guided by radar? It gives a pilot the ability to fly in all kinds of conditions, day or night, in clear weather or storm. In dense clouds that keep a pilot from seeing things in front of him, the radar screen shows what is ahead and all around. Radar penetrates the clouds and fog and shows the pilot what is out there.

Faith in Jesus Christ is the spiritual radar that helps us see through the clouds of life. If we see only with our eyes, we will miss the reality of God's mercy and the way to heaven through Jesus. His victory on the cross can be seen only by faith. Human senses are limited to time and space, but faith in Christ sees God in all that happens. Faith's radar penetrates the storms and heartaches of life so that we can see Jesus in the midst of it all, guiding us through.

Human hearts are amazingly alike. If you could speak honestly with people in America, China, England or Israel, you would hear their same needs and longings. Christians know that if people would trust in Jesus to guide them by His Word, they would be wiser than the wisest of the world. If we would see with the eyes of faith, we would know God loves us in Jesus, and wants us with Him in heaven.

Human wisdom is a poor guide when it comes to God. It is tainted with pride and vanity. We need to see the world through the eyes of the child who trusts God for all good things. The next time you fly, remember that your pilot is being guided by radar. Today and always, let yourself be guided by the radar of God's love for you in Jesus Christ.

"Show me your ways, Lord, and teach me your paths." (Psalm 25:4)

Our Lord Jesus is the best Pilot for life.

Corrie ten Boom, Dutch evangelist who survived the horrors of Nazi Germany, once wrote, *"Yesterday is a cancelled check, today is cash, and tomorrow is a promissory note to those who accept the victory of Jesus."*

Christians have difficulty understanding forgiveness and redemption. Forgiveness is erasing past sins; redemption is repayment of the debt of sin. Mankind is often able to accept forgiveness but not always able to accept redemption.

After one of her speeches, a man told Corrie ten Boom he believed he could be forgiven but not redeemed. *"The consequences of my sin cannot be erased,"* he said. He told of how he had fathered a child in his youth and how the living child and the memory of his sin would remain with him forever, thus never allowing him to be redeemed.

Corrie then explained, *"Jesus does not patch things up in our lives, but He does renew us."* If this man would ask Jesus to go back with him to that dark spot in his life, He would change its darkness into light. That was His purpose in coming to us, to deliver us from all sin. Corrie ten Boom continued, *"Do you understand that?"* and then answered her own question saying, *"Of course you don't!"* It was not a rebuke, but the plain truth.

Some concepts of God may be confusing, but they are still true. We will only understand God's redemption fully when we are in heaven and have new minds. But for now we can understand these things only by faith. Whoever accepts Jesus as the Victor over the past, present and future, will see the dark spots in life changed into the blessings of His light.

The devil wants us to dwell in darkness. He wants us to doubt God can change and redeem us. The devil may seem powerful, but remember, *Jesus is more powerful than the devil.* He is far greater than Satan because He has already defeated him. If we belong to Jesus, we are on the winning side in this very real struggle in the world.

"The LORD bestows his blessing, even life forevermore." (Psalm 133:3)

Give thanks for Corrie ten Boom's ministry and insight.

Several years ago there was a popular bracelet worn by many youth and adults with the initials, "WWJD." It stood for, "What Would Jesus Do?"

That thought is still a fine idea to keep in mind when making choices in life. We people of this era and culture have so many choices at our fingertips, so many that are good and also so many that are bad. We need the Holy Spirit to remind us to consider first what Jesus might do as we make our choices each day.

A pastor friend said he wished a bracelet also might be made that had on it "WDJD," "What Did Jesus Do?" We base our salvation not on our ability to make right choices, but on Christ's perfect work for us, His death and resurrection. All who believe in Him will not perish but have eternal life. What did Jesus do? He earned eternal life for us, and gave us the power of the Holy Spirit to make good choices each day.

What decisions are giving you struggles right now? A relationship? Job? Finances? Health? Peace of Mind? Ask the Lord to help you separate yourself from the emotions that accompany your struggle. Then ask yourself "What Would Jesus Do" in your situation?

Remember what He has already done for you. He has forgiven you your sins. He has given you a new life. He has blessed you with an eternal blessing that transcends all your earthly needs. He has given His life for you, and with the Spirit's help you can now live your life for Him.

Perhaps there's also a need for a third bracelet, "HCITH," "How Can I Thank Him?" All these things might seem silly, but any good thing that can remind us what God has done, anything that can help us respond to Him worthily, will be a good thing.

"God did not send His Son into the world to condemn the world, but to save the world through Him." (John 3:17)

HCYTH? (How Can You Thank Him?)

FEBRUARY 6

General John B. Gordon was a respected officer for the South during the Civil War. After the war, he decided to run for the United States Senate from his state. However, one man in the state who had served under him in the war, was angry with something he had done and was determined to see him defeated. Everyone knew this man would fight Gordon's bid to become a senator.

During the political nominating convention, this man angrily stomped down the aisle with his anti-Gordon vote in hand. But as he saw General Gordon sitting there, he saw how the man's once handsome face was disfigured with the scars of battle. The scars were marks of his willingness to suffer and bleed for a cause he had believed in.

The angry old soldier stopped and stared at Gordon's scars. After a moment, he sat down, clearly stricken with remorse. He finally said quietly, *"It's no use; I can't do it. Here's my vote in favor of John Gordon."* Then, turning to the general, he said, *"Forgive me, General. I had forgotten the scars."*

As a result of this change of heart, the former Confederate General was elected Senator from Georgia in 1873, and in 1879 he became the first ex-Confederate officer to preside over the United States Senate. General John B. Gordon later served as Georgia's Governor. What a difference it makes when people remember the scars!

The same is true of Jesus. With so many things to distract us, we don't often take time each day to reflect on what He endured on Calvary's cross for us. His death was not symbolic; it was real. When we are tempted to stray from the faith, or even to make light of His sacrifice for us, remembering the scars that show His sacrifice has the power to draw us back to Him.

"He was wounded for our transgressions and bruised for our iniquities; The chastisement for our peace was upon Him, and by His stripes we are healed." (Isaiah 53:5)

Christ's scars show us the depth of His sacrifice.

38

FEBRUARY 7

When my wife and I took a trip to Israel in 1999, many wondered why were going at such an unsafe time. Yet we were quite safe and never felt in danger. We travelled with Christians from Georgia, Canada, New Jersey and Colorado.

During our trip, our Jewish guide was Abraham who knew both the country and the New Testament well. We were safely driven through the busy and narrow streets by Doud, our friendly Moslem driver. Both of them said, *"God bless you"* to us as we parted, and I'm sure they meant it.

Many images remain of that trip, but one stands out. It was our last day and we were worshipping at the "Our Father Chapel" on the Mount of Olives. We were led by a Anglican Catholic man who wore a Jewish prayer shawl. As the service began, we heard the Moslem cry for prayer from a nearby minaret. It was quite a mixture of faiths in that moment!

It's tempting to think all religions are merely different forms of the same religion with different names for the same God. But this is not true. Jesus is the only Savior, and we must not confuse Him with false gods. Yet that moment reminded me that some of His people live in a divided land called Israel, and they worship in several different ways.

We briefly visited the Bethlehem Lutheran Christmas Church, an active congregation founded during the early twentieth century. Many of its members are from families whose ancestors have been Christians since the Fifth Century.

Being there helped us North American Christians to view the ancient land of Israel through "new eyes." Many Palestinian families have been Christian centuries before our barbarian ancestors embraced Christianity.

Interestingly, that church had two different hymnals in the pew racks, one in German and the other in Arabic. Even there, Christians have certain preferences for worship as they strive to hear the Word of God and keep it.

"Worship the LORD in the splendor of his holiness; fear him, all the earth." (Psalm 96:6)

God often brings greatly different people together!

FEBRUARY 8

It's been said, *"Worry gives a small thing a big shadow."* My mother said, *"Worry is concern without faith."* Christians need to be concerned about life, but we must still have faith that God will take care of us. As sinful people, however, we are all prone to worry.

Before taking our trip to Israel, I confess I was slightly worried about going. Things were all set, tickets were bought, bags were packed, and it was a time to depart. But newscasts told us the political situation there was tense, so it made us pause as we started. It helped us pray, too.

But the trip turned out well, moving us to go again the following year and take some friends with us, forming small tour. The memories of there places visited there and how our faith was strengthened will always be good ones.

A grandma was known always to worry openly about her family members. One of her granddaughters said, *"Granny, why do you worry so much? None of the things you worry about ever happen."* *"Yes, my child,"* she said, *"and that is precisely why I plan to keep on worrying – so that none of it ever happens!"*

Sometimes our worries are large, and not just about small things. Concern for our declining health, or lack of money for necessities, or worries over poor choices our loved ones have made, or a deteriorating world situation may make our problems seem great. This is when we must trust God the most.

May none of the bad things you worry about ever happen! God in His wisdom and love will never let anything happen that will harm your faith. Our faith needs to be tested and tried to make it stronger, and God lets that happen. But He will never tempt us so much as to harm our faith. *"The will of God will never take you where the grace of God will not protect you."* (source unknown)

"Trust in the Lord with all your heart and lean not on your own understanding." (Proverbs 3:5)

Keep trusting Him, and let Him take your worries.

There are rocks everywhere in Israel, especially around Jerusalem. Rocks there are plentiful and the basis of most building. Virtually all of them are from local quarries, and though stones are common, they are still precious to the Israeli and Palestinian people. Most buildings in Jerusalem are constructed of light colored native limestone, making their capital appear "Jerusalem the golden."

Rocks can be useful. You can shape them for building and you can even plant trees among them on the hillsides. Decaying rocks produce nutrient-rich soil for fruit trees, grain and vegetables. If it weren't for rocks, Israel would neither be so solid nor so beautiful. Because there are not enough trees for wood, and lumber is expensive, rock construction provides homes and buildings for the people there.

Jesus was a carpenter, and He probably worked in both wood and stone. Today most of the trees there have been removed because of Roman taxation and poor management, but the rocks are plentiful. Centuries ago when the land was stripped bare of its trees, God provided the rocks, so common and yet a blessing to all.

Are we not like the rocks? Who of us is not common like others around us? Who of us does not act sharp or hardened at times? Who of us is not molded and shaped according to His plan? Being shaped by God is what makes us useful, even beautiful. Some of us may believe ourselves to be more naturally attractive, but all of us are truly lovely when He shapes us and places us where He wants us.

The love of God in Jesus shapes us and the Holy Spirit helps us be open to the Good News of Jesus. Christ allowed Himself to be shaped into human form so that all who trust Him will be saved.

The Pharisees once said to Jesus, **"Teacher, tell your disciples to be quiet!"** But He said, **"If they kept quiet, the very stones would cry out."** (Luke 19:39-40)

Are there times when you feel like a stone? If so, what are you crying out for?

In every age great events have been derailed because someone concentrated on the wrong details. When Napoleon's armies invaded Russia in 1812, his soldiers seemed invincible on their march to Moscow. Then the Russian winter struck. Orders were quickly sent to his supply depot in France: *"Blankets, boots, food! Send all you have immediately!"*

But a supply officer said, *"You have the wrong forms. Give me the proper forms and you'll have the supplies. If you have wrong forms, there will be no supplies." "But the winter is bitter and men will die."* said the messenger. *"Will you refuse men the necessities of life because of wrong forms?"* The supply officer's reply? *"Wrong forms - No supplies!"*

So the Russian winter struck down Napoleon's army with a force ten times the power of swords or cannons. Nearly half a million French soldiers died or were captured with only twenty seven thousand men returning home alive. Part of the reason for this monumental loss was because someone concentrated on the wrong details.

We probably all know the Ten Commandments. But some say there is also an unofficial Eleventh Commandment that applies here: *"Thou shalt not sweat the small stuff!"*

This concept can be interpreted several ways: *"Thou shalt not stop something great just to get your own way."* Or, *"Thou shalt not be upset over little things and neglect bigger things."* Or, *"Thou shalt not sweat the small stuff!"*

Christians can get bogged down in unimportant details. Hundreds of millions are headed for hell while the Church haggles over policy. Millions need to see Jesus, but instead they see church leaders argue. When Christians spend too much time in their small corner with their own needs, they leave less time and effort for the lonely, the needy, or the lost.

"Seek first his kingdom and his righteousness, and all these things will be given to you as well." (Matthew 6:33)

What small stuff do you sweat, while ignoring the big stuff?

A commercial has these exact words, *"Protect yourself from the problems of this world with GOLD!"* The salesman tells you how easy it is to invest, clinks some new gold coins together and says, *"The right gold, at the right price, right away."*

Precious metals may be a good investment if you have the money. But does gold protect you from the problems of this world? That's questionable. Indeed, the quest for gold may have caused more problems than it has ever solved.

There is something far more precious than gold, something that can protect us during the world's problems. This precious item was contained in a traveling exhibit, it's probably also found in your home. It comes in several forms, sizes, colors and versions, and it's called, The Holy Bible.

An event called, "The Bible Through History" was held at the Glen Eyrie Conference Center in Colorado Springs. Dr. Joel Lampe, Curator of the Bible Museum in Goodyear, AZ, was there with his traveling exhibit to show how we've come to have the Word of God in our English Bible translations.

There were copies of Dead Sea Scrolls and cuneiform tablets, as well as authentic ancient Torah scrolls and old English Bibles. During displays and presentation, participants were able to hold a Geneva Bible printed in 1585, as well as an 1615 authentic edition King James Bible.

Old Bibles have great value due to age and authenticity, but their true value is in what they contain, the Holy Word of God and the Gospel of Jesus Christ. Not all the gold in the world would equal the value of the contents of those Bibles, or of the Bible in your home.

The Gospel has given life to countless people, rescuing them from eternal death and separation from God. It heals the wounds of sin and gives eternal life, which is far more precious than gold. You have a Bible in your home. Do you realize its true value?

"Blessed are those who hear the word of God and keep it." (Luke 11:28)

The Bible is "the right message, at the right price, right now."

FEBRUARY 12

Gilbert was eight years old when the Pinewood Derby races were announced. Like all the other Scouts he was given a sheet of sandpaper, a block of wood, four wheels, and told to go home and give it all to his Dad. That was not easy for Gilbert because his Dad didn't do things with him. The block remained untouched for weeks, so Mom stepped in and decided Gilbert should do the work. And he did.

Soon his block of wood became a Pinewood Derby car, crudely made, but ready to roll. Gilbert felt good knowing he had done it on his own. The big night came and his pride turned to humility when he saw the other cars. They were all made as a father-son partnership, with cool paint and sleek bodies. A few boys giggled as they saw Gilbert's scruffy car.

The races began and two by two the cars rolled down the ramp. Amazingly, Gilbert's car eliminated all his opponents except Tommy. Just before the final race Gilbert asked if he could have a moment to pray. The judges agreed.

Gilbert bowed his head for a few seconds, then said, *"Okay, I'm ready."* Tommy and his father cheered as their car sped down the ramp. Gilbert and his Father watched his block of wood race down the ramp, finishing a fraction ahead of Tommy's. Gilbert leaped into the air with a loud, *"Thank you!"*

The Scout Master came up to Gilbert with the obvious question, *"So you prayed to win, huh, Gilbert?"* *"Oh, no sir,"* he replied. *"That wouldn't be fair to ask God to help me beat someone else. I just asked Him to help me not to cry if I lost."*

Gilbert didn't ask God to fix the outcome, just give him strength to endure it. Gilbert's Dad wasn't there, but his mother was and so was his Heavenly Father.

Perhaps we spend too much prayer time asking our Father to rig the race, remove the struggles or help us win. Maybe it's better we seek His strength for the struggle. Perhaps we should ask God to give us the grace to lose with dignity.

"Ask and it will be given to you; seek and you will find; knock and the door will be opened to you." (Matthew 7:7)

Then we'd really be a winner!

FEBRUARY 13

I once received a phone call from a member telling me of the suicide of a student at a local High School. I decided to stop by the school to visit her son, arriving during lunchtime.

Scores of youth were in the commons area, standing in groups, sitting at tables or on the floor, and all seemed stunned by the news. Being sixty years old at the time, I wondered what it was like to be a teenager that day.

How many of those teens were without God? What did they hang onto if they didn't have faith in Jesus? Did their families help? Would they have a productive life in the future? Will they search for meaning in life like we did? Will their electronics make them happy? How many of them will come to faith in Jesus, and will the church interest them?

It was a sad hour of visiting and wondering what the future held for these young people who are our future workers, family members and, God willing, church members.

Years ago my wife, son and I had Christmas dinner with the family of the Defensive Coach for the Denver Broncos, who were members of our congregation. Charlie Waters, #41 of the 1970's Dallas Cowboys football team, was a legendary defensive safety during those glory years. He showed us some trophies and memorabilia, and it was a memorable Christmas Day, especially for our son Brian, a loyal Cowboys fan.

A year later, while living in another city, Coach Waters and his wife lost their real trophy when their oldest son died suddenly. It was their darkest hour, but they knew their Lord Jesus and they had Christian friends to hold them up. #41 had won many awards, but his son, a young believer in Jesus, received the greatest award of all, life forever with the Lord.

Believing in Jesus doesn't guarantee a heartache-free life, but it can give us strength to endure our problems that come. That High School student had probably lost hope in his life, but Cody was given eternal life because of Jesus.

"My times are in your hands; deliver me from the hands of my enemies, from my pursuers." (Psalm 31:15)

In Jesus Christ, God loves us no matter what.

45

A pastor once preached a sermon on sacrificial love, and told the following story: *"A father, his son and his son's friend were sailing on the ocean. A fast approaching storm swept them out to sea and the waves eventually capsized their boat."* As the pastor told the story, two teenage boys in the front row began to show their first interest in the sermon.

The pastor continued, *"Grabbing a rescue line amid the raging waves, the father was forced to make the most difficult choice of his life. To which boy would he throw the single lifeline? His beloved son was a believer in Christ and he wanted to save him. But his son's friend was not a believer. In that instant the father yelled, 'I love you, son,' and then threw the line to his son's friend!"*

The friend was saved, but his son disappeared and was never found. The pastor explained that he knew he'd see his son in eternity, but he couldn't bear the thought of his son's friend being lost forever.

The pastor likened this story to God's willingness to sacrifice His only Son so that we, the lost ones, might be saved. He urged all present to grab the lifeline God was throwing them.

At the end of the service the two teenage boys came up and one said, *"Come on, Pastor, what father would give up his son in the hopes the other guy would become a Christian?"*

An older gentleman next to the pastor overheard this and said, *"You're right. It isn't very realistic. But then, you see, I was that father, and the boy who caught my line is standing next to me. He's the pastor who just spoke to you."*

I have to admit I struggle with this story. I have two sons. How could a loving father not rescue his own son? I love my two sons so much that I would never want to lose one. But the Gospel message is that God threw the lifeline to us first, not to Jesus. Because He did, His own Son lost His life and we are saved.

"This is love: not that we loved God, but that he loved us and sent his Son as the sacrifice for our sins." (1 Jn. 4:10)

That's how much God loves you!

Ash Wednesday will soon be here. It's the beginning of Lent, the fifty-day period of repentance and reflection in preparation for Holy Week, when we remember Christ's suffering, death and finally His glorious Easter resurrection. Many attending Ash Wednesday worship will receive on their foreheads ashes made from last year's Palm branches mixed with olive oil. The forehead mark is usually a cross.

Ashes were a biblical sign of mourning and humiliation, applied to the body as a sign of repentance. Repentance means turning from sinful ways to God's ways. Repentance can be life-changing, but it is a notion foreign to much of the world. Grieving over one's failures is considered by modern people a negative or even pathological behavior. *"Life is meant to be enjoyed,"* they say, *"Any brooding over what's been done is bad."*

The day before Ash Wednesday is Shrove Tuesday ("fat Tuesday"), the day of the American Mardi Gras. Since 1699, it has been the annual time of over-indulgence and high living before Lent. Mardi Gras is celebrated as a short time of revelry before a longer time of repentance. People party hard so they'll have something to repent.

"Giving up something for Lent" is a modern form for fasting, a time of self-sacrifice intended to direct our thoughts to God. I once tried giving up reading the newspaper for Lent. While I enjoy this simple morning activity, like unhealthy food it can harm a person when taken steadily. Fasting is done when you replace what you've taken away with something better, like reading Scripture or these devotions.

Whatever Lent means to you, I hope you will take time to worship the Lord often during this time. No one to my knowledge has ever over-indulged in worship. Jesus Christ gave His life, His all, so that we may have a godly life here on earth and an eternal life there in heaven.

"Repent, for the kingdom of heaven has come near." (Matthew 3:2)

God bless you today and all through Lent!

FEBRUARY 16

It is said there are two kinds of Christians, Basement Christians and Mezzanine Christians. Basement Christians like to point out the pitfalls of life. If they're happy, they know it won't last. And if they see you being happy, they will warn you about it! They want to drag others down with their cynicism and dark negativity, because they believe too much light isn't good for one's faith.

Mezzanine Christians want to lift others up. They know there's sin in the world, but since Jesus is their Savior they enjoy each day of God's grace. They invite others to come up to where the view is great! *"God loves you,"* they say, *"so why always be sad?"* Most people are between the basement and the mezzanine and wonder whom they should heed.

Life is not just endless work and toil. We have a purpose for living, to rejoice in the life God has given us and to let our lights shine and show forth God's glory.

Whenever we show kindness, compassion, gentleness, sharing or caring, we're rejoicing and letting our faith in Christ shine. But faith can only shine if it is alive. The Holy Spirit gives us the spark that lights up our lives by showing us Jesus is our Savior. That's His purpose. He also empowers us to help light up the lives of others. That's our purpose.

A man once told me God had given him the gift of being able to look forward to see potential problems in life. I guess he thought pessimism was a spiritual gift!

Today don't be a Basement Christian. The world has enough of them already. Instead, try to share the joy of the Mezzanine Christians. Share your faith, lift others up by what you say and do. And if you're so moved, sing! Hum or whistle a tune at home or at work. You'll be amazed at what it will do for you and others around you.

"Rejoice in the Lord always, and again I say, Rejoice!" (Philippians 4:4)

Smile at people today. They'll wonder what you're up to!

FEBRUARY 17

Here's a lesson in stress management. Fill a cup with some water, as much or little as you wish. Now hold it out in front of you and guess the weight of the cup of water. Your answer will range from a few ounces to a pound. Some will say how heavy it is depends on the weight of the cup, while others say it depends on the amount of the water in it.

The heaviness of your cup will not depend on its weight alone, but on how long you hold it. If you hold your cup out in front of you for a minute, it will seem light. If you hold it out there for one hour (if you can actually hold it that long) you will have an aching arm. But try to hold the cup in that same hand for a whole day and you may need to call an ambulance. The weight remains the same, but time makes it heavier.

If we try to carry our burdens all the time by ourselves, sooner or later we will not be able to do so, being weakened and weighed down. To carry our burdens, we must rest for awhile before picking them up again. Laying our burdens down periodically refreshes and strengthens us.

Jesus had this in mind when He said, **"Come to me, all you who are burdened and weary, and I will give you rest." (Matthew 11:28)** He will help us carry our burdens if we will just let Him. We can give them to Him in prayer, for a short time or for a lifetime. Some burdens will not go away, but they will be easier to bear when we let Him help us.

Before returning home from work tonight, put that burden down. Don't carry it home with you. You can pick it up tomorrow. If you have the burden of poor health, lack of funds, a struggling relationship or any other kind of unrest, give that burden to Jesus. He will make it lighter by helping you carry it.

Then when you have rested you can pick your burden up again. You will find its weight lighter, and it may even be gone entirely. Life is short. Don't let your worries weigh you down without the Savior's help!

"Cast all your cares on Him, because He cares for you." (1 Peter 5:7)

Today let Jesus help carry your burdens.

Satan tempted Jesus saying, **"If you are the Son of God, throw yourself down."** (Matthew 4:6) This is the temptation to take the easy way out of a difficult situation. Jesus could have tried finding an easier way to save the world, but He didn't. God's road often seems narrow and bumpy, and Satan's road wide and smooth. It's our human nature to avoid the hard way. Do you feel bad? Take a pill. Someone bothering you? Sue him! Too much talk about sin? Find another church. Don't like your spouse? Get a different one!

In 1968 Sen. John McCain was a prisoner of war in the terrible "Hanoi Hilton." When he had been captive a year, he had dysentery, heat rash and a broken leg that wouldn't heal. One day the North Vietnamese prison commander made him a great offer. *"To show how compassionate we are, we're setting you free."* he said. *"You can go home now."*

Can you imagine his emotions? He would be free at last! But he also realized that they would use this as a public relations ploy now that Admiral McCain, his father, had just become Pacific Fleet Commander. His early release would demoralize the other prisoners, perhaps making them confess to something.

There was a code of honor among prisoners: "First in is the first to leave." Five others had been there longer than he had, so he said, *"I'm not going unless you set the others free."*

By saying "no" to freedom, Lt. Commander McCain said "yes" to four more years of beatings, torture and hardship. He could have taken the easier road, but he didn't.

It's tempting to find an easier way, like the Olympic athlete who uses drugs to win a medal. There are always easier ways to get a job done, but we lose when we try to trick God or His people. Jesus could have taken the easy road, but He chose the hardest. He "stayed the course," all the way to Calvary. Thanks be to God He did!

"Not my will but Yours be done, O God." (Luke 22:42)

God could have given up on us, but then where would we be?

In the early twentieth century, farmers in Georgia and southern Alabama were accustomed to planting the same crop every year, cotton. Year after year they'd plow up as much land as they could and plant it all to cotton. Cotton was their life, as it had been for over two hundred years.

But then the dreaded boll weevil devastated them with a severe crop failure. Farmers mortgaged their homes and planted cotton again, but again the weevil destroyed their crops. Realizing they faced economic disaster unless they made some changes, a few farmers decided to take a risk and plant something new.

The crop they planted was peanuts, which was resistant to pests and had a good price in the market. These farmers were successful. The peanut proved so hardy and profitable that they reaped great profits that year. They paid off their debts, other farmers also planted peanut crops, and soon prosperity returned to the area.

Today in the center of most towns in Georgia and Alabama you will find monuments to Civil War heroes. But in a few towns you will also find a monument to the ugly boll weevil. If it hadn't been for that nasty insect, they would never have found their new-found prosperity.

Even in disaster God can bless us, if we are willing to make some changes. Every moment of our suffering can be an opportunity for us to grow in faith. In a perfect world there would be no depression, pain or misery. But our world is sinful.

The Good News is that Jesus our Lord took our pain and suffering upon Himself on Calvary, so that all who trust Him are released from eternal suffering. Our life of faith in Jesus Christ may be not perfect, but it is forgiven, and that's what counts.

"Teach me Your way, O Lord; lead me in a straight path." (Psalm 27:11)

Thanks be to God He gives us certainty in uncertain times.

Returning from a brief pleasure trip years ago, I realized my body was crying out due to its bulk. It had been a wonderful Caribbean Cruise, but I had gained nearly ten pounds in just four days! I felt terrible. Reluctantly I turned to eating salads and lighter food. It was difficult because I'd always considered lettuce as food for hopping rodents with big ears, and people who fill their plates at a salad bar as cattle at a feed trough.

But it was time to do something, so I bellied up to the (salad) bar and munched lots of greens covered with low-fat, no-taste dressing. It made me realize why Dad always put molasses on the cattle feed.

Eventually this change of diet did some good, so long as I refrained from ice cream and sweets. But I drew the line at eating yogurt and guacamole. They told me those things were healthy, but as far as I was concerned, that stuff was not meant for human consumption!

Salad bars may be good for the waistline, but they can be deadly for our faith-life. Picking and choosing what you wish to believe from the Bible and leaving the rest can be disastrous. "Salad Bar Christianity" makes it too easy to omit what is most important, our salvation in Jesus.

History is full of instances where God's Word has been tasted, nibbled and eventually discarded for selfish or unholy purposes. We may have freedom to choose what we believe, but not all beliefs lead to heaven. Only Jesus does. This is as certain as death and diets.

Over the years different diets have come and gone, but the Gospel of Jesus remains unchanged, true and holy. We should not add to or subtract from the message of salvation in Jesus. We dare not cut corners on the message of God's love. We need all of what God gives us in the Gospel.

"I will forgive their wickedness and will remember their sins no more." (Jeremiah 31:34)

God give you His full joy today as you believe in Him!

A nurse escorted the anxious old man to the bedside of the young man. *"Your father is here,"* she whispered to the patient. She repeated the words and the patient's eyes opened. He was heavily sedated from the pain of a terrible auto accident. Barely able to see, he reached out his hand and squeezed the older man's hand. The nurse brought in a chair next to the bedside.

All through the night the old man sat there, holding the young man's hand, offering gentle words of hope. The dying man said nothing, just held tightly to the old man's hand. During the night his life slipped away.

The old man wept as he placed the lifeless hand back on the bed, and went to call the nurse. She did what was necessary and offered her sympathy to the old man, but he interrupted her. *"Who was he?"* he asked. Startled, the nurse replied, *"I thought he was your son."* *"No, he wasn't my son. I've never seen him before. I was looking for someone who was supposed to be on this floor and was directed to this room."*

"Why didn't you say something when you realized the mistake?" the nurse asked. He replied, *"He was injured so badly, and I was here ten minutes before I realized this wasn't the man I was looking for. But he seemed so sick and desperate, so I just stayed. I felt he needed a father by his side."*

So do we all. Our basic human needs are to be loved, approved of, valued and cared for. We can tolerate a mountain of trouble if we know someone loves us. Our Heavenly Father does, so He remains by our side and will never leave us.

The almighty God holds our hand when we're sick and quiets our hearts when we are troubled. Then He asks us to become His hands to hold the hands of others who are hurting, and His voices and feet to do His errands of mercy. We are His ambassadors of compassion.

"For we are his workmanship, created in Christ Jesus to do good works." (Ephesians 2:10)

Join me in some acts of kindness today, won't you?

53

Joe and Mary were quiet people in a faithful marriage that is rare these days. When Joe died, they had been married sixty-four years. A few years later at Mary's death, they were united once again.

Theirs was more than a marriage. They were best friends in a partnership for eighty-four years that began when they first laid eyes on each other in the First Grade. They were rarely apart after that and wouldn't have been in the same grade except that Joe had an illness that made him repeat the First Grade. If he'd have been healthy, they might never have become friends. Problems can lead to great blessings.

After graduating from high school, they tried dating others, but always came back to each other. After they were married, Joe joined her church. They traveled around with his job as a salesman, finally retiring in Colorado.

They were quiet, faithful church members, never leaders, but sitting in church most every Sunday unless health prevented it. They were always positive, loving and faithful to each other, rarely critical of others, and a real blessing.

Joe eventually went into the nursing home and Mary went to see him every day. At Joe's death, they'd found she had cancer, so she was too ill to come to his funeral. That was a very difficult day for her. But now Joe and Mary are together again, in the Lord's kingdom.

This kind of relationship is rare these days when people are told marriage is no big thing. Some have called marriage *"just frosting on the cake."* For Joe and Mary, however, marriage was the whole cake, and the frosting, pan, spoon and mixing bowl all rolled into one. Their relationship was their life.

These days many state laws allow marriage between any two people, regardless of gender. But God created us male and female and He gave us marriage. If you run short of someone to admire, if you want to see some true heroes of marriage, think of Mary and Joe.

"Where you go I will go, where you stay I will stay. Your people will be my people, your God my God." (Ruth 1:16)

Thank God for people like these two.

One rainy afternoon a man was driving along one of the main streets of town, taking those extra precautions necessary when the roads are wet and slick. His little girl was with him on a trip to the supermarket. Suddenly, his daughter spoke up, *"Daddy, I'm thinking of something."*

This kind of announcement usually meant she had been pondering some fact for a while, and was now ready to expound to her father all that her active six-year-old mind had discovered. He was eager to hear this.

"What are you thinking about, honey?" he asked. *"The rain,"* she began, *"Rain is like sin, and the windshield wipers are like God wiping our sins away."* Her Dad was impressed. *"That's really good, Honey."* He always thought she had been listening in church or Sunday School more than he realized. Children often do hear and understand more than we think.

His curiosity broke in. How far would his little girl take this revelation? So he asked, *"Do you notice how the rain keeps on coming? What does that tell you?"* The little girl didn't hesitate a moment with her answer. *"We keep on sinning, and God just keeps on forgiving us."* *"Do you think the wipers will ever stop,"* said her father. *"Nope!"* she said smiling! *"But in heaven there'll be no more rain!"*

Sounds like that little girl indeed had been listening to her Christian parents at home or to her pastor or teacher in Sunday School class. Jesus forgives us because He loves us and His love will never end.

Today if you experience the gift of rain, try to remember this little girl's words as you drive and perhaps turn on your auto windshield wipers. Then be glad that God's divine wipers will never stop cleansing your sins.

"You have hidden these things from the wise and learned, and revealed them to little children." (Matthew 11:25)

In heaven there'll be no more rain, only "Sonshine!"

One day a distinguished man approached a professor in a local cafe. *"You want to hear a great story?"* he asked. Though he really didn't want to, the professor listened.

"Several decades ago a boy was born to an unwed mother who never revealed the boy's father. He had a hard time growing up, because when he was in public, he was asked, 'Hey boy, who's your daddy?' At school, grocery store or even on the street, people of his town would ask, 'Who's your daddy?' The boy often hid to avoid going in public because hearing that question hurt so much."

"When he was twelve years old, a new preacher came to his church. One Sunday morning during the sermon, the new preacher put his hand on the boy's shoulder and said, 'Son, who's your father?' Everyone was very quiet, for now they thought they would finally learn the answer. The new preacher sensed something was wrong, so he said, 'Wait a minute!' he said. 'I know who you are. I see the family resemblance now. You are a child of God'."

"He patted the boy on his shoulder and said, 'Boy, you've got a great inheritance. Go and claim it.' That day the boy smiled and walked out the church a changed person. From then on, whenever anybody asked him, 'Who's your Daddy?' he'd tell them, 'I'm a Child of God'."

The gentleman got up from the table and said, *"Isn't that a great story? And you know, if that preacher hadn't told me who I was, I'd probably never have amounted to anything!"* After he walked away, the professor asked the waitress, *"Do you know who he was?"* The waitress grinned and said, *"That's Ben Hooper, former governor of Tennessee!"*

Because of Jesus, we are all children of our Heavenly Father. No matter what our earthly father may be like, we have a loving and providing Father who will never leave us nor forsake us.

"Whoever humbles himself like this child is the greatest in the kingdom of heaven." (Matthew 18:4)

I'm His child too. Are you?

A successful young executive was driving through a neighborhood street in his new car. Dressed in a tuxedo and headed for a date, he was watching for children and slowed down when he saw something ahead. Suddenly, a brick smashed into his driver's side door! He slammed on the brakes, and jumped out of the car and grabbed the guilty boy. *"What the heck are you doing?"* he shouted. *"That brick is going to cost you a lot of money!"*

The young boy was crying. *"Please, mister, don't hurt me. I'm sorry but I didn't know what else to do!"* *"What were you thinking?"* the driver demanded. *"It's my brother."* sobbed the little boy. *"His wheelchair tipped over and he's hurt and I can't lift him up! Please help me, Mister, please?"*

The young man went over to the little fellow's brother, lifted him back into his wheelchair, and put him back on the sidewalk. Then he took out his pocket handkerchief and dabbed at the fresh scrapes and cuts. The boy was bruised and shaken but he would be all right.

"Thank you and God bless you, mister. I'm really sorry about the brick," the boy said again. *"It's okay,"* said the young man, *"don't worry about it."* The young man stood there a few minutes, watching the boy push his brother down the sidewalk. He saw his soiled tuxedo, looked back at the boys and then felt a lump in his throat. Back to his car, the dent in his door looked bad, but he decided to leave it there awhile. It would be a reminder not to go through life so fast that someone in need had to throw a brick at him to get his attention.

God speaks to us often, sometimes quietly in our hearts, sometimes plainly through His Word, and sometimes rudely with a brick. It's our choice whether or not to listen. God loves all people, and He puts us here to show that love, even when we're all dressed up and in a hurry. Jesus didn't think to get His hands dirty over our sins, and all He asks is that we help others, **"The least of these." (Matthew 25).**

"Love your neighbor as yourself." (Luke 10:27)

Hopefully, He will share His love you, without needing a brick.

An orchestra had scheduled a concert and one of the movements featured a flute solo that was to be played as if it was a distance away. The conductor instructed the flutist to stand just off stage behind the curtain, and since the two would not be able to see each other, he was to listen carefully, counting the measures precisely in order to begin playing at the right time. Then the piece would be performed just right.

Concert night came and when it was time for the flute solo, the flutist was offstage and began playing exactly as he should. Lovely distant notes floated out beautifully from behind the curtain until suddenly there was a sour note and then the flute was silent.

The conductor finished the piece and rushed off stage to berate the flutist. *"Maestro,"* he said, *"everything was going beautifully when suddenly this big stage hand ran up, grabbed away my flute and pushed me back, saying, 'Shut up, you idiot! Don't you know there's a concert going on out there?'"*

Some people mistakenly believe that Christianity is a complex thing in which God imposes difficult rules and expectations on people. Therefore, they think, we all have to act in a certain way and not be creative and not do things differently than others are doing.

Actually, the opposite is true: Christianity is quite simple. It is all about our having faith in Jesus Christ. It's as simple as trusting in Jesus, the Son of God, for everything, and it's as complex as allowing Him to rule in our lives.

That kind of trust can show itself in different ways. Whether we choose to worship God by singing a hymn accompanied by an organ, by repeating a chorus with a praise band, or singing with only an African drum to accompany us, so long as we are doing so to give praise to our Lord Jesus, we are being the people God wants us to be.

"What does the Lord require of you? To do justice, to love mercy and to walk humbly with your God." (Micah 6:8)

God doesn't give us complex rules. He just wants our faith.

"Artful Eddie" was a lawyer who had it all. He was one of Al Capone's lawyers who fixed the Chicago dog races, overfeeding seven dogs and betting on the eighth. It was cheating, but it brought him money, wealth, style, and status. Artful Eddie cheated at all kinds of things.

But one day he walked into a police precinct and turned himself in. He squealed on Capone's betting ring and, as he expected, was soon silenced with a shotgun blast. Why? What was his motive? Surely he knew the consequences. Certainly he knew the mob would kill him for talking. Yes, Eddie knew the consequences of telling the truth, but he did it anyway. What could have moved him to do such a thing?

The answer was his little son Butch. Artful Eddie had spent his life with the underworld long enough, but for his little son Butch, he wanted more. He wanted to be a Dad his boy was proud of, and to do that he had to clear his name.

So, was it worth it? Did Butch turn out better than his Dad? He surely did! Had Eddie lived, he would have been proud of his boy. He'd have seen Butch get appointed to Annapolis Naval Academy and commissioned a World War Two Navy fighter pilot.

Eddie would have been proud that Butch downed five enemy bombers and saved the lives of hundreds aboard the carrier *"Lexington."* Artful Eddie's son also died, but he did it fighting for his country. To top it off, Congress awarded Butch our nation's highest military tribute, the Medal of Honor.

Today when people hear the name O'Hare around Chicago, they don't think of gangsters, they think of Butch O'Hare, son of Artful Eddie O'Hare. There's even an airport, O'Hare Field, named for Lt. Commander Edward Henry O'Hare, son of a gangster gone good.

"Greater love has no one than this: to lay down one's life for one's friends." (John 15:13)

Thank God for people who make sacrifices for their children.

We're now into the season of "Lent," a word from the Old English meaning "spring." Lent is the fifty day period before Easter, starting with Ash Wednesday and ending on Holy Saturday. During Lent, Christians are urged to repent of their sins and recall the suffering and death of Jesus Christ.

ASH WEDNESDAY - Ashes are an Old Testament sign of repentance. Ashes made from burning last year's palm branches and mixed with olive oil are placed on foreheads.

HOLY WEEK - Palm Sunday through Holy Saturday, it's the time recalling Christ's triumphant entry into Jerusalem on a donkey as foretold in Zechariah 9:9.

MAUNDY THURSDAY – *"Maundy"* is from the Latin term *"mandatum"* meaning *"command."* On that night, Jesus commanded His disciples regarding the Lord's Supper, **"Do this in remembrance of me." (Luke 22:17-19)**, and again, **"Love one another as I have loved you." (John 15:12)**

GOOD FRIDAY - The day commemorating Christ's crucifixion and death. Most believe it was called *"good"* since Christ's offering Himself as the sacrifice made it good. Some churches observe a Tre-Ore (three hour) worship service from noon until three o'clock, the time period Christ hung on the cross in darkness. Others have an evening Tenebrae service of darkness.

EASTER - This is the highest festival day of the Church Year, celebrating the resurrection of our Lord and Savior. His resurrection is proof He is the Son of God. If Jesus had not risen from the dead, there would be no Christian faith. The date changes each year, according to the Jewish Passover date, and can be as early as March 26 and as late as April 25. *"Easter"* is derived from a pagan fertility festival, which is the root of the secular rabbit and egg tradition. The Church *"christianized"* the pagan festival to neutralize its effect on society. In His resurrection, Jesus proved that He was the Son of God.

"If Christ has not been raised, then your faith is in vain." (1 Corinthians 15:14)

May God bless your observance of Lent and Holy Week.

FEBRUARY 29
(Leap Year)

I try not to worry about modern culture, but some trends are troublesome. One of those is warning us about all kinds of dangers lurking everywhere. We're constantly warned of global warming, overpopulation, water shortage, obesity, identity theft, illegal aliens, sexual predators, economic failure, energy shortages, transfats, religious extremism, etc.

Hearing such topics every day would make a newcomer to our planet think that life on earth is on the brink of extinction. But this is far from true. People of the world live better today than at any time in history.

It was not better in the days of the horse and buggy. There were far worse examples of war and genocide during Roman times, or even in the early 1900's. Diseases decimated populations, and wars destroyed cultures years ago almost as fast as they arose.

We have it far better today than we think. People have more time on their hands to write of gloom and doom. In any other age, we'd have been too busy chopping wood, working fifteen hour days, and inventing home remedies just to stay alive. Today's news travels fast. We know instantly what's happening everywhere, so we are prone to panic.

Since mankind sinned in the Garden of Eden, people have always lived with potential dangers. Note that none of those dangers listed above are spiritual or eternal. However, unbelief does bring eternal death that destroys forever. The soul that trusts Christ as Lord is not in danger of eternal death, for faith in Christ is the door to eternal life.

Jesus once said, **"Fear not those who kill the body but cannot kill the soul. Rather, fear the One who can destroy both soul and body in hell." (Matthew 10:28)** Jesus came to dispel human fear, but some people seem to prefer living in it.

Rather than crying out in fear, we should trust in Jesus, and turn our fears over to Him. By faith, let Him carry our burdens, whether real or imagined, and He will bring us safely through this abundant life unto our eternal home.

Smile and enjoy the day. It's not nearly as bad as people say.

DAILY WALK WITH JESUS in...
MARCH

+ + +

MARCH 1

A daily prayer book contained a message about being carefree saying, *"We all want to be carefree. Children expect to be carefree when school is out for summer vacation, adults expect to be carefree when they become empty nesters, and everyone looks forward to the carefree years of retirement."*

North of Phoenix, Arizona, there is a city named Carefree, probably named to convey the idea that you'll be carefree when you live there. Of course, we can't escape all the cares of life, no matter how much time, money or desire we may have. Life will always toss its troubles at us, no matter what.

1 Peter 5:7 says, **"Cast all your cares on Him because He cares for you."** Health cares, job cares, money, child or world cares - cast them all on Jesus, because He knows how to handle them. Some He will remove, others He will help us through, and some may remain a long time. But Jesus will help us handle them. He is our heavenly care-taker.

A man told how he struggled with the sudden death of his wife. *"I learned the meaning of the words in Psalm 23,"* he said, **"Even though I walk through the valley of the shadow of death, I will fear no evil."** *"The important word is 'through'. Some people get into the valley and stay there, not knowing how to get out. Jesus went through the valley and He will help us get through it."*

During Lent we remember how Jesus went into the valley and endured the pain, isolation, rejection and death that we deserved by our sins. He went there so we wouldn't have to stay there. He didn't stay there either, but came out alive on Easter Sunday. Jesus is our great care-taker, and He forgives our sins. Now we can be spiritually carefree in Him.

Jesus is our risen Lord who loves us, no matter where we are.

MARCH 2

In 1982, Roberta Gaspari was served with divorce papers. Her husband of ten years disappeared, leaving her with two sons and only her wits to live. She felt crushed but not for long.

She could earn money giving private violin lessons, but that would not provide enough. She went to the East Harlem School District and offered to teach violin to students for no pay. If they were pleased they could offer her a staff position. It was a hard sell, but she was given a trial period.

Soon Ms. Gaspari had over a hundred violin students, there in the middle of the East Harlem slums. Her skills and attitude not only taught young musicians, it changed lives. She was eventually offered a teaching position and her popular program brought in hundreds of students, some of whom were later accepted into Julliard and Eastman Schools of Music.

In 1993 she was shocked to learn her program was to be cut. With hundreds of students waiting to learn the violin, the school district had chosen not to fund her work. She offered to find funds to keep her program going, and school officials agreed but offered no assistance.

With some parents, she planned a benefit concert, and all went well until came the bad news. The hall they'd rented couldn't be used, and their concert was only a month away. Again, Roberta Gaspari felt crushed, but not for long.

Word of her plight came to another violinist who offered her the use of a hall, *"But only,"* he said, *"if I and some of my friends may play along."* It was Carnegie Hall! The man was violinist Isaac Stern, and his friends were Itzhak Perlman, Arnold Steinhart, Joshua Bell and other virtuosos. The benefit concert resulted in her East Harlem violin program being endowed, and it is still going today. The 1999 film, *"Music of the Heart,"* details her story more fully.

In our life's journey, we can't avoid feeling crushed from time to time. But Jesus walked that road for us and has earned us forgiveness and a new start. Trust Him for life!

"Make music to God on the ten stringed lyre." (Ps. 33:2)

Wherever you go, let Jesus be your traveling companion.

An elderly carpenter was ready to retire. He told his long-time employer about his plans to quit building houses and enjoy his family and free time. He would miss his work but they would get by. He just needed to retire.

The contractor was sorry to see him go, for he had been a faithful worker many years. He asked him if he would build just one more house as a personal favor. The man said yes, but his heart was no longer in his work. He resorted to shoddy workmanship, used inferior materials and worked too quickly. But after all, he thought, it was his last job and no one could fire him for bad work now.

When the house was finished, his employer inspected the house and handed him the keys. *"This is your house,"* he said, *"my gift to you."* The carpenter was shocked! If only he'd known he was building his own home, he'd have built it far better!

So it is with us. You and I build our lives one day at a time, often putting into it less than our best efforts. Then with a shock we realize we must live in the "house" we have built, and we cannot go back. We are the carpenters. With each nail we drive, each board we cut and each wall we build, we are constructing the house of life we live in. Today's actions and decisions will affect our lives tomorrow.

Give thanks to the Lord that He gives us a second chance through His forgiveness. If we had no living God who cares for us, then all our foolish decisions, rebellious actions and selfish attitudes would collapse our life around us. Without our Lord Jesus, our lives would be nothing but disaster. But with Him, we have a blessed hope for the future.

Trusting in Jesus, we are assured of eternal life, despite how poorly we may have lived our lives. By faith in the Son of God, even the most rickety of lives can be salvaged and made strong for eternity.

"Trust in the LORD with all your heart and lean not on your own understanding; in all your ways acknowledge Him, and He will make your paths straight." (Prov. 3:5-6)

Live your life wisely today!

MARCH 4

Why do bad things happen to good people? A few years ago Rabbi Harold Kuschner wrote a best-seller on this topic, and his premise was that there's no rhyme or reason to bad things happening. They just happen randomly, and we should learn to deal with them.

I don't think that's what another Rabbi, Jesus of Nazareth, would have said. He'd probably first have asked, *"Are you sure you're good people? Only God is truly good. Sin removes your goodness. But God can bring good out of the bad that happens to you. Just look at Job or Joseph."*

Things also looked pretty bad for Jesus, and yet think of all the eternal good that came from His death and resurrected life. His gifts are for each of us. We cannot presume to know how all the good or bad things in life will affect us. Only God knows that. Hopefully we will also know some day.

I'm surprised more bad things don't happen to us. We often think things are bad today, that government is out of control and society is sliding down a "slippery slope." But life has been much worse than it is today. In centuries past there was far more disease, danger to life and limb, and more insecurity in providing for people's needs.

If something bad happens to you or those you love today, try to find what God is doing in the midst of it. He loves His children and wants what is good for them. He said, **"I will not leave you as orphans; I will come to you." (John 14:18)** Jesus, the Son of God, is our Savior who loves and forgives us.

A pastor and his wife tried their best, but they had become so incompatible that she divorced him. During the years that followed, he led Divorce and Loss Recovery Workshops that helped dozens of men and women grow in faith through their losses. The lessons we learn from the bad things that happen can be the most important lessons of all. Many of them could not be learned in any other way.

"In everything give thanks, for this is the will of God concerning you in Christ Jesus." (1 Thessalonians 5:18)

Saying and believing that verse takes real faith.

MARCH 5

I once attended an adult discussion group where a dozen or more retirees gathered to share their ideas on the question, *"What is intelligence?"* While I doubt anyone left the meeting with a better understanding of the topic, we did have a better idea what each of us was thinking.

In that group I often found my Christian faith questioned. Some believed in Darwinism and other secular belief systems. Others believed there was no right or wrong, just choices. If I spoke of my faith, I found my ideas challenged.

That same winter I watched the movie, "Our Privileged Planet." In it, an astrophysicist and a philosopher showed the miraculous position our earth has in relation to the rest of our solar system and the universe.

If our earth were just a bit closer or farther away from the sun, complex life could not exist. If our planet were smaller or larger, or if the earth's crust were thicker or thinner, or if our atmosphere had a different mix of its life-giving gases, human beings and other life could not exist.

The film concluded that Intelligent Design must have made things the way they are, and I agree with this. Sadly, some of the scientists in that movie have since been ostracized by colleagues, and one was even fired for writing that scientists should consider the idea of Intelligent Design.

Such scientists are courageous, for they will be ridiculed publicly by others who believe that God does not exist. The negative reaction to Intelligent Design shows that wisdom often has little to do with intelligence.

Christians believe the Almighty Creator of the universe has placed us into an amazing moment on an amazing planet which is in the best place among the millions of planets in the universe. What's even more incredible is that our Creator God loves His creation. All who trust Him and have faith in His Son Jesus Christ will be given eternal life.

"I will astound these people with wonder upon wonder; the wisdom of the wise will perish." (Isaiah 29:14)

Wise and intelligent people will always acknowledge God.

MARCH 6

These words from Ecclesiastes 3 may be familiar: **"To everything there is a season, and a time for every purpose under heaven, a time to be born and a time to die."** The life circumstances that follow in this chapter describe birth and death, war and peace, laughter and sadness. I would add, *"There is a time to tackle a problem and a time to let it go."*

This has been made clear to me with my hearing. Years ago I began noticing ringing in my ears. My doctor said it was tinnitus, a condition caused by medication, nerve damage, infection, heredity or all of the above. All people have some ringing in their ears now and then, but tinnitus is a constant, loud inner ear noise that is heard all the time. There are over-the-counter treatments, but none of them really work.

Tinnitus usually leads to hearing loss. Hearing aids can help, but they don't stop the sounds. There is a recorded case in which tinnitus became so severe the patient asked to have some nerves severed to stop it. The surgery made the man totally deaf, but the ringing still did not stop. Imagine spending the rest of your life hearing only the ringing in your ears!

A person may know what a problem is, what causes it, or even what it may lead to in the future. But some problems never seem to go away. That's when we must learn to let them go and let God deal with them. I have learned some tricks to ease my tinnitus, but I have found giving it to God works best.

I am not suggesting we should deny a problem exists or not try to find a solution. Perhaps one day a cure for tinnitus will be found. Meanwhile, if I can do nothing to stop it, I must let my problem go and let God handle it. I don't always think about the ringing, but I know it's there, and so I ask for help to ignore it. I've learned to *"Let Go, and Let God."*

Jesus said, **"With God, all things are possible." (Matthew 19:26)** God can fix anything, even tinnitus. In the Garden of Gethsemane Jesus asked His Father to remove His suffering, but it remained, and so Jesus willingly let go and went the way of the cross for us.

With God all things are possible, including good hearing.

MARCH 7

One day a boy found the cocoon of a butterfly. As he was watching it, a small opening appeared and soon a new butterfly emerged after struggling to force its body through the small hole. Then it seemed to stop making any progress. It appeared to have gotten as far as it could.

The boy decided to help the butterfly, so he took a pair of scissors and snipped off the remaining bit of cocoon. The butterfly then emerged easily, but it had a swollen body and small, shriveled wings.

The boy continued to watch the butterfly, expecting at any moment that the wings would expand and it would be able to support the body fly. But it didn't happen. In fact, the butterfly crawled around awhile with its swollen body and shriveled wings and eventually died.

What the boy in his haste did not realize was that the restricting cocoon and struggle to get through the opening were God's way of forcing fluid from the body of the butterfly into its wings so that it would be ready to fly. In his impatience the boy had stopped a life-saving struggle.

Often our struggles are what we need in life. If God allowed us to go through life without them, it could limit or cripple us for the future, and we would not be as strong or as wise as we could have been. Without our life's obstacles, we might never "fly."

We may feel trapped by our circumstances, events or limitations, but within each struggle there are gifts from God: patience, courage, endurance, strength or hope. Without the opportunity to face those struggles, we would remain adolescents in our faith.

"We know that suffering produces perseverance; perseverance, character; and character, hope." (Romans 5:3-4)

What struggles are you having right now? What problem can you ask God to help you with?

MARCH 8

He had been looking forward to this moment all week, and after six hard days it finally arrived. It was Visitation Day! The man with the keys arrived to swing open the large, heavy doors. The cold, gray hallway sprang to life in the warm glow of light. He was happy that the time had finally come.

Families and individuals began to arrive. He peered from the corner of the room, longing for the first glimpse of his loved ones. He lived for these weekends, and he loved their visits, so he watched intently as their cars arrived.

Finally the people were there, some a little late, people for whom he would do anything. They embraced, talked of love, ate a light lunch, and reminisced how things used to be. At times they broke into singing, laughter and some even applauded. But all too soon it was over. They had come for barely an hour this week and were already leaving.

A tear came to his eye as his loved ones departed to their homes and restaurants. The man with the keys closed the doors, and it was suddenly very quiet again. He heard the key turn in the lock marking the end of that special day and stood there, wondering if the visit had helped anyone. He could only hope it had.

His name was Jesus. He knew some of His loved ones would not contact Him again until next week, if then. As the last car pulled away from the parking lot, Jesus began to wonder once again if His saving work would be beneficial to them, so He began His preparation for the next Visitation day.

Is the time we spend with Jesus just a quick Sunday visit? Is there more time we could give Him? It's nice we come Sunday, but could we have a daily visit with Him also? He's there waiting for us, anytime, anywhere, for any reason. The joy of a daily visit will be ours as well as His, and it will make our day brighter and more fulfilling.

"Come to me, all you who are weary and worn, and I will give you rest." (Matthew 11:28)

The benefits are wonderful. He guarantees it.

70

MARCH 9

Mike Christian was a young man from Alabama who enlisted in the Navy and became a pilot. In 1967 he was shot down over Viet Nam. After being captured, he and other prisoners periodically were allowed to get packages from home, containing handkerchiefs, scarves and other items. Mike found a bamboo needle and worked several months to make an American flag which he sewed inside his shirt. Every afternoon he and his fellow prisoners would hang the flag-shirt inside out on the cell wall and say the Pledge of Allegiance.

One day the Vietnamese guards searched their cells, discovered Mike's shirt with the flag and removed it. That evening they hauled him out and beat him severely, in view of the other prisoners. When they threw him back in the cell with the others, his face was so swollen he could barely see. His fellow prisoners cleaned him up as best they could on the concrete slab with a little water and only a few naked light bulbs hanging overhead.

After they'd cleaned him up and some time had passed, one of the prisoners looked at him in the corner of the room. There, sitting beneath a dim light bulb with a small piece of red cloth, another shirt and his bamboo needle, nearly blinded by his beating, Office Mike Christian was sewing another flag. He could have let the beatings crush his spirit, but he refused to let that happen.

What are you pledging your allegiance to these days? What disappointments have nearly crushed you? What are you willing to endure for the sake of your faith?

The next time you see a flag, give it your respect and let it remind you of the privilege of taking a stand for your country, and especially for the truth that Jesus is your Lord and Savior.

"In the Cross of Christ I glory, towering o'er the wrecks of time." (from the hymn)

I pledge allegiance to Jesus Christ!

MARCH 10

Sometimes people today wonder about the necessity of a strong military. They may point to other uses for tax funds to educate the young or help people in need.

A few years ago, I received a message from a pastor who had been an Air Force technician before he went to the seminary. He was also the first boy I confirmed as a new pastor. Pastor Al sent me this bit of insight about the need for a strong military in America. I thank him for the wisdom. He wrote,

"Years ago in Alaska I saw a sign on the wall of the Ready Room of an F-106 interceptor group. Their job was to intercept Soviet Bombers coming over the pole into the U.S. This is what the sign said:

> *"War is an ugly thing, but it is not the ugliest of things. A depraved consciousness that believes there is nothing worth fighting for, nothing for which you are willing to pay the ultimate price, is much worse. Indeed, there are eternal virtues greater than ourselves, greater than our wants and desires. And the only way a man who is unwilling to pay the price for those virtues will enjoy them, is by the efforts of those who are better than he."*

Pastor Al said this was a reminder to the soldiers in the Ready Room as to why they were there, as well as an indictment on all who believe the military is unnecessary.

Among my ongoing prayers is that Americans will not grow weary of the struggle against evil in the world, but will stand firm against it. I don't want war to continue, but it's not good for our soldiers to come home without finishing the job.

However, with today's faceless enemy, we're not sure when to lay down our arms. I invite you today to pray for our service men and women as they work to protect our nation from its enemies.

"Put on the whole armor of God that you may be able to stand against the schemes of the devil." (Ephesians 6:11)

May God grant that our soldiers can all come home soon!

Sometimes the truth hurts. No matter what you or I may want to hear, some unwelcome truths can cut like a knife. One time comes vividly to mind.

I had officiated at the funeral of a "biker" whose friends told the funeral director, *"Just find some preacher for the service."* The church parking lot held as many motorcycles and pickups as the fifty or sixty attendees inside. I gently told them of the Gospel of our loving Lord Jesus, and His acceptance of all who came to Him in faith. At the coffee time afterwards, no one from the group spoke to me except one man who walked over and quietly said, *"Your zipper's down."* Not the truth I expected!

Unexpected truths may not be what we want to hear, but they may be what we need. A person who works in public can expect feedback that won't always be positive, despite our efforts or the truthfulness of our message. Writers periodically get criticized, and though it may sting, it is what is needed. How we react to criticism will determine our maturity and strength.

Jesus was gentle with most people, yet harsh with those who should have known better. His strong comments to the Pharisees and occasionally His own disciples came because they needed to be jarred from their entrenched ways. Calling the Pharisees "hypocrites" was a stinging rebuke to those unwilling to change. But it was the truth.

Jesus didn't come into this world to be critical, but to fulfill God's eternal plan of forgiveness. His road to Calvary was for our salvation. He came to show us God's accepting mercy, not just how to follow rules. What He said and did for all people was meant to help, not hurt.

When we trust our Good Lord for all things, we will be truly blessed. When we realize what He has done for us on Calvary, it should soften those unwelcomed truths so that they can benefit us the most.

"You will know the truth, and the truth will set you free." (John 8:32)

How can you show His love to others today?

MARCH 12

What can God do with fifty-seven cents? Near the end of the Nineteenth Century, a little girl was turned away from a church because it was too crowded. *"They won't let me go to Sunday School,"* she sobbed. Seeing her unkempt appearance, the pastor guessed the real reason. So he took her by the hand, led her inside and found a place for her in a Sunday School class. The child enjoyed it so much that she wondered aloud about children who have no place to learn about Jesus.

A short while later, this child died and her parents asked the kindhearted pastor to conduct her funeral service. In one of her pockets was found a crumpled small red purse. Inside was fifty-seven cents and a note which read, *"This is to help build the little church bigger so more children can go to Sunday School."* The pastor carried this note and the red pocketbook into the pulpit and told the story of her wish. He challenged his people to raise money for a larger building.

A newspaper reporter learned of the story and published it. It was read by a realtor, who offered the church a piece of land worth thousands of dollars, and his price would be just fifty-seven cents. Church members and friends made other donations, and within five years the little girl's gift had increased to $250,000, a huge sum for that time.

Today if you visit Philadelphia, go see Temple Baptist Church, with its seating capacity of over three thousand. Also visit Temple University, where hundreds of students are trained in the Bible. Notice also the Good Samaritan Hospital and a nearby Sunday School building which trains hundreds of Bible scholars each year.

In one of the rooms you will find a picture of a little girl whose fifty-seven cents started that remarkable place. Beside it is a portrait of her pastor, Dr. Russell H. Conwell, author of his book, Acres of Diamonds, the true story of a brave little girl.

"Test me in this," says the LORD Almighty, "and see if I will not throw open the floodgates of heaven and pour out so much blessing." (Malachi 3:10)

God can do miracles through those who have great faith.

Throughout history, men and women with great ideas have faced opponents. Whether it's creating a nation, inventing a product or making a family, visionary people have faced roadblocks by those who believe their ideas are better.

Ken Follett's novel, <u>Pillars of the Earth</u>, is about the struggle to build a cathedral during the Middle Ages. Things were done by hand then. Every stone was quarried, hauled, cut, shaped, lifted and set in place by hand or with crude machinery. Despite protection of Church or noblemen, the builder was opposed by those who didn't want him to build.

Thus, the cathedral was started then burned, rebuilt then smashed, rebuilt and destroyed, but always rebuilt again. The book's cathedral took fifty years to build. Some cathedrals took hundreds of years to complete.

I once preached a midweek sermon series on the "Seven Last Words from the Cross" and the sixth Word was, **"It is finished!" (John 19:30)**. The Greek word, "Tetelesthai" means His work was done. His life, His ministry, His New Kingdom, His keeping God's Law, His taking on Himself the sins of the world - all these monumental things were over. **"It is finished!"** meant achievement, not defeat. It was completion not quitting. It's like saying, *"I'm finally done!"*

A mother who has raised her large family, a man who has finally paid off his house, a doctor who can practice medicine after years of study, a middle aged woman who is finally getting married, or a man who retires after working fifty years - all these know the meaning of, **"It is finished!"**

Some things in our lives never seem to get done, but Jesus' task is. **"It is finished!"** He cried. Nothing more is needed for salvation. No human effort, no sacrifice, obedience or act of mercy can add to what He has already done. He endured the cross on Good Friday, and in three days the world would know it. He finished the task and we are the beneficiaries.

When He said, **"It is finished!"** He did so for us and for our salvation.

Give thanks to God that we have eternal life by faith in Christ.

An adult daughter with a physical deformity asked her father why life was so difficult. She did not know how she was going to make it if things kept going so badly. Her life seemed to be just one problem after another and she was weary of it.

Her father took her to the kitchen, filled three pots with water and turned on the burners. When the water pots came to a boil, he placed carrots into one pot, eggs into the second, and into the last pot he placed coffee beans. The daughter watched impatiently, wondering what he was doing. After a time he put the cooked carrots on a plate, the eggs in a bowl and poured some of the coffee into a cup.

"What do you see?" he asked. She replied. *"Carrots, eggs, and coffee."* He asked her to feel the carrots and how they were now softer. He broke an egg and showed her it was now hard-boiled. He asked her to take a sip of coffee, and she found it was strong but good.

Her father explained that each item faced the same adversity, boiling water, and each reacted differently. The carrot went in hard but came out soft and weak. The egg went in a fragile liquid in a thin shell but came out hardened. The coffee became strong and rich as it boiled. *"Your life recently has been like a boiling pot. Which one of these are you right now?"* he asked.

When adversity knocks at our door, how do we respond? Do we wilt like the carrot, or get hard like the egg? Or will we be like the coffee which changes the water while releasing its rich flavor and aroma? Does adversity make us weaker, more hardened or richer? How do you handle adversity? Are you a carrot, an egg, or a coffee bean?

Jesus accepted His trials and made the best of them. He did not become weak, nor did He harden Himself against His enemies. His life was a triumph over Satan. Jesus changed the world forever through His death and resurrection.

"We are troubled on every side, yet not distressed; we are perplexed, but not in despair; persecuted, but not forsaken; cast down, but not destroyed." (2 Cor. 4:8-9)

Lord, grant us such a faith as this, amen.

"The Straight Story" is a movie of a true story about Alvin Straight who drove a garden tractor across Iowa to visit his brother Lyle. The brothers hadn't spoken in years, but when Alvin heard Lyle had a stroke, he wanted to make things right before either of them died. Due to poor health and poverty, Alvin couldn't drive a car or fly, so he drove his garden tractor two hundred miles across Iowa.

Along the way Alvin met a runaway girl with whom he shared a warm fire one night. The girl told him she didn't need family and was never going home. Alvin told her of a game he used to play with his children. He'd give them each a stick and asked them to break it, which they did. He then said to put many sticks together and try to break them, but they couldn't.

The individual sticks were each person alone, he said, but the bundle was family. Alone we can break, but there's strength in family. In the morning the girl was gone, but where she slept lay a bundle of sticks. She'd decided to go back home.

The Bible tells us in Psalm 68:6, **"God places the lonely into families."** Today's secular culture often tries to convince us there are too many people on earth, or even that the earth would be better off without any people. The more people there are, they say, the worse it is for the world. It also tries to tell us people should deal with problems by themselves.

God gives us biological families and extended families, where brothers and sisters are related, or our family is made up of friends, church members, fellow workers or neighbors. God put people on earth to enjoy it and care for each other. Our loving God places the lonely into families for our good.

People are not the problem. Sin is, and God has a solution to Sin. His Son Jesus died to forgive it. He rose again to show us that believers, too, shall rise. Give thanks for your family. Mend fences where you can, and don't be isolated. Be thankful for the bundle God gives to keep you from breaking.

"It is not good for a person to be alone." (Genesis 2:18)

I'm looking forward to God's great Family Reunion!

MARCH 16

Years ago my older brother died of a heart attack while singing in a choir in church. While it was a good way for a Christian to die, his passing was a great loss to our family and to the small community where he lived and worked. Brother Fritz died at age sixty-six.

When Fritz found something he liked, he stuck with it. Consider these numbers: twenty-five years managing a business, twenty-five years as church Financial Secretary, thirty-three years with the Barber Shop chorus, thirty-eight years as auctioneer, forty-six years in his church choir, and sixty-six years a member at the same congregation. Small wonder, then, that in that same year he and his wife would have celebrated forty years of marriage.

In these days of insecurity, when families seem to move every few years, and some change spouses often, it's nice to know there are some people who stay put. Fritz was one of my heroes, not because he fought a battle, but because he kept a lot of them from happening.

He also served for two years in the Army occupation forces in Germany and died as Commander of his local American Legion Post. He did just about everything in his hometown except run for office, saying he'd rather do the work than be in charge. He was a good man in a time when we need more good men to look up to.

If you know anyone like Fritz, tell them you appreciate them. I don't think I ever told him how important he was to me, the older brother I looked up to, the brother everyone would love to have. I preached at his memorial service, and though difficult, it was also an honor. Family members need to grieve the loss of loved ones, and that's what a memorial service is for. I was able to do that and more.

"A friend loves at all times, and a brother is born for a time of adversity." (Proverbs 17:17)

Thank You, Lord, for our family, amen

MARCH 17

It's St. Patrick's Day but most of us know little about St. Patrick himself. His brief writings, Confession and Letter to Coroticus, are the basis of what we know of him. Confession was written to recount his personal call to convert the Irish people. His Letter to Coroticus, an Irish warlord whom Patrick was forced to excommunicate, is a wonderful illustration of his skill as a preacher. But it doesn't tell us much about him.

St. Patrick was born and named Patricius in the Fifth Century somewhere in Roman Britain to a wealthy family. He was not religious as a youth and may even have renounced the faith for a time. While in his teens, Patrick was kidnapped and transported to Ireland, where he was enslaved by a local warlord until he escaped six years later.

Patrick returned home, took training and vows for the priesthood, and eventually returned to Ireland as a missionary to his former captors. It is not clear when he actually came back to Ireland, or for how long he ministered there, but he was definitely in Ireland for a number of years.

By the time he wrote his two short works, Patrick was recognized by Irish natives and the Roman Church hierarchy as the Bishop of Ireland. He made clear his commitment to Ireland and intended to die there.

Patrick was said to have used the three leaves of the Irish shamrock to explain the Holy Trinity. This is all we know about him, and yet he is honored the world over as a remarkable man of God. March 17 is celebrated as his birthday in Ireland and other parts of the world.

God uses all kinds of experiences to bless His people. Patrick could have sworn off his captors. Instead, he cared enough about them to go back and share his faith in Christ. That's what he believed Jesus wanted him to do. Jesus loved him with an everlasting love on the cross and open grave, so he wanted to share that faith and love with others.

"For all the Saints, who from their labors rest." (from a hymn)

It's amazing how God uses our experiences to help others.

MARCH 18

William Cowper (1731-1800) was a beloved English poet and hymn writer, but few people knew he suffered fits of melancholy and attacks of spiritual despair. One episode led him to attempt suicide, despite his dedication to Jesus and the Church. In those days, as now, mental illnesses caused people to do things they normally would not do. Mental illness affects both believers and unbelievers.

On one of these occasions during a dark night of his soul, Cowper set out from his home in London with the intention of jumping into the Thames River to drown himself. Instead, he got hopelessly lost in the dense fog and wandered blindly for some time.

Eventually, lost and confused, he walked into a house to get out of the fog. The house? It was his own! God had guided him through the fog and brought him back to those who loved him. Moved by his experience, he sat down and penned the words of this beloved hymn, and later on dozens of others we have heard or sung so often:

"God moves in a mysterious way His wonders to perform;
He plants his footsteps in the sea, And rides upon the storm.

Ye fearful saints, fresh courage take; The clouds ye so much dread
Are big with mercy, and shall break In blessings on your head."

If it seems you are heading into a dark night of your soul and feel that God is far away, be assured He knows where you are. He is standing in the shadows, waiting to help. Just as He knows every sparrow that falls, He knows all about you and your needs. When we entrust our life to God, by faith in Jesus we will be able to make it through the fog of this earth to our heavenly home.

"Weeping may endure for the night, but joy comes in the morning." (Psalm 30:5)

May you know God is with you always, today and every day!

MARCH 19

We all have family or friends that we remember, and we know why they are memorable. Sometimes we remember the things they said, and at other times we recall the kind of persons they were. How will people remember you? How would you like them to remember you?

Rev. Sabine Baring-Gould, author of "Onward Christian Soldiers," was pastor of the North Devon Church in England. He enjoyed showing visitors around the church yard, pointing out things of special interest. He always pointed out the tomb of one of his predecessors, located next to the churchyard wall. The tombstone had been erected by grateful members of the parish, and near the bottom it listed many ways in which this pastor had faithfully fulfilled his ministry of caring, loving service to the members and people of the community.

Baring-Gould would ask visitors if they noticed anything unusual about the grave, someone would remark, "*There is no name on the stone! Who was he?*" "*That's the point,*" the pastor said. *"Generations of children have sat on the bank above the stone, and their dangling feet gradually wore away the pastor's name on the top line, leaving only a listing of the things he did below. His grave marker doesn't say who he was, only what he did."*

People may not remember well who we are or what we have said. But if there are some acts of loving service, some kind words of encouragement, or some good or courageous works of mercy that we have contributed to their lives, those become our true memorial.

I read somewhere, *"Nothing done for a child is ever a waste of time."* That's true of what Jesus has done for us, whether we are young or old. Nothing Jesus did for us was a waste of time. It was all for our eternal benefit.

**"Onward then ye faithful, join the happy throng!"
(from the hymn, "Onward Christian Soldiers")**

May you bless someone today by what you do or say.

There are times in life when winning is not the goal as much as just finishing the race. I wasn't much of an athlete in high school, and the time I got the most applause from a crowd was when I thought I did my worst.

I was running the hurdles on a cinder track, and halfway through the race I lost my balance and fell down. I got up, jumped another hurdle, lost my balance and fell down again. I limped across the finish line to a surprising amount of applause. It was probably because I finally had finished and they wouldn't have to see me fall again.

Being a winner in life may only be getting up when you fall or keeping going when you want to quit. Violinist Itzhak Perlman once had a string break in the midst of a concert solo, but he finished the piece anyway, playing with only three strings and adjusting notes as he played. He later said, *"Sometimes it is the artist's task to find out what music you can still make with what you have left."* That's a great thought from a man unable to walk during his life due to polio.

Perhaps you have taken a fall in life in the form of a huge mistake, a terrible decision, or a time when the cinders of life ground into your legs. If so, it is up to you to get up again, admit your mistake, take responsibility for your decision, and keep on going. If you do, then you are not a failure.

We all fall down in life, and God knows we do. He sees us hit the track on our face or trip over our own feet. But He is always there to pick us up again. He may not stop us from falling, nor promise it won't happen again. But if it does, He will be there for us then, also.

Jesus said, **"Come to me, all who are weary and tired, and I will give you rest." (Matthew 11:28)** His rest refreshes us, and with it will come the chance for a new start. Jesus loves us no matter what and His love will never fail. Today may you find the strength to get up again, and to know the joy our Good Lord will give you to get going again.

"Take my yoke on you and learn from me" (Matt. 11:29)

Find out what music you can make with what you have left.

There is a lot of fear in our world today. Some fear our country is going over the edge economically and politically. The current war against terrorists is complex and never-ending. Churches need help, families need help, even the world itself cries out through its earthquakes and storms.

Yes, there is plenty to fear in our world today. There is crime, battered women and children, cancer, AIDs, and greed. We wonder why politicians want to fix things in the world before they fix things in our own country. Sometimes we feel like a prisoner to forces around us we can't control.

Our Lord and Savior Jesus Christ became a prisoner. In the Garden of Gethsemane, He willingly gave Himself up to the authorities and then walked the way of sorrows to the cross of Calvary. His suffering and death bought us back from the brink of hell.

Jesus didn't run and hide in the face of fear. He didn't avoid danger, but rather put Himself in harm's way for our sakes. Because He did, He's won the battle against Satan, and we have the prize of peace with God.

Jesus is Lord of all, all people, all the world, all the universe. He is also Lord of our fears. His gift to us is His peace, something so precious. It is peace of mind, peace within our soul, a peace that is ours because He Himself is for us, not against us.

No matter how badly life may be treating you right now, no matter how rotten the world may look, no matter how lousy you may feel, remember: God is for you! Who cares who's against you? Don't be afraid. Trust Him, keep praying and watch how things will get better.

"If God is for us, who can be against us? He who did not spare his own Son but gave him up for us all, how will he not also with Him graciously give us all things?" (Romans 8:31-32)

I will try not to be afraid today and hope you will try, too!

MARCH 22

Years ago I saw something unforgettable, a Holstein cow standing in the middle of a California freeway! She should have been in a pasture or feedlot with other cows. Instead, she was munching grass on a narrow portion of the median between the east and westbound lanes of Freeway 91 near Riverside. How did she get there?

One thing was sure, that cow had a problem. If she were to walk one way, she'd be hit by westbound traffic, and if she went the other, some eastbound truck would run her over. In front were oleander bushes and in back was an overpass, so the only thing she could do was to stand where she was and munch grass.

St. Paul told the Christians in Asia Minor something similar. He said, **"That is how you should stand firm in the Lord!" (Philippians 4:1)**. Rather than making a change, he wanted them to stand firm. He wanted them to hold fast to the Gospel, the teaching of salvation by God's grace through faith in Jesus. If they did, they would have eternal life, and they would not be lost eternally.

Veering to the right can lead to legalism and a religion of rules. Going to the left can lead to a life of lawlessness, ignoring God's commands or twisting His Words to justify our actions. It's best to stay in line with Jesus. Holding fast to the Gospel of His forgiveness is the safest way.

I never heard what happened to that cow, but standing firm was the only chance she had of staying alive. I'm sure someone from one of the nearby farms came to her rescue. There are many huge dairy farms in southern California and cows are valuable there.

"Be patient and stand firm, because the Lord's coming is near." (James 5:8)

Stand firm in the Lord! That's good advice for us all.

Do you have enough in life? How much do you need? When is enough, enough?

An elderly mother and her daughter were saying a tearful goodbye at an airport. As she boarded the plane, the mother said, *"I love you, and I wish you enough."* A passenger later asked the woman why she had said, *"I wish you enough."* She said, *"It's a custom in our family to say this when parting. When we say 'I wish you enough' we are wanting the other person to have a life filled with just enough good things to sustain them."* She then recited:

I wish you enough sun to keep your attitude bright.
I wish you enough rain to appreciate the sun more.
I wish you enough happiness to keep your spirit alive.
I wish you enough pain so small joys in life will appear larger.
I wish you enough gain to satisfy your wanting.
I wish you enough loss to appreciate all that you possess.
I wish you enough hellos to get you to the final good-bye.

For many of my years officiating at my weddings, I have prayed for the couple using words adapted from the Bridal Prayer of Louis B. Evans who wrote, *"Give them enough joys to keep them hopeful and enough trials to keep them faithful. Give them enough happiness for daily joy and enough sorrow for daily trust. Give them enough strength for persistence and enough tears for tenderness."*

Do you have enough of what is important? If you want more of anything, will it be worthwhile? Will what you seek be lasting and will it sustain you? In John 14:8, Phillip said, **"Lord, show us the Father, and it is enough for us."**

Jesus did show His disciples what God the Father is like, for He said, **"I and the Father are one." (John 10:30)** Jesus, the Son of the Father, willingly gave His life on the cross for us so we can have enough of what we really need. Today may you have enough faith, hope and love in Jesus Christ to sustain you, and thus be blessed by God in your life.

"Whoever has seen Me has seen the Father." (John 14:9)

With faith in Christ, you already have enough!

MARCH 24

My eldest son was talented in track. During his senior year in high school, Chuck and the other runners were lined up for the 110 meter high hurdle race. It was the first track meet of the season and was held at ten thousand feet, high up in the Colorado mountains. There had been light snowfall, but the clouds finally lifted that morning and it was brisk with a slight wind at their backs.

My son had the center position in this first race of the season. Just as the sun broke through, the starter gun fired and the athletes raced down the field, some smoothly, others not, but for all, an amazing thing happened. All the runners finished in record time. Every runner had his personal best! My son's was the fastest time in the state in years. State record time in the mountains! What a way to start the year!

But then someone counted the hurdles, and measured the distance. The course was wrong. It was too short! Instead of 110 meters, they'd run only 100 meters. Their "record times" didn't count because the race was wrong. When they corrected the error and re-ran the race, no records were set. My son became the state champion in the high hurdles that year, but he did it by running the rest of the season on the correct course at the correct distance.

Our accomplishments won't count if we are doing them wrong or taking shortcuts. Only when we are doing things right, running the correct course and staying within the rules can we achieve anything worthwhile.

Some people think all religions lead to heaven, but that's not true. The only way to eternal life is through faith in Jesus. Only by trusting Him can the race of life lead us to our heavenly goal.

"Run in such a way as to get the prize." (1 Corinthians 9:24)

Let's fix our eyes on the prize, Jesus Christ, who for the good of all, accomplished our salvation.

MARCH 25

Every early Easter morning in Salem, North Carolina, thousands of people make their way to the courtyard of a 200-year-old church founded by the Moravians, followers of John Hus, early German reformer whose teachings were similar to those of Martin Luther. Before daylight, members of various brass bands play hymns. Those not playing listen to the mystical sounding music which echoes all over the city.

At the first hint of the rising sun, a hush falls over the vast crowd. When the church bell tolls six AM, the Bishop emerges from the church and announces loudly, *"Christ is Risen!"* and the crowd thunders back, *"He is Risen indeed!"* The bands then lead the crowd in singing the hymn, *"Christ the Lord Is Risen Today,"* while everyone stands there in the church courtyard.

Then, in total silence, everyone processes to "God's Acre," an ancient cemetery nearby, where polished gravestones are covered with flowers. Even the oldest graves dating back three hundred years are decorated with forsythia, jonquils, tulips, and lilies. The service concludes there with more singing and a remembrance of those who have died since the previous Easter.

In those few moments of awesome silence and sweet floral beauty, it's as if the living are united with the dead. A witness wrote, *"When you are in the midst of all this majesty and beauty, you cannot fail to believe in the resurrection."*

Easter will soon be celebrated in churches across the world, and Christians all will share the joy and hope of the resurrection. The resurrection of Jesus Christ from the grave is the central teaching of the Christian faith.

Christmas is good, but Easter is great! Gifts or songs of a newborn child can make us happy, but Christmas has no meaning without Easter. Easter is proof that Jesus who was born is the Son of God, our living Lord and Savior.

"If Christ be not raised, then our faith is in vain. But Christ has truly been raised from the dead!" (1 Cor. 15:17,20)

I hope you're in a Christian church the Sunday after Easter, too.

MARCH 26

One winter I moved my family to southern California, a difficult move for a Midwestern family. But the Lord Jesus gave us hope through new friends such as Pastor and Mrs. Dave Prust. Dave was associate pastor at a nearby Church and his sense of humor and warmth always made us feel welcome.

A few months after we'd met, Dave was diagnosed with aggressive leukemia. After weeks of treatment at City of Hope, he was strong enough to preach one last sermon at his Church. I took that Sunday off to hear him preach on Romans 5, **"We rejoice in our sufferings, knowing that suffering produces endurance, and endurance character, and character hope."**

Pastor Dave died six months later. In the midst of my anxieties, God sent a dying man to give me hope. In the midst of his illness, God gave Dave hope. All our hope came from God's love in Jesus. Dave showed us that when you're on the freeway of life, God is always there to give you direction. Our hope comes from Jesus, son of man and Son of God.

In Christ our sufferings can produce endurance, the ability to hold on a little longer. Endurance produces character, that inner strength we didn't know we had. Character produces hope, the expectation that something better is soon to come. All this comes to us from God, such as it came to Job in the Old Testament. All suffering has purpose, especially to bring us closer to God.

Every year during Lent I wear a cross over my gowns that Dave's wife gave me. It is a carved wooden crown of thorns and it hangs by a rawhide strong. If you look closely, you will find the cross bears tiny teeth marks of his little daughter Rachel, who often nibbled on it when he held her as he greeted people. Today Rachel is a grown woman with a family of her own. And every year in Lent, I remember Dave as a man who God sent to give me hope.

"Hope does not disappoint us because God's love has been poured into our hearts." (Romans 5:5)

Thank God for people who give us hope.

MARCH 27

"No man is an island, no man stands alone;
Each man's joy is joy to me, each man's grief is my own.
We need one another, so I will defend
Each man as my brother, each man as my friend.
(by John Dunn)

Are you part of a family? If so, how's your family life? We all need to belong to an earthly family and also to a heavenly one. We all need to belong to a family somewhere, no matter how small, because we need to keep connected.

Today we easily can become disconnected. Work, hobbies, interests or retirement take people far away from beloved friends and family. But being miles apart doesn't have to mean separation. You and I can find a community wherever we are. That's why we decide to join clubs, societies, and churches. We all need to belong somewhere. Even today's electronic gadgets and social networks are there to help bring people into communities.

We especially need to belong to a community of God's faithful people, the Church. That's our true spiritual family. When a Christian steps inside the doors of a Church, there actually can be a sense of coming home.

God calls us to come home to His family. Some people believe belonging to a church is unnecessary, that they can "get religion" from nature, reading the Bible alone or watching church on TV. But rarely do they actually try it. It's easy to neglect God when you're not with others. People need human contact to nurture faith. Our faith rarely grows stronger when we are alone. That's usually when our faith gets weaker.

We need one another, and we need to be with our Christian brothers and sisters. There we can love, help, grow in faith and do the many good things with and for others that we cannot do alone. Don't try to be an island, for you do not stand alone.

"What a friend we have in Jesus, all our sins and griefs to bear." (from the hymn)

Today give thanks for your extended family.

MARCH 28

When Lazarus died, his sisters Mary and Martha said to Jesus, **"Lord, if You had been here, my brother would not have died!" (John 11:21)** There was disappointment in those words. Jesus was their friend and they felt He'd let them down when they needed Him most. They had asked Him to come right away when Lazarus was sick, but it was four days before Jesus walked the two miles to their home. By that time, Lazarus was dead and buried.

People can and will disappoint us in life, partly due to their frailties and partly from our expectations. We expect certain things of others, but some of our expectations are unrealistic. We expect people not to fail us. We assume others always will be there to help us and see us through our troubles. Yet who besides God can fix our problems?

You and I should trust God completely, but we should trust people only provisionally. God is holy, but people are not. They are weak and sinful. People cannot always live up to what we expect of them. Only God is without sin, and only He can be trusted for all things. Trusting God completely and trusting people provisionally makes sense. Anything more sets us up for disappointment.

King David, a man who often disappointed others, wrote, **"Do not put your trust in princes, in mortal men, who cannot save." (Psalm 146:3)** We must take care to avoid unrealistic expectations of others and also of ourselves. We will not always succeed as we hope to. Other people cannot fix all things for us. We need to be part of the solution. Our faith cannot be dependent on the Church or a church worker, only on Jesus Christ.

Remember that Jesus has made us a promise He will never break. He said,

"'Never will I leave you, never will I forsake you, says the Lord'." (Hebrews 13:8)

Thank You, Jesus, that You never fail us!

MARCH 29

In 1981, a young single mother stared down at her six year old son, dying of leukemia. Though devastated, she was also determined. One day she asked, *"Billy, what would you like to be when you grow up?"* *"A fireman, Mommy."* he whispered.

Billy's mother went to a fire station and met Fireman Bob. She explained her son's wish and asked if they could give him a ride in a fire engine. Bob said, *"We can do better than that. Have Billy ready Wednesday morning, we'll make him an honorary fireman for the day. He will eat with us, go out on calls, everything. Give us his size and we'll get him a fireman's uniform with boots and a hat."*

Three days later the firemen picked up Billy, dressed him in his uniform and let him sit on the back of the hook-and-ladder truck and "help steer it" to the fire station. Billy even went out on a fire call that day. He sat in the different trucks, a paramedic's van, and rode in the Fire Chief's car. A reporter ran a segment on him for the evening news. Billy rallied and it looked as if his health might improve.

A month later Billy's vital signs began to drop, and the Head Nurse called his family members, saying he'd probably not last the night. She also called the Fire Chief and asked if he could send a fireman to be with Billy in his final hours. The chief replied, *"We'll be there in a truck in five minutes. And ma'am, will you please announce over the PA system that there will be a test run and there is no fire?"*

Minutes later a hook-and-ladder truck arrived with flashing lights. Firemen extended the ladder up to Billy's third floor room and some firefighters climbed through his room window. Each one hugged him and told him he loved him. As the little boy struggled to breathe, the Fire Chief said, *"Billy, the Head Chief Jesus is waiting for you."* Later that night Billy closed his eyes for the last time, a proud little fireman.

"Be devoted to one another in love. Honor one another above yourselves." (Romans 12:10)

Hats off to our firefighters for caring. High hats off to Jesus, the greatest Chief!

MARCH 30

During his heyday, Nikolai Bukharin was as powerful a man as there was on earth. The Russian Communist leader of the Bolshevik Revolution was editor of the Soviet newspaper Pravda and a powerful member of the Politburo. He had achieved one of the highest positions in the Soviet Union. When Nikolai Bukharin spoke, people listened.

He was once addressing a huge assembly on the subject of atheism. On this particular Easter Sunday he hurled insults against Christianity. When he was finished, he demanded, *"Are there any questions?"*

Silence filled the auditorium when a man walked up from the crowd to the lectern and stood next to the communist leader. He surveyed the crowd to the left and then shouted in Russian the ancient Christian greeting: *"Christ is risen!"* The whole crowd arose to its feet and thundered the response: *"He is risen indeed!"*

I don't know what happened to that man after that. He probably paid a big price for his courage. I can only imagine what would happen today if someone made a witness like that after a public speech by an American president. He would be pummeled by the newspapers. I am certain this Russian man was harshly punished.

But the man had made his point. The resurrection of Jesus Christ is the central point of human history. Without it, the world would be doomed. But since Jesus has come, nothing has ever been the same.

Easter is the time to celebrate Christ's new life amid the world's death and destruction. It is a time to be renewed by the promise of our own resurrection. Thanks be to God that Jesus did rise from the grave. He gives us courage for life now, and the promise of a future life to come.

"Christ has been raised from the dead!" (Romans 15:20)

Give thanks for willing witnesses to the faith!

92

The following words were written by a Confederate soldier as he was recuperating from his wounds in a makeshift hospital. The soldier died there, and these lines were found among his possessions:

> *I asked God for strength, that I might achieve,*
> *I was made weak, that I might learn humbly to obey.*
> *I asked for health, that I might do greater things,*
> *I was given infirmity that I might do better things.*
> *I asked for riches, that I might be happy,*
> *I was given poverty, that I might be wise.*
> *I asked for power, that I might have the praise of men,*
> *I was given weakness, that I might feel the need of God.*
> *I asked for all things, that I might enjoy life,*
> *I was given life, that I might enjoy all things.*
> *I got nothing that I asked for, but everything I had hoped for.*
> *Almost despite myself, my unspoken prayers were answered.*
> *I am, among all men, most richly blessed.*

I have pondered these words many times since first reading them. Here was a mortally wounded man who had given his life for a lost cause. He knew his time was short, and yet he didn't dwell on his failures, but on what he had learned from his experiences.

He did not get what he wanted in life, but he realized he had gotten what he needed. His legacy to us comes in the last two lines, *"Almost despite myself, my unspoken prayers were answered. I am, among all men, most richly blessed."*

His prayers were answered by God, and thus He was richly blessed. You and I may never have to face the horrors of war such as this man did, but we can still find ourselves, *"most richly blessed."*

"My times are in Your hands, O Lord." (Psalm 31:15)

May we all have such faith in God's will for our life!

APRIL

+ + +

APRIL 1

April 1 is a day to pull harmless jokes on those around us. The origin of April Fool's Day is unclear. Until the Sixteenth Century, the western world used the Julian calendar which began each year on our March 25, usually during Holy Week, so some New Year's festivals were pushed back to April 1.

When the Gregorian calendar came into use, it moved New Year's Day to January 1. Some think April Fool's Day was to trick people into thinking April 1 was still New Year's. Others made April Fool's Day a carry-over from the Romans' riotous end-of-winter celebration, Hilaria, held March 21.

We live in a highly educated time of history. People pride themselves in finding explanations for almost everything. But of all the explanations of human wisdom, none explains the presence of evil in the world. How did evil get here? And since evil is so obvious, why do "evolving" people keep doing such terrible things to each other? Despite our advances, many bad things in the world seem to be getting worse.

Make no mistake about it, evil does exist. People believe God exists, also, even if they don't acknowledge Him. Evil is not some trick God has played on us. It's the work of Satan, another personality who truly exists and hates God. God's love is more powerful than Satan's evil, and that's good news.

April 1 is a time to give thanks that Jesus is God's true and living Son. His death is a historical fact, and so is His resurrection. Christ's perfect life on earth, His atoning death and His new life again have defeated the forces of evil. God loves us, and that's the greatest fact of all.

"The fool says in his heart there is no God." (Ps. 14:1)

Jesus is alive, and that's no joke!

95

APRIL 2

One year on Palm Sunday, my son's father-in-law passed away unexpectedly. He had not been feeling well and thought it was the flu. He had seemed in good health, so his passing at age seventy-two was a shock to all who knew him. He was a quiet Christian man whose father was a Lutheran pastor.

I asked my son whether their small children knew their Grandpa had died. He said they did know because they had heard their Mom crying on the phone and asked why. *"But I don't believe they understand what's really happened,"* he said.

A short time later Chuck told me their six year-old son had asked, *"Does Grandpa like his new room?"* The question stopped my son cold. It seems he had told the boy that when a person dies believing in Jesus, God gives him a new room to live in, a room up in heaven just like he wants it. Thus came his question, *"Does Grandpa like his new room?"*

My son talked with him about this and then asked him what he would like to have in his new room in heaven. He said without hesitation, *"Escalators, fans and lots of stuffed animals."* Those three things had recently fascinated him, and he wanted his room filled with them.

What would you like in your new room? How would you explain a Christian's death to a small child? How would you explain to a child the blessings of heaven and eternal life with Jesus? Are you ready for your new room?

During Holy Week we are assured again that Jesus did all that was necessary so that we can all go to the new room God has prepared for us. Although a death in the family can be a somber reminder each year, but it can fill us with joy because a Grandpa and Dad, a husband, uncle or friend, now has a new heavenly room prepared for Him by Jesus, our Risen Savior.

"In my Father's house are many room. I am going to prepare a place for you." (John 14:2)

In my room I want a recliner, a large print Bible, and a door leading to all my loved ones.

APRIL 3

Cactus flowers are blooming in Arizona this time of year. Lovely and fragile pink, yellow, white and red flowers dot the tips of the green and gray cactus pods, and for a short time they make us forget the sharp needles that protect them.

There are hundreds of varieties of cacti, from the tiny half inch lilliput cactus to the forty foot giant saguaro. All are succulent plants, retaining water in their leaves and stems, adapting themselves to the desert climate. Cacti are found as far north as Canada and are native mostly to the Americas, though a few varieties live in dry parts of Africa and Sri Lanka. Most common is the prickly pear with hundreds of varieties.

Oh yes, they all have cactus needles! Sharp spines from a thirty-second of an inch to four inches long can penetrate cloth and skin. Cacti live mostly dormant lives, taking in water and food when it's available, using what it has stored up when it is not. A mature saguaro can drink up 500 gallons of water in a week during the monsoon rains, storing it for the coming dry weeks. Birds, butterflies, bats, bees and small animals depend on cacti for food and housing.

I have a dozen and a half varieties of cacti in my garden at our Arizona winter home, all received from neighbors. A cactus cutting can set down roots in a few months and grow in the hardest of desert soils. It will live a long time without water, In the spring, cactus flowers beautify the desert.

God has created such an amazing world. Despite so many who accept the theory of evolution, Christians believe the world didn't come by chance but by God's Intelligent Design. Belief in God is not a complex thing.

With God all things are possible. He created all things and wants people with Him. But sin and evil have come into the world, so God sent His Son Jesus to take away the punishment that sin and evil require. What remains is for us to trust in Jesus, and the Holy Spirit helps us do that. God makes all things possible, including accepting sinful people into heaven.

"The earth is the Lord's, and everything in it, the world, and all who live in it." (Psalm 24:1)

To believe in God, we just need to get out of His way.

APRIL 4

The end of the winter season at an RV park often brings items left next to the garbage dumpsters. These are unwanted items that usually still work, and are left for someone else to take. People in RVs are good at recycling.

One April day as I dropped off some scraps of wood, I picked up a small item sitting on the ground. It was a nearly new red Dirt Devil corded hand vacuum. I took it home and, as I suspected, it just needed a good cleaning to make it work like new. It had an adapter hose for narrow spaces, just what I need for getting the dust out of our window tracks.

The next day I drove past the dumpsters and there sat another vacuum, this time a black upright Dirt Devil. Again I took it home, emptied the dirt chamber, and cleaned the filter. Now we have an upright vacuum that is better than our old model for picking up the desert dust. The next day I put our old, but still working, vacuum by the dumpster for someone else to use. It was soon gone.

Both of these abandoned items had the same problem - their owners forgot to empty the dirt. It made me think of our need for spiritual cleansing through confession and absolution. If we don't get all our "sin dirt" removed by forgiveness, soon nothing in our life works well.

Calvary is God's eternal garbage dumpster. When Jesus died, He got rid of all our sins. The Bible says He has removed our sins from us, **"As far as the east is from the west." (Psalm 103:12)** That makes Jesus our divine Garbage Man, and what He removes is gone forever.

The next time your life seems out of kilter, check whether or not you need to do some personal house-cleaning. It's always good to clean up regularly.

"If we confess our sins, He is faithful and just and will forgive us, and cleanse us from unrighteousness." (1 John 1:9)

Jesus empties our Devilish Dirt. Now there's an interesting theological concept!

APRIL 5

A friend wrote that her grandparents were married for over half a century and played their own special game. The goal of their game was to write the word "SHMILY" in a surprise place for the other to find. They left SHMILY around the house and as soon as one discovered it, it was the other's turn to put SHMILY somewhere for the other to find.

They wrote SHMILY with their fingers through the sugar and flour containers. They smeared it in the dew on the windows or mirrors. SHMILY was scribbled on the lunch sack and Grandma once unrolled an entire roll of toilet paper and wrote SHMILY here and there until the very last sheet.

SHMILY messages were found in the car and on the bed pillows. It was in the dust on the mantel and ashes of the fireplace. Her grandparents knew the meaning of love. SHMILY was more than a flirtatious little game; it was their way of life. Their relationship was based on a devotion and affection and they held hands every chance they could.

Even at their advanced ages they stole kisses, finished each other's sentences and shared the daily crossword puzzle. Before meals they bowed and gave thanks, marveling at their blessings, a wonderful family, good fortune and each other.

When Grandma got cancer, Grandpa helped all he could. He painted her room yellow so that she could always be surrounded by sunshine. They still went to church every week until Grandma couldn't leave home anymore.

When Grandma died, SHMILY was scrawled on yellow and pink ribbons of her casket bouquet. As the crowd thinned and family members gathered around Grandma one last time. Grandpa stepped up to her casket and sang to her. Though they already knew, he told his family that SHMILY meant, *"See How Much I Love You?"*

God shows us His love every day in many ways. See it in the smiles of loved ones, in the yellow daffodils, the blue sky or white snow. God's most wondrous SHMILY was written on the open tomb as the angel told the women,

"He is not here; He is risen." (Matthew 28:6)

See How Much He Loves You? ("SHMHLY")

99

APRIL 6

Are you happy? We often try to convince ourselves that life will be better after certain things happen. For instance, after we get married and have a baby we're sure we'll be happy. When we are frustrated that our baby is so helpless, so we think we'll be happier when he's grown.

We're sure we'll be happier when our spouse solves that problem, or when we get a new car, or when we can take a long vacation, or get out of debt, or change jobs, or get better neighbors, or something else.

The truth is, however, there's no better time to be happy than right now. Or at least we can be content. Life will always be filled with challenges. We need to realize this and decide to find our contentment. Happiness is more a result of our decisions than our feelings.

Many of us think happiness exists outside ourselves. But there will always be some obstacle in the way, something to happen first, some unfinished business to complete before life will become truly good. We don't realize that obstacles are part of what life is made of.

So stop waiting for happiness to come until you finish school, or lose ten pounds, or the kids leave home, or you get married, or the car is paid off, or until you retire. Now is the time you can be content. Happiness is a by-product of life, not a major goal. Happiness comes during our journey with Jesus. It is His gift along the way, not the final destination.

St. Paul learned about happiness and contentment, and he wrote about it with these words from prison: **"I have learned to be content whatever the circumstance. I can do all things through Him who gives me strength."**(Philippians 4:11, 13)

Happiness is fleeting and is more about excitement, fun, and material things. Contentment lasts longer. It's finding joy in life and satisfaction in work, nature and life. If we strive to be happy we will be less content. If we strive to be content will be more patient, caring, and happier.

Like Jesus, **"Who for the joy that was set before Him endured the cross, despised the shame, and is seated at the right hand of the throne of God."** (Hebrews 12:2)

Pray that this attitude becomes your attitude.

APRIL 7

Carol and I once took a short trip to England. Low airfares and a few extra vacation days moved us to go where we'd wanted for years. We packed a lot of travel in those six days, seeing major London sites, Bath and Stonehenge, Oxford, Warwick Castle, Stratford on Avon. And we saw a lot of people driving on the "wrong side of the road."

Everywhere we went, newspapers bore headlines of a tragedy back home that happened just as we left, the murder of many students at Columbine High School. We found the English people to be friendly, and when we told them we were from Colorado they all expressed sadness over the tragedy and gave us encouragement.

We stayed five nights at a Bed and Breakfast in Kent, forty miles east of London. It was a converted rectory from the mid-1800s, and Carol was sure it still had some of the original dust.

Sunday we worshipped at All Saints Church in Birling, one of four small churches in this Anglican Parish. The locals called it the "new" church, though its original building was from the 1400s. The Trottiscliffe church was the "old" one, originally built in 788 AD, under King Offa of the Saxons. The Trottiscliffe church has held its 1200th anniversary.

There were only ten other people with us at All Saint's Church that morning, but all greeted us warmly. During prayers the Deacon prayed for the people of Denver. Something about that prayer will always remain with me, not the words, but the memory those few English Christians included us Americans in their petitions during a time of need.

Some may recall the powerful witness of Cassie Bernall, who was killed that day after confessing her faith in God. God uses many means to bring hope to the lost of this world. Our world looks grim at times, but God has a purpose in everything. We must seek to find that purpose, no matter how bad things may get. We must learn to accept that God's will is best for us.

"The Lord gives strength to His people; the Lord blesses His people with peace." (Psalm 29:11)

May God help us find hope even amid senseless violence.

A group of some forty soldiers walked into the Atlanta, Georgia, air terminal, and the civilians there stood up and cheered. It was spontaneous and a great moment to be there.

From the crowd a young girl ran up to one of the soldiers who knelt down and said, *"Hi."* The little girl asked if he would give something to her daddy for her. The soldier, in his early 20s, said he would try and give her daddy the gift. The little girl hugged him and kissed him on the cheek.

The girl's mother stepped forward and explained that her husband was a Marine in Iraq for eleven months and how much Courtney missed him.

The other soldiers huddled together and one pulled out a cell phone. He talked on the device a minute or so, and then walked back to Courtney, bent down and said, *"I just spoke to your daddy and he told me to give this to you."* And he gave her a kiss on the cheek. He said, *"Your daddy loves you so much and he is coming home very soon."* Then the soldier stood and saluted Courtney and her mother. There were few dry eyes among the crowd in that moment.

The applause resumed as the soldiers headed toward their gate. The young soldier turned at the last moment and blew Courtney a kiss as a big tear rolled down his face.

We need to remember our soldiers and service personnel every day and pray for them and their families. We thank God for their sacrifices. Regardless of what some may say, these men and women are true heroes.

If our soldiers, sailors and airmen were not defending our freedom, we would certainly fail at defending it ourselves. The enemy is close to the gate, and he has the money, will and ways to destroy us. May God give us protection to keep that from happening.

"Serve one another humbly in love." (Galatians 5:13)

We live in the land of the free, only because of the brave.

After the resurrection when Jesus' disciples saw Him alive again, several of them decided to go fishing, perhaps in an attempt to get their lives back to normal, the way things used to be. When the resurrected Christ saw them in the boat, He challenged them to try something new, to **"fish out of the other side of the boat." (John 21:6)**

When the Lord first comes into your life, nothing is normal, the way it used to be. Old challenges seem less important. Old friends may not understand us. Sin isn't as much fun, and our consciences keep us from participating in many of the old ways.

Sometimes Christians need to get out of the ruts of this world, to hear again the voice of Jesus calling us to try the "other side." The gods of this age, such as power, pleasure, possessions or play, can distract us and keep us living in the old ways, promising much but delivering only dust and ashes. But Jesus calls us to something better, to try the "other side."

Perhaps now is the time for you to try the other side in your life. Whether our gods come in the shape of a dollar bill or a football or a shapely person, whether we're falling apart or think we have it all together, no matter the circumstances, we need to follow the Lord's advice and try the other side.

That side is His side, and it is the one that delivers what He promises: love, joy, peace, patience, kindness and all the other fruit of the Spirit. Trying the side of Jesus may change things, maybe even turn your life upside down, but it will be the best thing that has happened to you in a long time.

"But the fruit of the Spirit is love, joy, peace, patience, kindness, goodness, faithfulness, gentleness and self-control. Against such things there is no law." (Galatians 5:22-23)

Worship the Lord with His people somewhere this Sunday.

Each year on "Baptist Day," the University of Chicago Divinity School invites a distinguished person to lecture to its students and faculty as they enjoy a picnic lunch on the lawn.

One year, invited guest Dr. Paul Tillich spoke there for two and one-half hours "proving" that the resurrection of Jesus was false. He quoted scholar after scholar and book after book, concluding that since there was no proof for the historical resurrection, the resurrection must be emotional mumbo-jumbo. It was based on a false notion that someone was capable of rising from the dead.

When he asked if there were any questions, an old preacher stood up and said, *"I have a question."* He held up an apple and began eating it. *"Dr. Tillich, is the apple I'm eating bitter or sweet?"* Tillich paused a moment and said, *"I cannot possibly answer that question, for I haven't tasted your apple."* The old preacher dropped the core of his apple into his paper bag and said calmly, *"Neither have you tasted my Jesus."*

Our relationship with God rests on faith, not on proof. It rests on faith that God's Word is true and trustworthy. Dr. Tillich tried to prove Jesus' resurrection was false with his "proof" of what others said. He and the others forgot that the faith of Christians rests on faith alone.

This Easter Sunday, Christian believers all over the world will gather again to re-affirm their conviction that Jesus of Nazareth is King of the Jews and Lord of the whole world. That is the meaning of the four letters we often see artists use to depict Jesus. "INRI" in Latin means *"Jesus Nazarenus Rex Ioudiorum,"* meaning, *"Jesus of Nazareth, King of the Jews."* The Son of God, has indeed risen. May you also worship Him Easter Sunday, and the next Sunday after that.

"Taste and see that the LORD is good." (Psalm 34:8)

Jesus Christ always outlasts His skeptics.

APRIL 11

After worship one Sunday my wife and our youngest son and I enjoyed a brunch at a cafe. It was our son's birthday and we were glad to be with him and talk of his new position with an organization that helps people with seizures. But as we enjoyed our food, we weren't thinking about those who made our lunch possible, the night workers, delivery people, garbage men, government workers, medical workers, soldiers, police and all others helping in our nation. They are all part of a life we take for granted.

We modern Americans have so many amazing things. We turn on a light switch, knowing we will get light. We turn on a faucet to get clean, safe water, heated with natural gas or cooled in our refrigerator which is filled with healthy food easily purchased in well-stocked grocery stores.

We take our medicines that are safe and we slip into comfortable, inexpensive clothing made halfway around the world. We sit in a favorite chair made in South America reading a book or watching a television made in China. All of these things are there for us, and we don't think a thing about them until something doesn't work as planned.

Computers, cell phones and automobiles take us places unimaginable only decades ago. We have so much and yet can become easily upset when things go awry. Sewers can clog, products can disappoint, and plans may not work out. But all in all, we have such abundant blessings in our lives.

We live in a nation free from tyranny. There are times of sadness or disappointment, but there is so much less evil to contend with here than in other places in the world. God is good to us, far better than we deserve. The next time you complain about a product, service or politician, think where you might have been born or live, rather than in the United States of America. Then think what life would be like if you did not have the hope of eternal life in Christ Jesus our Lord.

"But godliness with contentment is great gain. For we brought nothing into the world, and we can take nothing out of it." (1 Timothy 6:6-7)

God is good!

Easter is life-changing. It outlasts all of history's fleeting movements. It was May Day, 1990, during the last celebration of its kind. The USSR was celebrating its military might with a review of the troops in their annual May Day parade. The fall of the Berlin wall the previous November had cast a shadow over this parade, because things were changing. No longer was Communism the powerful force it had been. It was dying, and its people knew it.

As the parade neared completion, an amazing display brought up the end. For the very first time in any May Day parade since the 1917 revolution, a huge cross was carried by two large priests and several parishioners who held it upright with ropes. They had marched on foot the entire parade route holding up that cross.

As they approached the review stand where Premier Mikael Gorbechev and other dignitaries watched the troops, tanks, rockets and military might, they heard chants of protestors: *"More food! More Justice!"*

At that moment one of the priests carrying the cross shouted in a booming voice, *"Mikael Gorbechev!"* The Soviet president turned as the two priests lifted the cross higher, casting a thin shadow across the review stand with its photos of Marx, Lenin and Engels. The priest again shouted, *"Mikael Gorbechev!"* Then he added, *"Christ is arisen! Christ is arisen!"*

Over two thousands years ago, Christ's resurrection changed the world. Nothing was ever the same after Jesus of Nazareth arose from the dead. Modern history begins from that point. People were given hope that through Jesus Christ, death no longer holds a permanent curse over them. Through His resurrection, God promises that we, too, shall rise.

The resurrection of Jesus Christ overshadows all politics, all nations and all peoples. Christ is risen!

"Christ has indeed been raised from the dead." (1 Corinthians 15:20)

He is risen indeed!

We never know what effect our small acts of faith may have on others or even on the future. In Matthew 14, Jesus had been teaching a large crowd in a remote area, and during a break His disciples told Him that He should send them away because they were hungry and needed to find their own food. Jesus said, **"You give them something to eat."** (Matthew 14:16) They said they didn't have money enough, and all they could find were five small loaves of bread and two dried fish. **"How far will this go among so many?"** asked skeptical Andrew.

You know the rest of the story. That little lunch fed five thousand people with food to spare because it was blessed by Jesus. The famous lunch probably came from a small boy who heard the disciples saying they had no food and offered them what little he had. Lest you think you don't have much to offer Jesus, consider this story.

Edward Kimball, a Boston Sunday School teacher, decided to visit a young man in his class to see if he knew Christ. His visit led to the conversion of Dwight L. Moody. Moody became the most famous evangelist of the Nineteenth Century who had a major impact on evangelist Wilbur Chapman. Chapman shared his faith with Billy Sunday who received Jesus as Lord, joined his campaign and helped lead thousands of others to Christ.

Billy Sunday launched his own national ministry with great results in cities like Charlotte, North Carolina. At one of his revivals, Billy Sunday was assisted by evangelist Mordecai Ham who invited a young man there to receive Jesus as His Savior. That young man was Billy Graham, the most prominent world evangelist of the Twentieth Century.

If you think you don't have much to offer, remember Edward Kimball who spent an afternoon witnessing to a young man from his class. God has a special way of using our small, routine acts of faithfulness to accomplish great things.

"Lord, teach us to pray." (Luke 11:1)

What small but important act of faith might you do today?

APRIL 14

I was once driving the Interstate in a spring snowstorm. It was dark and traffic had slowed to a crawl. Only a few crazy drivers sped past the rest of us who moved along at the right speed for the conditions. It gave me time to ponder things, such as the several bumper stickers on the car ahead.

The driver had an interesting view of life. One bumper sticker read, *"Prodigiously Pondering Paranoia."* Another, *"Meddle Not in the Affairs of Dragons."* A third recalled Star Trek TV series (*"Boldly going where no man has gone before."*) This sticker read, *"Boldly Going Nowhere."*

"Boldly Going Nowhere" is interesting. Today everyone is going somewhere, day or night, and often a bit too fast. But *"Boldly Going Nowhere?"* Had he had no destination, plans or goals? Was this his motto, or just a bumper sticker?

A car ahead of me slid into the ditch on the slick road. I slowly rounded the curve when I suddenly remembered that a new donut shop had opened, and I could have one of their donut delights as I drove.

Alas! Their parking lot was full, and the drive-through lane was ten cars deep. Not even 10:30 PM and a Colorado blizzard could keep some people from the delights of their favorite new donut store!

I passed up the shop, deciding to come another time, perhaps tomorrow morning before Easter Sunrise service. No one will be there then, I thought. Such thoughts made me wonder if I, too, was *"Boldly Going Nowhere."*

A friend brought me six fresh donuts the following morning. She'd stood in line a half hour to get them. They were very good, but not nearly as good as her thoughtfulness.

We are all boldly or timidly going somewhere, and Easter Sunday's Resurrection Good News gives us hope it will be heaven, not perdition. Jesus' payment for our sin was enough. His resurrection assures a place with God. May each one of us find hope and joy and peace in these resurrection days.

"I know that my Redeemer lives." (Job 19:25)

CHRIST IS RISEN! HE IS RISEN INDEED!

Sometimes one day in a month can have many meanings. Today is "Tax Day." It can come during Holy Week or even fall on Easter. In our family, it's also the birthday of a loved one, Miranda, my mother-in-law, who was born on April 15th, and is now with the Lord.

Miranda was a devoted wife, career nurse, doting mother, proud grandmother, wise sister and aunt, reluctant farmwife and dedicated Lutheran woman. She was also a gemologist who enjoyed examining and grading the diamonds and other gems she sold from her small Iowa store. Her father had died when she was very young so she developed a strong sense of independence, duty and purpose as she lived out her faith and life. To me her greatest legacy is her daughter, my dear wife Carol.

We may wonder what difference we make in the lives of others. God brings many special people into our lives, people who don't merely cross our path but who truly make a difference, people who make our life better, more fun, more interesting. Miranda was such a person.

If you have one of those special people in your life, tell them that you care about them. Tell them today. Make a phone call or send a card. An Email is okay, but hearing your voice will be better. Christ makes our life richer through people who live out their faith and show us God's love every day. May you be one of those persons who enrich the life of someone else you meet today.

If April 15th is a day that raises your blood pressure, remember the good country you live in. Taxes are no fun to pay, but through them we receive many blessings. Let's therefore pray our elected leaders use them wisely and productively.

"By this everyone will know that you are my disciples, if you love one another." (John 13:35)

Happy Tax Day! Is that possible to have?

APRIL 16

Our first reaction to adversity is fear or sadness. When Judy Robles was just sixteen years old, she gave birth to her first child by Cesarean section. In the recovery room she asked what the baby's gender was and if the baby was okay. The doctor said he was a boy, but later her parents told her the news: her tiny son had a birth defect and would never walk like a normal child. That night and for many nights after, young mother Judy cried.

But Judy Robles was not crying on a special spring weekend in 2011. Her son Anthony, an athlete at Arizona State, had become a champion. It was Anthony's last match of his career and the crowd gave him a standing ovation as soon as his dominating win was complete. *"I'd prepared for this moment all year,"* he said, *"and I was scared. As soon as I hit the first takedown, I said, 'Okay, back to business'."* Anthony defeated the two-time national champion from the University of Iowa.

Robles has greater upper body strength than most of his opponents, and his style forces them to stay low. *"I didn't get into wrestling for the attention."* he said, *"I love the sport and am pleased when I can help motivate others to do things they wouldn't have thought possible."* In the medal ceremony he stood tall as he received his award as the NCAA Wrestling Champion at 125 pounds. You see, Anthony Robles was born with only one leg.

Anthony's success is not only in his overcoming adversity, but also in achieving his goals. Our success in life is not dependent on how we start life, but what we do during life and how we finish it. Jesus of Nazareth had a fine beginning but a terrible ending. Yet even death on the cross did not define His life. His resurrection did. His loss of life on Friday was prelude to His regaining it on Sunday. Jesus is not remembered for His dying, but for His rising again.

"I lay down my life, only to take it up again." (John 10:17)

May we, too, rise above our struggles, and with the help of God join the Saints in glory.

Christianity does not hold the Resurrection to be merely one of its important beliefs, it is the most important belief of all. Without the Resurrection, there'd be no Christianity. Martin Luther once wrote, *"The Gospel does not explain the Resurrection. The Resurrection explains why we have the Gospel."*

Easter is not only about Christ's resurrection, it's about our own resurrection, too. St. Paul wrote, **"Since death came through a man, the resurrection of the dead comes also through a man. For as in Adam all die, so in Christ all will be made alive." (1 Corinthians 15:21-22)**

Winston Churchill planned part of his own funeral, which took place in 1965 at Saint Paul's Cathedral in London. He asked to have included many great hymns of the church, as well as the Anglican funeral liturgy. He also asked that after the benediction had been said, a bugler, positioned high in the front dome of Saint Paul's, would play "Taps" whose lyrics are,

> *"Day is done, gone the sun*
> *From the lake, from hill from sky.*
> *All is well, safely rest, God is nigh."*

It was to be a touching moment, but the drama was not over. As soon as "Taps" ended, a bugler on the opposite side of the great dome immediately played "Reveille."

> *"It's time to get up. It's time to get up.*
> *It's time to get up in the morning!"*

Those who attended his funeral said this touch of "Churchillian" humor was his testimony that the end for the Christian would not be "Taps," but "Reveille!" When a believer comes to the end of life, he knows God is there to give eternal blessings from His Lord Jesus Christ.

"The trumpet will sound, and the dead will be raised imperishable, and we shall all be changed." (1 Corinthians 15:52)

In Jesus Christ, it's time to get up!

In 1 Peter chapter one, the apostle wrote, **"Blessed be God and the Father of our Lord Jesus Christ! By His great mercy we have been born anew to a living hope through the resurrection of Jesus Christ from the dead."**

In 1994, Sarajevo was under siege. Mortars and artillery fire had transformed the once beautiful city into rubble. Sarajevo's citizens were frightened, weary and increasingly despondent. One February day, a mortar shell exploded in the market killing sixty-eight civilians and wounding many more.

That same day a cellist with the Sarajevo symphony could no longer deal with the death and destruction. He took his cello to the market place, sat down amidst the rubble and played a short concert. Then he picked up his instrument and left. He came back to the market the next day and every day thereafter, for sixty-seven days, each time playing a concert as his gift of love to the city. He said he did it because he felt his community needed hope.

Hope is music of the heart. It is a gift given each of us to see us through the night. Once you've lost hope, you have little left. Hopelessness tries to kill everything it touches, but a living hope in Jesus Christ gives us strength to continue, whether it be in a marriage worth saving or a life worth living.

When all things around us are in chaos and ruin, hope is the music that still goes on. In this vast and infinite universe, you and I are not alone. During those times when all may seem to be crumbling down around you, listen for the music in your heart, the song of hope given you by the Lord. Listen carefully, for it is there, played for you by the Lord Jesus who loves you.

Then in some place, public or private, and in some way, raise your voice to God in your own music of hope.

"Remember Your mercy, O Lord, and Your steadfast love, for they have been from of old." (Psalm 25:6)

May you all have a living hope in Christ because He is risen!

APRIL 19

One Thursday in late April, a nasty windstorm moved through our dry area. It reminded me of a much bigger storm that happened when I was a five year old boy on our farm.

On a hot August day the western sky had turned pitch black and my father came running into our house shouting that a big storm was coming. He went back outside to close doors and tend the livestock while my mother hurried to close doors and windows in the house.

When the wind came, the trees around our house bent over almost flat, and I remember watching as the storm clouds blew over a big tree in our east pasture, a tree so huge I never imagined it could fall. It was a fearful time, but I still remember some details although it happened sixty years ago.

My teenage older sister, however, was more calm. While the rest of us hurried about in fear, Marian sat down at the piano and played a song. Then she came over, took my hand and said something I've never forgotten, *"Stick to me like a tick, and you'll be just fine."* She held me close till the storm was over so I wouldn't be afraid.

When you're unsure of what's happening out there, it's best to stick close to those who love you. But when you're all alone with nothing to lean on, like that mighty tree by itself in the pasture, the winds of life can blow you down, no matter how strong you might think you are. It is best to have someone strong to lean on, someone who will always be there. The best "Someone" is Jesus.

Stick close to the Lord and His people and you'll have the best chance of withstanding whatever storms bring. There's strength in being with the people that God gives us, but if we try to live our life all alone, we may be blown over.

"Stand firm and hold fast to the teachings we passed on to you." (2 Thessalonians 2:15)

Praise God for giving us loved ones who care!

I have an old piano that I fixed up. I bought it for fifty dollars and put another hundred into it. I repaired the internal parts as the best I could, gave it several coats of black paint on the outside, repaired the keys and tuned it the best I could. It didn't sound very good, but after all that work, it sounded good enough for me.

Alas! A professional tuner came and said my old piano was so bad it would never be worth tuning. I told him it was worth a lot to me because it still made music, and the way I played, who needed a better one? He chuckled, but still wouldn't tune it. No matter. My old piano is still valuable because of all the work I've put into it. I have some tuning tools and make it sound the best I can.

My old piano reminds me of myself, and maybe of you. We've been cracked and broken and worn down by sin, but God has repaired us in Jesus. We've made some ugly sounds at times, but we know we will be tuned perfectly by the One who loves us.

Despite all our chips and cracks, we have been covered with God's perfectly restoring righteousness. Though we may feel worthless, by the grace of God we can still make a little good music for ourselves and others.

God doesn't ask us to be in perfect condition, just repairable. With faith in Christ, we are valuable to the Heavenly Tuner. We may feel cheap, but to Him we are precious. He repairs our cracked frame, covers our chipped exterior and helps us make sweet music in our lives.

If you wonder whether or not you're good enough, just think of that old piano. I value it because of what I did for it in repairs, just like God values us because of what He did for us in Jesus.

"They sing to the music of timbrel and lyre; they make merry to the sound of the pipe." (Job 21:12)

Rejoice in the One who loves us because of all He's done for us.

APRIL 21

It often gets up to a hundred degrees during April in Arizona, so it was no surprise that my wife and I enjoyed the series, "The Frozen Planet." Each program showed the amazing abilities of God's adaptable creatures in the frozen north and south poles of our planet, or on mountain peaks.

One episode centered on a mother polar bear and her growing cubs who struggled during the plus fifty degree summer days and flourished during the minus fifty degree winter days. Even being from Minnesota didn't help me relate well to those temperature extremes.

Another program showed a variety of Arctic birds helping their little ones learn to fly by flying underneath them for "lift" so they wouldn't land on the tundra and become a fox's lunch. The parent bird made sure the juvenile made a water landing so it would stay alive and be able to fly again.

We are living on a most wonderful planet, despite what doomsday prophets may tell us. We are residents of a privileged planet God has created which allows humans to prosper and flourish as in no other age and on no other planet. Despite fears of global warming or a weakened America, we live in the most amazing time of history. For this we give God unceasing thanks and praise.

We should also be actively sharing the story of our faith in Jesus. The Sunday before in church we'd heard the President of my alma mater, Concordia Seminary in St. Louis, urge us to do just that. Despite what we may be led to believe, he said, today is a good time to be a Christian. It is a great time to be a pastor or a layperson who tells of Jesus. It is an fine time to let the Holy Spirit do His work of bringing people to faith.

In the desert it can reach one hundred ten degrees in the day and forty degrees at night, a seventy degree difference - amazing! But we sinners, though worthy of hell, are made saints by the death and life of Jesus. That's even more amazing!

"To everything there is a season and a time to every purpose under heaven." (Ecclesiastes 3:1)

Thanks be to God for His amazing mercies new to us each day!

For several of the last years of my ministry before retirement, Carol and I went every Tuesday afternoon to a local Nursing Home for a weekly worship service that I led there for the residents. One of the people we looked forward to seeing was a fellow who looked like Mr. Magoo, a bald and squinty-eyed fellow with a quirky little smile. His name was Robert Little, but we called him "Sarge" because of his gruff voice and the fact that he was an army sergeant in World War Two.

One week Sarge didn't come to the service, and I realized he hadn't come the week before either. After the service I asked about him. The news was not good. Sarge had died and was already buried.

They said the last time he felt good was at my Tuesday service a few days before he died. They said after we'd left he had sat in his wheelchair by the piano, humming some of the hymns we'd just sung. Two days later he died, and it was a shock to all. Many staff and volunteers had grown attached to Sarge and they missed him. One can only hope some of the Gospel messages he'd heard during my services there had helped to strengthen his faith in Christ.

Sisters Mary and Martha of Bethany were shocked when their brother Lazarus died suddenly, but they believed Jesus could help them. They and all their friends were all amazed when Jesus raised their brother from the dead. The message and joy of Easter are still with us. We know He will also raise all believers, in the last day. For that, we rejoice and give thanks to our loving God.

"I am the Resurrection and the Life. Whoever believes in Me, though he dies, yet shall he live, and whoever lives and believes in Me shall never die." (John 11:25-26)

May you live and believe in Jesus for eternal life!

APRIL 23

A few years back, one of my colleagues preached a sermon on the theme, "EASTER or EASIER?" His concept was that with the addition or removal of a small line above the "I," the word changes completely. "EASTER or EASIER?" The difference between the two was found in the cross. Do we Christians want to live the EASTER life or do we want to live the EASIER life?

Our modern-day conveniences make life enjoyable. Gone are the days of hauling water, chopping wood, butchering meat and sewing all our clothes. Those things are now optional, replaced by ready-made items or inventions. Gone are the days of one-dimensional communication when we spoke into the telephone. That's all been replaced by cell phones, Skype, satellites and electronic messaging.

Gone too, it seems, are the days of mutual respect, security and honor. These have often been replaced by fear, suspicion and relative values. We're seeing that more choices and easier communication are not making our lives better. Maybe we should stop trying to make things easier, and make them more like Easter.

In the days leading up to Easter, Jesus did what was necessary, not what was easiest. He did what God wanted Him to do, walking a human road littered with rocks of discontent, hatred and sin. He did not dodge life's troubles or pain, but endured them all, knowing the end result was worth it. He chose the road to EASTER, not EASIER, and so can we.

I try often to make things easier for myself, but know the litter I remove from my road today will be replaced by more tomorrow. If, however, I walk each day with the Lord at my side by prayer and faith, the road won't be as difficult. The two men on the road to Emmaus **(Luke 24)** felt burdened until they realized the Lord was with them. The events had not changed. What mattered was who was with them on the road.

"Did not our hearts burn within us while He talked to us on the road, while He opened to us the Scriptures?" (Luke 24:32)

May we all feel His presence and walk beside Him today!

117

There is a time for risky love. There is a time for extravagant gestures. There is a time to pour out your affections on people important to you. When the time comes, seize it, and don't miss it!

The young boy watched as students taunted another boy, and his insides churn. It was his friend they were mocking. He knew he should stand up for his friend, but the mean guys are also the cool guys, and he wants them to accept him. If he speaks up, they'll never let him into their group. So, because he cares what they think, he does nothing for his friend. *"Someday those cool guys will accept me,"* he thinks.

The young husband looks into the display case thinking, *"She'd like that bracelet, but it's expensive, and she already has one. She's practical and will understand if I get her some nice towels. Someday I will get her a bracelet like that."*

The young widower is going through his wife's dresser. In the bottom drawer he finds a pink negligee he had given her, still in the box. She said she was waiting for a special occasion. *"Someday I'll wear it,"* she said. "Someday" was an expression they both often used.

But sometimes "someday" does not come. "Someday" is the enemy of love. Someday is the snake who hisses, *"Someday you'll go visit those folks. Someday you'll take her on a cruise. Someday you'll tell your brother you admire him. Someday you'll have more time to play with your kids."*

But we know the truth. "Someday" never comes. The price of practicality is often higher than the cost of extravagance. I should know. The boy watching his friend mocked, that was me. The young husband buying towels, that was me. The widower discovering his wife's unworn negligee, that was me.

Jesus risked His all to show us His love. The reward of love is always greater than the cost. The missed moment never brings joy later. Do it now! Give it, call him, tell her, just do it! A seized moment brings joy, but a neglected one regret.

"This is the day which the Lord has made." (Ps. 118:24)

Carpe Diem – Seize the day!

In the Civil War, during the Second Battle of Bull Run, Captain F. W. Clark and his men were surrounded by Confederate troops. In a fierce battle, his small detachment was nearly wiped out, and Captain Clark was reported missing and presumed dead.

Clark's family was devastated. He was the last male left. All their other able-bodied men had gone off to that tragic war and died, so the family sent word asking for the return of his body if it was found.

Captain Clark, however, was not dead. After hiding for a week behind enemy lines, he struggled into the Union camp in time to be handed a letter from his family asking for the return of his body. Clark himself wrote the reply: *Still have use for the body. Will return it in person. Kindest regards, F. W. Clark.*

Two weeks later, a very much alive Captain Clark had a joyful and tearful reunion with his loved ones. At least one of their men who went to that bloody and cruel war came back alive, and they were filled with joy.

On that first Easter Day, Jesus Christ came back, very much alive. He could simply have arisen from the dead and gone straight to heaven, but He showed Himself alive to hundreds of people to prove it was true. Just as He came to His disciples, so now He comes to us, His present day disciples, to you and me.

When you feel God has disappeared from your life, it's great to know He has come back. He comes back to each of us through His Holy Word of promise given by the Holy Spirit. He comes back to us every time we receive Holy Communion, or hear the Gospel of His forgiveness of our sins.

"Praise be to the God and Father of our Lord Jesus Christ! In his great mercy He has given us new birth into a living hope through the resurrection of Jesus Christ from the dead." (1 Peter 1:3)

Thanks be to God that He did it for us all in Jesus!

I am one of those people who still picks up a penny. I am amazed some folks won't even pick up a dime. Some will laugh at this and say that my kind are dinosaurs, but maybe this story will help you understand why I do this.

A man and his wife were invited by his wealthy boss to spend a weekend at his lake home. The boss was generous and took them for dinner at a fine restaurant. As the three of them were about to enter, the boss reached down and picked up a penny off the sidewalk! *"How absurd!"* thought the man's wife. *"What does he need with a single penny?"*

Throughout dinner, this bothered the man's wife. Finally, she could stand it no longer. She causally mentioned that her daughter once had a coin collection, and asked if the penny he'd found was valuable. The wealthy man pulled out the penny and held it out for them to see. *"Look at it."* He said. *"Read what it says."* She read, *"United States of America." "Read further,"* he said. *"One cent?" "Keep reading." "In God we Trust?" "That's it!"* he said.

"The name of God is holy, even on a coin. In 1864 'In God We Trust' was first stamped on US coins, but we never seem to notice it today. Every now and then God drops me a message telling me to trust Him. Who am I to pass it by? So when I see a coin, I stop and pray, then I pick up the coin as a response to God. Fortunately for me, God is patient and pennies on the street are plentiful! Then I put that penny together with others and give them to someone in need."

When you see a penny on the street, do you pass it by? Maybe it's the Lord's way of reminding you to trust in Him. Sometimes I even find a nickel or dime, and each one has the same motto: "In God We Trust."

Some days we may feel like we are like that penny, dropped or cast aside, too insignificant for others to notice. But Jesus sees us and He immediately comes to us. He sees our value, cleans us off and treasures us as His own.

"Every Sunday each of you must put aside part of what you have earned to give when I return." (1 Corinthians 16:2)

A penny for your thoughts?

APRIL 27

In 1932 a young Chicago musician traveled to St. Louis for a revival. He hated to go because his wife was ready to deliver their first child. He kissed her goodbye and left town in their Model A Ford. The next night, as he was being applauded for a song, he was handed a telegram. *"Your wife just died in childbirth,"* it said. Despite the applause, he could hardly keep from crying.

When he went back home he learned he had a baby son, but that same night the baby died, and his world fell apart completely. For days he closeted himself away from the world, angry at God, angry at himself for leaving, and lost in grief. An old friend invited him to the neighborhood music school where he sat down at a piano and began to play a new melody over and over again. Then the words also fell into place.

Precious Lord, take my hand, Lead me on, let me stand,
I am tired, I am weak, I am worn.
Through the storm, through the night, Lead me on to the light,
Take my hand, precious Lord, lead me home.

The young man later wrote, *"The Lord gave me these words and melody. He also healed my spirit. I learned that when we are in our deepest grief, when we feel farthest from God, this is when He is closest, and when we are most open to His restoring power. So I go on living for God willingly and joyfully, until that day comes when He will take me and gently lead me home."*

That young man was Thomas A. Dorsey. Some have mistakenly thought he was one of the Dorsey brothers. However, this man, the real Thomas A. Dorsey who wrote this fine song, was a little known black pianist from Chicago. And he left us with lovely tune and a great message, born out of his own time of struggle and renewed faith.

"Even though I walk through the valley of death, I will fear no evil." (Psalm 23:4)

God will lead us through the dark valley to the Light of His Son.

APRIL 28

One morning as we were getting ready to return from our winter residence in Arizona, I walked around Palm Creek, our RV park, and I was struck at how empty it was.

From December through March it is anything but empty. Palm Creek has over two thousand spaces and in the winter season it is home to over three thousand people. In those full days people are everywhere, playing, biking, walking, golfing, napping and laughing.

Right then, however, just three weeks after it had been full, two-thirds of the spaces and homes were empty. Two thousand people had left, and the park felt empty.

"Empty" is not a positive word to me. An empty bank account is daunting. An empty chair means someone has left or even died. Sometimes we are empty of emotions, such as when the tears of loss drain us. Empty nesters acutely feel the loss of children no longer at home. "Empty" is not a word we normally like to hear.

Unless, of course, we hear it in connection with Christ's tomb. On Easter morning the disciples found it empty. His body was gone. **"He is not here - He is risen. Come and see the [empty] place where He lay." (Matthew 28:6)** Now the word "empty" is something good, a word that has wonderful and eternal meaning!

An empty home can leave us sad, but the empty grave of Christ brings us hope and joy. There's nothing negative about "empty" when it means Jesus is alive. With faith in Jesus, our life is full and wonderful.

Because He lives, I can face tomorrow,
Because He lives, all fear is gone.
Because I know He holds the future.
My life is worth the living, just because He lives.
   (from the hymn)

May the empty tomb fill you with joy because you believe!

The true story is told of a time when great physicist Albert Einstein was traveling from Princeton on a train. When it came time for the conductor to come down the aisle to punch his ticket, Einstein couldn't find his ticket. He searched through all his pockets but the ticket wasn't there either. He looked in his briefcase, then on the seat and the floor beneath him, but he could not find his ticket.

The conductor said, *"Dr. Einstein, we all know who you are. I'm sure you bought a ticket. Don't worry about it."* Einstein nodded appreciatively.

The conductor continued down the aisle punching tickets. As he was ready to move to the next car, he turned around and saw the great physicist down on his hands and knees, looking under his seat for his ticket. The conductor went back and said again, *"Dr. Einstein, don't worry, I know who you are. You don't need a ticket. I'm sure you bought one."*

Einstein looked at him and said, *"Young man, I too, know who I am and that I bought a ticket. What I don't know is where I am going!"*

Imagine that! The brilliant physicist could not remember where he was going. Do you know who you are, and where you are going? Never forget who Jesus is, where He was going, and what He did for you.

In the Old Testament book of Genesis chapter 16, Hagar had run away from her mistress Sarah. In the midst of a desert, God sent her an angel who asked where she had come from and where she was going. We, too, need to ask ourselves periodically where we have come from and where we are going.

We are children of the Living God, and God's Son Jesus went to the cross for us and for our salvation. All who trust Him in faith are going to a place in eternity with God. I pray that all who read this message will trust Jesus as their Savior.

"Where have you come from, and where are you going?" (Genesis 16:8)

In Jesus, we know who we are and where we are going.

One friend asked another, *"How is it that you are always so happy? You have so much energy, and you never seem to be depressed."* With her eyes smiling, she said, *"I know the Secret!"* *"What secret is that?"* Her friend replied, *"I'll tell you all about it, but you have to promise to share the Secret with others."*

"My Secret is this: I have learned there is little I can do in my life that will make me truly happy. I must depend on God to meet my needs, and then I am happy. When a need arises in my life, I trust God to supply it. I have learned most of the time I don't need half of what I think I do. And God has never yet let me down."

The questioner thought, *"That's too simple!"* But reflecting on her own life she recalled how she once thought a bigger house would make her happy, but it didn't. She had thought a better paying job would make her happy, but it hadn't.

When did she realize her greatest happiness? While sitting on the floor with her grandchildren, playing games, eating pizza with them and reading them a story. Those times were simple gifts that brought happiness. God gave her grandchildren and being with them were her happiest times.

Now you know the Secret too. We can't depend on people or possessions to make us happy. Only God in His love and wisdom can do this. Just trust Him! Now the Secret has been passed on to you, so, what will you do with it?

Perhaps you also might want to share the Secret, that God in His love and wisdom will take care of You. But it's not really a Secret. We just have to believe in His love and trust Him for all things!

"The Lord bless you and keep you." (Numbers 6:24)

"It is no secret what God can do.
What He's done for others, He'll do for you.
With arms wide open, He'll pardon you.
It is no secret what God can do."
        (by Carl S. Hamblen)

DAILY WALK WITH JESUS in ...

MAY

+ + +

MAY 1

Today is May Day which has been celebrated in Europe since before the Christian era. Ancient Romans celebrated the flower festival "Floralia" during this time, and in other cultures May 1 was the first day of summer. Although May Day isn't popular in America, it is still observed in some European schools and churches with dancing at the Maypole, crowning the "Queen of May" and giving May baskets.

People enjoy having festivals, feasts and dancing. We've made holidays in honor of saintly men and women or in memory of heroes or great battles. Christians celebrate holidays to honor God or to remember the faithful who have led exemplary lives and taught us about faithful endurance.

One day in May an elderly lady finished her shopping and found four young men in the act of getting into her car. She dropped her shopping bags, drew a pistol from her purse, and shouted, *"I have a gun, now get out of that car!"* The four men ran like the wind.

Shaking in fear, she picked up her shopping bags, went to the car and tried to insert her key in the ignition. It wouldn't work. She tried again and realized she was in the wrong car! She went to the police station and was told in another room were four frightened young men reporting a car jacking by an old woman with a gun! No charges were filed.

We all admire someone who is willing to defend life and property. Jesus was willing to take up our defense as He gave His life on Calvary. His sacrifice earned us forgiveness of sins so that we can trust in Him for our salvation.

"The fear of the LORD is the beginning of wisdom." (Psalm 111:10)

Praise God for giving us courage and joy!

125

In a western movie called, "Broken Trail," an old cowboy named Prentiss Ritter is called upon to speak at the burial of a young friend. He spoke these words, *"We are all travelers in this world. From the sweet grass to the packing house, birth till death, we travel between the eternities."*

Though not a Christian sentiment, his words were correct. We are all travelers in a world that offers no lasting peace or rest apart from Jesus Christ. We Christians travel between the past and the future, awaiting our eternal home with Jesus with the hope that will last beyond this life. We trust that God will be with us wherever we are.

Whenever the troubles and struggles of life threaten us with anxiety or despair, we remember that we are loved by a Savior, the Lord Jesus, Son of God and master of Eternity. He offers us hope for this life and an even greater hope for the life to come, a life in heaven filled with joy and peace which comes to all who trust Him in faith.

In Hebrews 11:13, the writer, speaking of many heroes of faith, such as Enoch, Noah, Abraham and Sarah, says, **"These all died in faith, not having received the promises, but having seen them afar off and were assured of them."**

The men and women of God who did not know Jesus, but who still trusted that God would someday send a Savior, were truly heroic in their faith and will have a special place in heaven. We look forward to meeting them in God's presence.

You and I live in the present days, but we also look ahead by faith to being with the Lord. Jesus said, **"I am the Bread of Life. He who comes to me will never go hungry, and he who believes in me will never be thirsty." (John 6:35)**

One day all believers will experience eternity when faith becomes sight, the day when we will see the Lord in all His glory. Such a hope lifts us out of the sadness of the past to the joy of a bright and cheerful future life.

"He who believes has eternal life." (John 6:47)

For time and eternity, Jesus is all we need.

About this time of year the Church observes an important but neglected holiday called Ascension Day. On Good Friday Jesus left His disciples through His death on the cross, but He came back on Resurrection Day. Forty days later He left them again on Ascension Day when He returned to heaven.

Do you ever wonder where Jesus is right now? We believe He is in heaven, in a place and an existence not controlled by time and space. You and I are limited by time. We can live only in the moments of today. But Jesus lives in today, in yesterday and in tomorrow, all at once because He is not limited by time. Jesus truly is "timeless."

You and I are also limited by space. We can only be in one place at a time. But being God, Jesus is not limited by space, so He can be in a thousand or million places at once. That means He can truly say to every Christian, **"I am with you always."** **(Matthew 28:20)** He can say that to tens of millions of people at the same time and can mean it!

This is difficult for humans to understand. However, consider the computers we use. Their ever-increasing power of huge storage space and rapid calculations should help us believe in a God can know all things and be everywhere. The Creator is always greater and more capable than His Creation.

As Jesus ascended back into His heavenly home, the Bible says a cloud took Him from their sight. At times it may seem a cloud takes Jesus from our sight, too, a cloud of bills or worries or work, even a cloud of temptations.

If you ever wonder where the Lord is, remember that He has not moved away. He is still with you and will be with you always. We have His promise on that, and Jesus always keeps His promises.

Jesus may have disappeared into a cloud at His Ascension, but He is still here, as near as a prayer, as close as a fellow Christian, as near at hand as our Bible.

"I will never leave you nor forsake you." (Hebrew 13:5)

No matter where you are, Jesus our Savior will never leave you alone.

127

MAY 4

While walking through a new subdivision near our home, I saw mud and clay everywhere from the bulldozers as they cleared the land to lay out new streets and foundations. Construction sites were littered with lumber, stones and all sorts of trash, and it was quite a mess. Even the newly started houses looked ugly with their insides exposed as they were being framed together.

Yet this mess is necessary to have a finished product. When completed, those homes will be beautiful. New landscaping will make them look as if they are pictures in a home design magazine. Everything will be clean and neat for the new homeowners when they move in. During construction, however, the mess seems unmanageable.

Our daily walk with Jesus can be much the same. In life we must occasionally go through a messy period of confusion or disharmony. It is in those times that God is building a new part of life for us. He might be removing some old boards in our lives and replacing them with new ones. He might be adding another room. He might even be changing the shape of our lives altogether. But unless a messy time takes place, we will never see the new and improved version.

The Lord's goal for us is to become more like Himself. To achieve a change for the better will require removing all that is not from Him. It can be a painful and messy process, but in the end it will be worth it.

If God is allowing a messy period in your life right now, remember that this time may be necessary in order to ensure something better for you. Like a woman once said, *"I embrace the mess!"* You don't have to like it or revel in it, but you can accept it and not consider it a tragedy. Learn from what is happening to you so you can experience the fulfillment of His purposes for you in these times.

"My help comes from the Lord, Who made heaven and earth." (Psalm 121:2)

Embrace the mess, and then expect wonderful things to emerge from it.

Today is my birthday. When we lived in California, I learned of the Cinco de Mayo celebration among Hispanics. It is a celebration of Mexican heritage and a commemoration of an unexpected victory of the Mexican army over French soldiers at the Battle of Puebla on May 5, 1862.

Jesus' Words in Matthew 11:28, **"Come to me, all who labor and are heavy laden, and I will give you rest,"** are some of the most encouraging in the Gospels. If you are tired, come to Jesus. If you feel the weight of the world on your shoulders, come to Jesus. If the heaviness of life is crushing you, come to Jesus. Come to Him and He will give you rest.

Because He is truly human, He understands completely the burdens of humanity. He understands the burden of our sins and the devastation they cause. Sin can destroy families, churches and weaken countries. But Jesus has already defeated sin. Satan was beaten on the cross! We do not have to carry the burden of our sins any longer. Jesus did that for us completely on Calvary. When God finishes something, it is truly finished! We do not have to defeat Satan, because Jesus has already done that.

There is no burden Jesus cannot help us carry. Several boys in a small town were playing on abandoned railroad tracks. They decided to see how far each of them could walk while balancing on a single track. One big boy walked a long ways before falling off. A smaller fellow barely walked a few steps before he fell, so they laughed at him. But one of them said to the little guy, *"Hold my hand,"* and the two boys walked the tracks together, holding hands side by side, one on one track and one on the other. Two of them together did what one could not do alone.

Jesus walks beside us, too. He holds our hand when we are shaky and leads us when we are unsure. He will even carry us when we are too weary. It's His promise, and Jesus never goes back on his promises.

Jesus, teach me how to help someone when they are tired and weary. Amen.

We never know what good will come from our deeds of kindness. God can use the smallest thing we do in the mightiest way. We need to remember this, especially when we are tempted to neglect the small things, because we think they won't matter. Here is a true story to illustrate this:

A poor Scottish farmer named Fleming was working his land one day when he heard a cry for help coming from a nearby peat bog. Running to the site he found a young boy mired in the mud, terrified and vainly struggling to free himself. Fleming threw the lad a rope and saved him from a slow and terrifying death.

The next day an elegant carriage came to the Scotsman's humble home and a nobleman stepped out, introducing himself as the father of the boy Fleming had saved. *"I want to repay you,"* he said, *"for saving my son's life."* *"I cannot accept payment for what I did,"* Fleming replied, waving off the offer.

Just then the farmer's son came to the door of the family home. *"Is this your son?"* the nobleman asked. *"Yes,"* the farmer replied proudly. *"Then let me take him and give him a good education. If the lad is anything like his father, he'll grow to a man you can be proud of."*

And that he did. In time, Farmer Fleming's son graduated from St. Mary's Hospital Medical School in London, and went on to become known throughout the world as Sir Alexander Fleming, winner of the 1945 Noble Prize for his discovery of medical uses for penicillin.

At about that time the nobleman's son, now an adult, was stricken with pneumonia. What cured him? Penicillin. The name of the son whose life was saved by penicillin? Winston Churchill, the future Prime Minister of England.

"Therefore, as we have opportunity, let us do good to all people, especially to those who belong to the family of believers." (Galatians 6:10)

Give thanks for the miracles of medicine!

We live in an age where speed is considered necessary. We have microwave ovens, quick computers, fast cars, cell phones and instant foods. But have you noticed that God is not always in a hurry? It took decades for Moses to get ready to lead the people out of Egypt. It took Joseph twenty years before he became second in command in Egypt. Jacob worked fourteen years before he was released from Laban's control, and Abraham and Sarah were nearly one hundred years old before their son was born. Why isn't God in more of a hurry? Because He waits for the right time to do His work.

God called each of these servants to accomplish a certain task in His Kingdom, yet He knew they could not do it if they were not ready. Therefore He waited for just the right time in order to bring their mission to fulfillment.

You and I are more often focused on the DESTINATION than we are on the JOURNEY. When we experience God's presence daily through Word and prayer, one day we will wake up and realize that God has done something special in our lives. The destination is not always the point of life. The journey is how we come to know Him more fully.

In this journey we become acquainted with His love, grace and power. In the journey we learn His wisdom and provisions, as well as the faith it takes to achieve them. The DESTINATION is not always the goal. Our JOURNEY can be just as important in our life.

When Joseph came to power in Egypt, his wealth and authority were not important to him. He had surrendered himself to God, so that he was not anxious about tomorrow and or his circumstances. He knew God was faithful and would always be there to help him, no matter what.

So it can be with you and me. We must wait for God's timing and accept wherever we are in the journey. When we learn to find contentment where we are, then we can experience God's love in ways we never thought possible.

"I am Your servant, O God." (1 Kings 18:35)

May God bring you His joy in your JOURNEY with Him!

MAY 8

Have you ever felt like something was missing in your life and you didn't know what it was? One day years ago I needed to use my old chain saw, so I took it out, fueled and oiled it and tried to start it. This saw had been getting harder to start during the past several years, so I pulled and pulled on the starter rope, but to no avail.

After no success, nearly breaking the rope and wearing out my arm, I sat down and tried to figure out what would make it run. My eye was drawn to a small set screw next to the choke. I'd never touched that screw before but knew it had something to do with the fuel mixture. So I turned it a quarter turn to the left, pulled the rope and the engine roared to life! In ten years it had never run any better. All it needed was the correct fuel mixture. That tiny fuel valve must have been gradually closing over the years of use.

So it can be with us. Without realizing it, our personal "fuel valve" can slowly close down, shutting us off from what we need in life. Missing worship a little more, praying a little less, buying more stuff, and giving less to worthy causes, serving personal needs more while helping others less - all these acts can eventually can choke off our spiritual life and relationship with God. They're usually done in small increments, tiny selfish steps that seemed right at the time, but slowly replaced what we should have been doing.

If you sense something missing in your life, don't just keep doing things the same way. Take time to look at your whole life, what you are doing, who your friends are, what you're not doing and what you should be avoiding. Then let God draw you to see what's wrong. This takes prayer.

God will give you what you need if you let Him, a life dedicated to better priorities, more faith and worship, more forgiveness and compassion. But you must find the plugged "valve" so the fuel of God's love can flow into your life.

"Show me Your ways, Lord, teach me Your paths." (Psalm 25:4)

Sometimes it takes a sore arm and some frustration to realize how life works.

132

We all need hope, and we also need someone to help us get it. I read a story about the benefits of having a positive attitude in the face of seemingly hopelessness.

Jim, a metro bus driver, one day realized he needed to change his boring life, and decided he'd try to make a difference in the lives of the people on his route. Many people rode his bus each day with sad faces. While his own job gave him little hope for advancement, he thought perhaps he could give his riders something better.

Jim began cheerfully to greet each person who got on or off his bus. He rarely opened the rear door, so they all had to walk past him in front where he'd say, *"Good morning, and how are you today?"* or, *"Have a fine day and be careful."* He treated them like friends, not just bodies to haul around.

When the doors closed, Jim sometimes greeted them over the loudspeaker, and as they rode along he often told them of sales at this or that store. Sometimes he even shared a positive thought to ponder. He smiled and looked each passenger in the eye, and they began to smile back.

Soon his bus, partially filled with sullen people, was full of riders nearly every day, and some chatted with each other as they rode. Word got around that the passengers on his bus would be treated well, so people went out of their way to take his bus rather than another. They knew they would leave his bus feeling better. Having a "dead end" job didn't stop Jim from bringing a little joy to his riders.

Jesus was always kind to people He met. His kindness changed their lives. He let His love show through to all, the young or old, rich or poor. It takes no talent to be negative. Anyone can be grumpy and find fault. It does, however, make a big difference if we show a cheerful attitude. The world and also the church have enough cynics. Let's not add to their numbers.

"Blessed is the one who is kind to the needy."
(Proverbs 14:21)

Give hope to someone you meet today!

Just before returning from Arizona one year, Carol and I drove out into the desert to see the giant Saguaro cacti in bloom. Native only to the Sonora Desert, the Saguaro is the largest of all cacti, growing up to 50 feet high, weighing up to three tons, and living one hundred fifty to two hundred years. It can only start to grow from seed, unlike most other cacti which can take root when parts are just stuck in the ground.

The Saguaro uses desert moisture wisely and thrives where others perish. In the springtime its large white blossoms open on top of the cactus arms, and when pollinated, produce juicy red fruit for birds and animals. They can also be prepared in special dishes by the Tohono O'odham (People of the Desert), a native American tribe of the Sonora.

A few years ago, the Desert People built a casino in Maricopa. The Akimel O'odham (People of the River), had already built a casino just south of Phoenix. People go to casinos thinking they will be winners, but usually end up losers. It is a rare casino visitor who comes away winning more than was spent, and most stay until all their gambling money is gone. The enjoyment of being in a casino doesn't last long.

Some will say, *"It's just for fun."* If you enjoy gambling for fun, that's your choice, but be careful. But if you think you will come out a winner, you'll be disappointed. Just because we are allowed to do something doesn't mean we should. Legal or lawful actions need right motives or purposes.

Jesus taught us that all our blessings come from God. His disciples urged believers to be good stewards, working to earn a living, investing wisely, and using what they'd been given to help others in the best way.

"All things may be lawful, but not all things are helpful, and not all lawful things build you up." (1 Corinthians 10:23, paraphrased)

May God move us all to be good stewards of what we've been given.

MAY 11

What makes us value the things we have? My wife once watched a TV show in which an expert appraised the value of old things people brought to him. This episode featured a Van Briggle vase made about ninety years ago and the owner was told it was worth over a thousand dollars.

The next day as my wife was putting some items in a box for a church garage sale, she came across a heavy old wine-colored vase, one she had never really liked. Recalling that TV show, she turned it upside down and discovered it, too, was a genuine Van Briggle. It might even be worth some money. She decided to sell it, so she had it appraised. Amazingly, that ugly old thing sold for three hundred dollars!

What makes God value us? Why should He care about sinful, greedy, cranky people? He has to do everything for us. He creates us through our parents and protects us as we grow. He must provide us with everything we need. While He gives us freedom of choice, our sinful natures often choose the wrong ways or things.

He must even give us faith through the Holy Spirit, because our sinful nature prevents us from believing in Him. He opens the doors of heaven through Jesus, and even has to push us through! God listens to our prayers that often sound like they're from ungrateful, whining children, and yet still He provides for our needs.

With all the trouble we are, what makes us valuable to Him? It's because the Divine Parent doesn't turn His back on His child. The Creator won't reject His creation. We may run away or reject Him, but He doesn't reject us. His love includes everyone, and it will never fail us, despite what we may do. Praise God He values us much more highly than we value Him.

"O Lord my God, I will give thanks unto You forever."
(Psalm 30:12)

I'm always amazed at God's love!

135

Human life is frail. It is also pressure-sensitive. Did you know that humans can live under water only to a relatively shallow depth? Even with the aid of sophisticated air systems and high-tension steel, people can descend safely to only about twelve hundred feet beneath the ocean's surface. Beyond that, air systems can't keep us alive, and even steel begins to buckle due to the extreme pressure and the weight of the ocean water. The finest nuclear submarine at three thousand feet under the sea will break apart and be crushed.

Yet at twelve thousand feet under the ocean's surface, life still exists. The amazing humpback whale, a mammal like us who breathes air like we do, has been tracked through electronic devices to dive down to twelve thousand feet!

Why doesn't it get crushed? Somehow, God in His infinite wisdom has equipped those magnificent creatures to be able to withstand the greatest of pressures on the outside, because they are balanced by equal pressure on the inside. I have no idea how that's possible, but it works.

With life's pressures all around us, you and I need similar help with balance from God. Through the Holy Spirit and His Word, God's strength is within us when we have faith in Christ. With Jesus Christ in our hearts, life's pressures on the outside can be handled.

It's little wonder that we often collapse, and that so many homes and lives break apart. So many people do not have Christ within them. Millions of people are living hollow lives, empty of God, and so they can collapse under pressure. We need to share with them that our living Jesus Christ is the remedy for a hollow life. Jesus will fill us with His strength and courage if we but ask Him.

He died that we might live, and He lives that we might not die eternally. That is Good News because it is a balance that will give us eternal life.

"Great is the Lord and most worthy of praise." (1 Chronicles 16:25)

Today be glad you're living above sea level!

When we moved to our present home and were making the last of several trips with cars filled with boxes, it occurred to me how exhausted we were from carting around all the things we think are important. Our backs and arms ached from lifting, and our legs were weary from going up and down steps. It seemed we'd never get that last box packed and the basement emptied, and we both longed for a well-ordered house once again.

But finally it was all done, and I turned onto the highway toward home with that last load. Up ahead was a hitch-hiker walking in the rain and probably carrying everything he owned in his pack. I didn't stop for him as I had no room, but I wanted to. I've always felt a little sorry for hitch-hikers, but that afternoon for just a few moments I actually envied him. He was walking, but he didn't have seven rooms full of stuff to unpack. He probably had no house payments either. All he had to do that day was keep walking and hope someone would give him a ride.

My feelings of envy didn't last long when I thought of the warm bed I would sleep in that night with someone I love. Though surrounded with unpacked boxes and many hours of unpacking ahead, we had a wonderful place to call home. All that traveler could have hoped for was another ride or a dry place to spend the night.

No matter how weary we may grow, no matter how faint we may feel, we must remember, 1) Our struggles won't last forever, and 2) by God's grace in Jesus we have a new home at the end of our journey, a home with the Lord.

Jesus is our caring Lord. In Him we are forgiven. In Him we have a family that loves and cares for us. No matter where you go, when you have faith in Christ, the minute you walk through a church door, you are with family. True, the family may argue and fight now and then, but it's still the family of God that tries to care for its own.

"Rejoice over her, you heavens! Rejoice, you people of God!" (Revelation 18:20)

Give thanks for your home, no matter how old or new it is.

When I was seventeen, I wrecked my Dad's 1953 Pontiac. I had driven to town, and late that night on the way home I got sleepy at the wheel, came too close to the center line and sideswiped an oncoming car. A few inches closer and we both could have been seriously injured or killed. Neither of us were hurt, and the cars were both damaged but drivable. Because it was late, we took each other's name and phone number and drove home.

I woke Dad up that night with fear and trembling and told him what had happened. *"Are you hurt?"* he asked. *"No, but the car is,"* I replied. *"Go to bed and we'll see to it in the morning,"* he said. The next morning he said, *"I was wondering when you'd do something like that. All the other boys did, and I figured you would too, sooner or later."*

What I discovered was that my father had actually expected me to have an accident and had already made the decision to forgive me ahead of time. To the best of my recollection, Dad never showed any anger for what I had done. I never had to pay him for the car repair and he never lectured me.

Our Heavenly Father has done the same. He has a plan of forgiveness for us before we sin. That's God's way, the way of grace and patient love for us we don't deserve. God provides us with His forgiveness even before we need it. That's what makes His grace so amazing.

When close friends or family die, we are sad. But if they are believers, we rejoice that we will be able to see them again in the big heavenly reunion God has planned for us someday. I enjoy reunions, because we see once again those people who are so important in our lives.

"While we were still sinners, Christ died for us, the Godly for the ungodly." (Romans 5:8)

May God give you joyful memories with your parents and other loved ones.

MAY 15

It was eight o'clock in the morning as the young man stood next to a trash bin at a train station playing his violin. Dressed in jeans, T-shirt and baseball cap, he played for forty-five minutes, expertly rendering six classical pieces as more than a thousand people passed by him in Washington, DC.

Of all who passed by, only six people stopped to listen for more than a moment, and they were usually children whose parents urged them to move on. Only one man stood and listened for several minutes.

No one knew that the fiddler standing there outside the Metro station was Joshua Bell, one of the finest classical musicians in the world, playing some of the most elegant music ever written on a priceless Stradivarius violin. Only days before, Bell had sold out a Boston concert at a hundred dollars a seat. That day a few folks tossed change into his violin case and kept moving.

This event happened in 2007 as an experiment by a local newspaper. Joshua Bell, born in 1967, is now the musical director of St. Martin in the Fields of London. The music he played was by Bach, Brahms and Bruch on his 1713 violin valued at over $4 million and once owned by virtuoso Fritz Kreisler. Yet hardly anyone stopped to listen.

Would you have stopped? I am ashamed to say I probably would have kept walking also. If we do not have even a few moments to spare to hear one of the best musicians in the world playing the best music ever written on one of the finest musical instruments ever made, how many other excellent things are we missing in life?

Jesus stands at the door of our hearts and awaits our response. Will we invite Him in or are we too busy to notice He's there? His invitation has eternal consequences, because in Him, we have eternal life.

"Behold, I stand at the door and knock. If anyone hears My voice and opens the door, I will come in to him and eat with him, and he with Me." (Revelation 3:20)

Listen for the music God is making for you today.

MAY 16

Back when telegraph was the only means of long-distance communication, a young man applied for a job as a Morse Code operator. He entered a large, noisy office with several telegraphs clacking loudly. A sign on the receptionist's counter instructed applicants to fill out a form and wait until they were summoned. The young man completed his form and sat down with the other male applicants.

After a few minutes, he stood up and walked past the desk into the inner room. The other applicants looked up in wonder. Why had this man been so bold? They hadn't heard any summons yet, so how could he go in so soon? Within a few minutes the young man emerged from the inner office escorted by the interviewer who said, *"Gentlemen, thank you very much for coming, but the job has been filled by this man."*

One applicant grumbled, *"That's not fair - He was the last one to come in, and we never even got a chance to be interviewed."* The employer responded, *"All the time you've been sitting here, a telegrapher inside has been ticking out a message in Morse Code that said: 'If you understand this message, come in - the job is yours.' None of you understood it except this man, so the job is his."*

People do not audition or interview to become Christians. God accepts all who come to Him with faith in Jesus, His Son. No one who seeks God will be turned away.

Believers in Christ can hear the voice of their Lord. They respond by trusting Him and bearing the fruit of good works in life that shows their faith. These "Fruit of the Spirit" are God-given Christian attitudes that help us each day. If the Holy Spirit is in our hearts, these fruit will show themselves in our lives some way.

"The fruit of the Spirit is love, joy, peace, patience, kindness, faithfulness, goodness, gentleness, and self-control." (Galatians 5:22-23)

May we all hear God speaking to us and be fruitful in life.

Troubles can cloud the clearest sky. Picture a lovely Sunday afternoon with sun shining, birds singing and spring in the air. Yet it's hardly noticeable because you're really upset. Something bad has happened and no amount of goodness or beauty can change your mind, no joy can make you feel better. When you and I concentrate only on our personal troubles, nothing else seems to matter, regardless of how lovely or good our surroundings may be.

The two men walking home to Emmaus were thinking only of the death of their friend Jesus. **"We had hoped He was the one who was going to redeem Israel,"** they said. **(Luke 24:21)** It is a disappointment when someone we count on fails us. It deflates our hopes, defeats our expectations, and turns life inside out.

A friend disappoints us, the job ends, a relationship fails, or a medical report makes us fearful. Such things may leave us grasping for something to fill the void. *"I had such high hopes for this job." "I really thought I knew her." "I can't believe he'd react that way." "I thought I knew him better." "I can't believe she'd do that."*

The two Disciples going home to Emmaus felt much the same. **"We had hoped He was the One."** But then Jesus joined them and everything changed. **"Why the long faces?"** He asked. **"Didn't He say this would happen? Stop feeling sorry for yourselves - lighten up! It's not as bad as you think!"** (Luke 24:25-26, paraphrased)

People don't always like hearing this. If we feel bad, we want someone to commiserate with us. But at such times truth is what we need, not more misery or grumbling. The truth of Jesus wakes us up to what's important. At the low points of life, we need to listen to Jesus, not more complaints.

After Jesus left them, they said, **"Did not our hearts burn within us as He spoke to us on the way?"** I guess you could call that "heavenly heartburn."

If you're feeling down, pray that Jesus will join you and lift you up.

MAY 18

God can teach us patience and thankfulness in many ways, even through technology. One Friday morning I was about to reprint my sermon when I discovered my printer wouldn't print. Two hours of trying to fix it later, I gave up, convinced God didn't want me to change my sermon. The following week I called a friend who suggested turning the printer off to clear its memory, and it worked. What a concept! Just turn the machine off and on again. A little rest can fix all kinds of problems, even in a machine.

But I wasn't done with technical problems that week. The next day it was my home office copier which gave me an error message: *"E-37, Turn Copier off, then on again."* I did that, but got the same message. I did it again and again, but got same message each time. No amount of rest time made that copier work. Thank the Good Lord for my copier repairman. He came and fixed it in five minutes.

Later the next week I had trouble with the church copier, too, but it took four visits before it started printing correctly again. Fortunately the repairman trimmed his final bill, or our small church would have had to pass the plate a second time on Sunday morning to pay for it.

Patience only comes after going through tough times. As they say, *"Good judgment comes from experience, and experience comes from bad judgment."* I have found this to be very true, especially when dealing with electronic things.

Jesus is the Holy One who can fix things in our life. His death and resurrection have repaired all our lives. He is the holy Repairman available any time who knows how to fix our problems. Best of all, He does so without cost, for He has already paid the price on Calvary.

"Weeping may come at night, but joy comes in the morning." (Psalm 30:5)

Jesus is our personal repairman. His services are available 24/7 and they're always free!

There is an old fisherman's prayer, *"Dear God, be good to me; the sea is so wide and my boat is so small."* You and I need to pray that prayer often, whether it's during a time of personal or family crisis, a time of great need in the home, church, workplace or nation, or a time of personal calm and peace.

In our lives we people are all on a long and difficult journey across a very wide sea. It is easy to get lost. Even a good boat gets tossed about by the winds of fear and trouble. Sometimes we act like we're the only boat in the sea and fail to look to other boats that could help us in the storm. We may spend our time pointing out the mistakes of other boats, or fall asleep at the rudder and let our boat drift into uncharted and dangerous waters.

Always we should remember that we have an infallible Chart and Compass in the form of God's Word. It's very easy to go out beyond His Beacon and take our direction from the whims of the latest charts written by enlightened captains of human wisdom. *"Dear God, be good to me; the sea is so wide and my boat is so small."*

Sometimes we act as if we're steering a battleship or a destroyer, charging others in the fleet. At times our boat gets stuck in the mud, and yet we cry, *"Don't rock the boat!"* when that may be the only way we'll get out of the mud. We act as if our boat is merely for our own pleasure and not also for rescuing others. Or we sail in circles, going nowhere. *"Dear God, be good to me; the sea is so wide and my boat is so small."*

Our hope does not lie in the strength of our boat, or the skill of our sailing, but in the Ruler of wind and waves. Jesus Christ, the Captain, promises to bring us through the dangers of the wide sea, through the storm and into the calm of His safe haven. It is because of Him that we can have godly joy amid any gloom and fear all around. *"Dear God, be good to me; the sea is so wide and my boat is so small."*

"God is our refuge and strength, an ever-present help in trouble." (Psalm 46:1)

Let's all pray that prayer on our voyage often.

143

A baby once asked God, *"They tell me You are sending me to earth, but how am I going to live there, being so small and helpless?"* God answered, *"Your angel will be waiting for you and will take care of you."*

The baby further asked, *"Here in heaven I don't have to do anything but sing and smile to be happy."* God said, *"Your angel will sing for you and will also smile for you, and you will feel your angel's love and be very happy."*

Again the baby asked, *"But how am I going to be able to understand when people talk to me if I don't know their language?"* God said, *"Your angel will tell you the most beautiful and sweet words you will ever hear, and with much patience and care will teach you how to speak."*

"But," said the baby, *"what am I going to do when I want to talk to You?"* God said, *"Your angel will place your hands together and will teach you how to pray."*

"Who will protect me?" asked the baby. *"Your angel will defend you against all danger,"* said God. *"But I think I will always be sad because I will not see You anymore,"* said the baby. God said, *"Your angel will talk to you about Me and will teach you the way to come back to Me, and I will always be close by."*

Then the child asked, *"Please tell me my angel's name."* God said, *"When you get to earth, you will simply call her by her name, 'Mother'."*

Jesus honored His mother and made sure her needs were met when she was old, just as she had done for Him when He was young. The apostle John took care of her and provided for her needs. Tradition says they lived many years in Ephesus which is located in modern-day Turkey.

You and I should also honor our mother and father as we are able, especially if they are in need. Jesus places us into families where we can show His mercy and grace to all.

[Jesus said] "Behold, your mother." (John 19:27)

God gives us many kinds of angels when we need one.

MAY 21

What are you willing to die for? For what cause or person would you be willing to sacrifice your life? You might ask Hilbert Schauer who grew up in Kansas during the "Dust Bowl" depression. Being from a rural family, he saw the hopelessness that came from crop failures, bank closings and dust sifting through the cracks into his home. The dust bowl hit his family most terribly when Hilbert's father died from dust pneumonia, leaving a large family behind.

When America was attacked in World War Two, Hilbert entered the Army and was commissioned an officer in charge of a company of black soldiers. Though he'd hardly even seen a black man before the war, he was now ranking officer in a company of them.

His company's assignment was the difficult task of munitions disposal. They were to get rid of unexploded bombs, shells, grenades and any other unneeded things that blew up. Some in his company, including officers, died in their duties, but Hilbert made it through the war okay.

After the war he became a lawyer, was appointed a district court judge, and eventually served on the Colorado Supreme Court many years until he retired. If asked, *"What are you willing to die for?"* Hilbert could have given several answers. He is a fine Christian man and a fellow member of our church who has helped to establish three Lutheran congregations.

We might also ask, *"What was Jesus willing to die for?"* Would the people He died for be the good people, the noble, the well educated or the wealthy? Or was He also willing to die for the poor, the sick and the sinners?

We know from Holy Scripture that Jesus died for all people, the rich or the poor, the wise and the wise guys, the good people and the bad. Jesus was willing to die for them all. Praise God that includes you and me!

"He died for all, that those who live might no longer live for themselves but for Him who for their sake died and was raised." (2 Corinthians 5:15)

Think about this as we approach Memorial Day.

145

MAY 22

A nobleman went hunting with his Christian servant who had been witnessing to him by telling him of the goodness of God's plans. During the hunt, the nobleman was attacked by an animal and lost a finger. He angrily told his servant, *"If God is so good, I would not have lost my finger."* The servant replied, *"Despite this, sire, I can only tell you that God is good. He knows why this has happened to you."* In anger over this response, the nobleman had his servant imprisoned.

Later the nobleman went hunting again and this time was captured by pagans who practiced human sacrifice. Just before being offered on a pagan altar, it was noticed the nobleman was missing a finger, so he was let go. He did not meet the pagans' requirement to be of sound limb and body.

Upon his escape and return to his castle, the nobleman had his servant released from prison, and said, *"Your God is good, for I was spared."* He then added, *"But why did He allow you to be put in prison for so long?"* The servant replied, *"Sire, if I had not been in prison, I would have gone with you, and I would have been sacrificed, for I have all my fingers!"*

You and I may complain about our lives and the negative things that happen to us. But we must remember that nothing is random for those who believe and trust in Jesus. Everything has a purpose, so every morning it's good for us to offer our day to God. Ask Him to guide our actions, inspire our thoughts and ease our negative feelings.

St. Paul tells us in Romans 8:28, **"We know that in all things God works for the good of those who love Him, who have been called according to His purpose."**

We often hear this Bible verse paraphrased, *"All things work together for good."* If you read the verse again, you can see that paraphrase is not quite accurate. All things do work out for good to those who love Christ and have faith in Him. Faith makes things work out for our good, faith in Jesus Christ.

Do not be afraid, for God is never wrong!

MAY 23

Helen Roseveare was born in 1925 in Hertfordshire, England. She entered Cambridge University and there came to know Christ as her Savior. She became a medical doctor and in 1953 left for the Belgian Congo as a missionary. Soon after she arrived, she met a young man named John Mangadima, and he wanted her to teach him how to be a doctor. Helen agreed and in exchange, he taught her the Swahili language.

In 1960, the Belgian Congo declared its independence and faced a bitter civil war. In the midst of riots and lawlessness, Helen continued her work. But then she was beaten, raped, arrested and held captive by rebel soldiers. She was freed months later and returned to England. Fearful and horrified, she vowed never to return to the Congo.

After two months at home, she received a letter from John Mangadima who told her that her work was not finished. By faith, Helen returned and in her last years on the mission field, she established the Evangelical Medical Center Hospital, a training college, and four bush clinics. Helen Roseveare is still revered among Congolese Christians today.

Are you experiencing difficult times? Our Christian walk through life is never easy, but if we hold fast to Jesus Christ and the hope He gives us, He will reward our faithfulness and bless others through us. Today in prayer, thank the Lord that He will give you strength to face whatever comes. Then remain steadfast in Him.

A personal note: Carol and I have a lovely adopted grand daughter who was born in the Democratic Republic of the Congo, formerly the Belgian Congo. She was abandoned at birth and taken by a stranger to an orphanage from which my son and his wife adopted her. Perhaps the work of Helen and John laid the groundwork for her coming into our family.

"I thank Christ Jesus our Lord who has enabled me, because He counted me faithful." (1 Timothy 1:12)

We give thanks for the work of all Christian workers in Africa, and pray for their safety in these dangerous times there.

In the 1950's Carl Stuart Hamblen, songwriter and radio host, was noted for his partying and womanizing. He never turned down attending a party, and his songs reflected this.

One day a young preacher was holding a revival nearby. Hamblen invited him on his radio show but first decided to attend one of his revival meetings. Early in the meeting the preacher announced, *"There is one man in this audience who is a big fake!"* Hamblen was convinced he was the one the preacher was talking about, so he got up and left.

A few nights later he showed up drunk at the preacher's hotel room in the middle of the night, demanding that he pray for him. The preacher refused, saying, *"This is between you and God, and I'm not going to get in the middle of it."* But he did invite Hamblin in and told him about Jesus. Hamblen ended up on his knees, tearfully receiving Jesus as his Savior.

When Hamblen quit drinking, "the fun life" for him also stopped. His Hollywood friends left him and he was fired because he refused to accept a beer company as a sponsor. He tried writing Christian songs but the only successful one was, *"This Old House,"* written for his friend Rosemary Clooney.

His friend John said, *"All your troubles started when you got religion. Was it worth it?"* Stuart said, *"Yes."* John said, *"You liked booze so much. Don't you ever miss it?"* Stuart said, *"Nope."* John said, *"I don't understand how you could give all that up."* Stuart said, *"It's no big secret. All things are possible with God."* John said, *"That's catchy. You should write a song about that."* And that's just what he did:

> *"It is no secret what God can do;*
> *What He's done for others, He'll do for you.*
> *With arms wide open, He'll pardon you;*
> *It is no secret, what God can do."*

The preacher who led him to Christ was Billy Graham. His friend John Wayne later quit drinking and was baptized.

"I can do all things through Christ who strengthens me." (Philippians 4:13)

It is no secret – God can work miracles!

Today we are told we must be tolerant of everyone and everything, whether we agree with it or not. But people tend to be more tolerant of what benefits them. However, the dictionary defines tolerance as *"an attitude of patience and fairness towards those whose opinions or practices differ from ours."* Tolerance is supposed to free us of bigotry, but it doesn't always work, especially when it's forced on us.

On my deck for several years stood an old exercise bike I bought at a garage sale. It moved my arms and legs well enough, but the only exercise I got from it those days was moving it around when I swept the deck. One day I was moving it and out fell two quarters and a dime. I shook the thing and out came more coins. I found over $6 in nickels, dimes and quarters in that old thing! The few dollars I paid for it came back to me with interest. I became much more tolerant of the exercise bike, at least until I gave it away. I didn't ride it that often, even after it gave me all that money.

One of the strengths of the Christian faith is its ability to bring different people together, people of different color, culture or ethnic origin, those who might otherwise be separate from each other. In Christ, barriers can be torn down. **"In Christ, there is neither male nor female, Jew nor Greek, slave nor free." (Galatians 3:28)** Such results are good, but they don't always happen easily.

Sunday morning still remains one of the most segregated times in America. The Gospel of God's love in Christ brings people together, but peoples' sins can also separate us. Despite the separation of our sin, the Gospel of Christ bridges the gap. Following Jesus changes people, making them more caring.

God wants us to be tolerant of all people, but never tolerant of the wrong things that people do. God loves us, but not our sin. I don't know what happened to that old bike, but I value exercise more now than I did before. Now if I would just do it more!

Thank the Lord that He loves us, no matter what!

MAY 26

Some amazing stories have come out of that terrible storm that struck New Orleans a few years ago, the one called Hurricane Katrina. One man told of swimming away from his house, his two children clinging to his back, and paddling through the flood debris to the roof of the tallest building nearby. Others soon joined them on that rooftop.

After reaching the place of safety, the man realized they were on a church roof. He said to the others on the roof, *"I guess we're on holy ground."* A woman with them pointed at the steeple and said, *"I know this place. I believe my grandfather and grandmother helped build this church!"* After two days, they were rescued from the roof of that House of God.

That person's grandparents never could have imagined that God would use their work to save their grandchildren and others in a flood. They may have prayed for their souls, and encouraged them to trust in Jesus, but I'm sure they had no idea their building would help save them with its tall roof. Those folks had no idea how God would use the work of their hands, and neither do we.

We all need a church to build. We all need a steeple to look up to, or even a roof to climb on. We need it for ourselves and also for those who come after us. I'd surely like to know what happened to those people on that roof, especially their children. It would surely show God's plan for them.

I can almost imagine that, on some future day, God will use one or more of those children for something very good, to serve people in need or otherwise be a blessing for others, like the builders of that church. God will use His children in unexpected ways to help others, if we will just let Him.

"We are His workmanship, created in Christ Jesus for good works." (Ephesians 2:10)

May God move us all to build a church for our current generation and for future ones, too.

150

My father was born in 1898. He lived to be ninety-seven years old and was forty-six when he first picked me up as his youngest newborn. Dad lived by his hands, and I remember seeing them in the nursing home as wrinkled and thin, not as the strong hands that drove tractors, handled tools, milked cows or gave a strong but gentle handshake. He was my father, twenty little ones in our family called him Grandpa.

My father's hands did many things: They put food in my mouth and clothes on my back, tied my shoes and pulled on my boots. They were a bit clumsy around women, but gentle to infants and children. They shook my hands when he was proud of me, and wrote me letters in a fine cursive script.

His hands held children, helped neighbors and on rare occasions were clenched in anger. They held me close when I cried, combed my hair and steadied my hands around tools. They reached out to hug me, my wife and my children. With them my father showed us how to love our wives and how to fold our hands in prayer.

With his hands, my Dad lived and worked, and with them he made a living on this earth. He enjoyed shaking hands with people. I wonder if in heaven he has been able to shake the hand of Paul or Peter or Martin Luther, or even God. He was husband, father, friend, grandfather, and neighbor, and his kind of hands were familiar to us all.

Now my hands hold my grandchildren. They are no longer as strong as before, but they're still useful. Someday I hope to shake my father's hand again, and my Heavenly Father's hand, too. My grandchildren, young and inexperienced, fit well into the hands of their Grandpa. Their hands are small and perfect. Mine are rough and spotted but they hold those little hands tenderly.

Jesus' hands became our blessing, for with them He was held to the cross that removed the sins of the world.

"The hand of God was on His people." (2 Chronicles 30:12)

Whose hands have blessed you in your life?

A number of years ago former U. S. Senator Mark Hatfield was touring Calcutta with Mother Teresa, visiting a "House of Dying" where sick children were cared for in their last days. They also visited the dispensary where the poor lined up by the hundreds each day to receive medicine and medical aid.

Watching Mother Teresa minister to the people left to die, Hatfield was overwhelmed by the magnitude of the suffering. *"How can you bear the load without being crushed by it?"* he asked her. She replied, *"My dear Senator, I am not called to be successful, but I am called to be faithful."*

God doesn't tell us we must be successful, but we are called to be faithful. He calls on us to do our best and He will take care of the results. Any meager successes we may have come from Him. He just bids us be faithful and loving in whatever we do.

God has always been faithful with us. Our faithful Lord Jesus went the distance on earth and gave His life on the cross of Calvary that we might live. By His wounds we are healed.

Whoever believes Jesus is Lord will be saved. Jesus said whoever helps the least of God's people, helps God Himself. May we all believe that Jesus is our Lord and, as much as humanly possible, may we remain faithful to Him.

We need not be as charitable or courageous as Mother Teresa, but we can show kindness to those in need. We need not be able to preach like Billy Graham, but we can tell what Jesus means to us. We may not have a voice like an angel, but we can sing God's praises in worship.

What can you do to show your gratitude to the Lord for what He has done for you? The following words of King David show his response:

"What shall I render to the Lord for all His benefits to me? I will lift up the cup of salvation and call on the name of the Lord, I will pay my vows to the Lord in the presence of all His people." (Psalm 116:12-14)

God can help us do our best, despite our weaknesses.

MAY 29

A pastor friend of mine shared that he went to visit his mother who had just had a stroke. She had been the compassionate caregiver in his family, caring for her ninety year old father until he passed. But now she lay in bed, her left side paralyzed and struggling to understand why. Their ensuing six day visit was marked with a bad day, then a good day, alternating regularly almost like clockwork.

She passed away, and as he later looked back on those days, he told me, *"The bad days were actually the best, for on those days we called on the Lord in prayer more fervently and submitted to His will more completely than we did when she had a good day. But the Lord knew how much we could take, so each bad day was followed by a good one."*

It takes faith to realize bad days can lead to good things. It is in our pain that we cry out to God, and it is in our valleys that the mountaintops become meaningful. Thanks be to God that He gives us strength to see the good in the midst of the bad that happens.

My friend also related a day he climbed to the top of a "fourteener," one of the fifty-four Colorado mountain peaks of fourteen thousand feet in height. He said it took him six hours to hike the eight miles, but he stayed on the summit only fifteen minutes. Those fifteen minutes were enough, he said, to make the rest of the strenuous climb worthwhile.

Happiness often comes in unusual and unexpected experiences, and though it may be short, the joy life produces is worth the effort. God knows we need some happiness, so He gives it to us in surprising ways. Happiness can even come through someone's death, especially the death of God's Son Jesus by which all our sins are forgiven and removed. But remember, His resurrection followed. It's a risen Lord we worship, not a dead martyr.

"But now Christ is risen from the dead, and has become the first fruits of those who have died." (1 Corinthians 15:20)

That's great news, don't you think?

It was graduation night, and they entered in tandem, nearly a hundred graduating seniors filing into the crowded auditorium to take their places of honor. With maroon gowns and traditional mortarboard caps, they looked almost as grown up as they felt.

The crowd was filled with Dads swallowing hard, and Moms brushing away tears. The class this year had been told it could not pray during the commencement because of a court ruling. The principal and several students were told to stay within the guidelines of that ruling. They could give inspirational and challenging speeches, but no one was to mention God, or any divine guidance or blessings on the graduates which had been done in former years. The speeches were nice, but routine, at least until the final speech was given and received a standing ovation.

The final student walked up to the microphone. He stood still and silent for just a moment smiling, and then it happened. All ninety-two students, every one of them, suddenly SNEEZED! The student on stage said loudly, *"God bless you, each and every one of you!"* And he walked off stage. The audience exploded into applause for the graduates who had found a unique way to invoke God's blessing on their future, despite a high court's disapproval.

This incident actually happened, and I wish it would happen more often. The young graduates walking our stages are in need of God's blessings now more than ever. They need people willing to take the stand for their faith in God. And not just any God, but in the triune God of the Holy Bible.

Prayer in schools may not be necessary, but to deny it when others want it is wrong. If you happen to attend any kind of graduation this time of year, whether high school or college, think of this story. Then, if you feel like it, sneeze real loud! Maybe someone will mention God's name in a blessed way.

"In the congregations I will bless the Lord." (Psalm 26:12)

God bless all our graduates!

Things in our world aren't always what they seem. We may read into the events of life what is not there. One Sunday Carol and I went to a trendy Pizza Bistro, and I noticed some of the waiter staff wearing Tee Shirts that said on them, "Legalize Marijuana." I suppose that message shouldn't have surprised me since their clientele was mostly young, but I didn't particularly like seeing it in print. Then I re-read the T-shirt and realized it said, "Legalize Marinara." It wasn't about the green weed, but the red sauce. That clever slogan caught my attention.

Things may not be what they seem in our daily life either. Our path of life may seem incredibly bumpy. A loved one goes astray, or the doctor says it's cancer, or elected officials disappoint us, or financial worries threaten to overcome us. We may think, *This isn't the path I should be taking. There must be a better way than this!*

That's when we need to remember that God is with us on the path. When we think our path of life is too steep or harsh, remember that God knows the path we are on, and His Son has taken that path already. Matthew 28:20 tells us, **"Lo, I am with you always, to the end of the earth."** Joshua 1:9 reminds, **"Be strong and courageous. Do not be terrified, for the Lord your God will be with you wherever you go."**

We can courageously take the path God has given us today, trusting He is with us each step, and He knows it will be blessed. God knows our path already and He will not lead us astray. Out of all possible paths, He knows the best one for us to take, and He will be with us to the end.

As the beloved hymn says:
> *Be still my soul, the Lord is on thy side.*
> *Bear patiently the cross of grief or pain.*
> *Leave to thy God to order and provide;*
> *In every change He faithful will remain.*
> *Be still, my soul; thy best, thy heavenly, Friend*
> *Through thorny ways leads to a joyful end.*
>   (from "Be Still My Soul")

MEMORIAL DAY

Dr. Joe Morgan was speaking to a crowd near the Pearl Harbor Memorial, recalling the attack of the Japanese in 1941. Joe had been stationed on Ford Island, in the center of Pearl Harbor. At 7:55 AM, he heard planes flying overhead. This nineteen year-old Texan, who had joined the Navy to "see the world," was confused as machine gun bullets rained down. As he watched his fellow sailors fall and die around him, his confusion turned to fear and hatred as he saw the Japanese "Rising Sun" symbol pass overhead on plane after plane.

He settled into a machine gun nest and managed to shoot down several Japanese planes. Although Joe was a Christian, he found himself hating the Japanese nation and its people that been responsible for killing over twenty-four hundred people at Pearl Harbor that day.

During that night, Joe said a prayer that changed his life. He promised God that if he survived the war, he would become a preacher. He kept his promise to God, but he never got over his hatred towards the Japanese.

In 1954, Joe became a pastor of the Wailuku Baptist Church in Maui. Two years later, he heard that Mitsuo Fuchida, commander of the naval air forces that attacked Pearl Harbor, was in Maui, so Joe went to hear his speech.

He listened with awe as Fuchida told of his becoming a Christian. After Fuchida's talk ended, Joe went up and introduced himself. Fuchida immediately bowed low to him and said one word in Japanese, *"Gomenasai." "I am sorry."*

What happened next was as an important moment for Joe as any other in history. Two former enemies shook hands, and Joe felt all his anger toward the man and his country leave. God replaced his rage with the peace of forgiveness. Morgan and Fuchida shook hands as brothers in Christ.

Forgiveness is a gift we give. It does not need the other person's contrition or sorrow. It only needs our willingness to let go of what will hurt us if we keep it. God gave us His forgiveness, despite our sins and failures. We can do no less.

"Love your enemies." (Matthew 5:44)

Gomenasai, dear Lord Jesus!

156

DAILY WALK WITH JESUS in...

JUNE

+ + +

JUNE 1

Have you ever considered how important you are to others? One winter I decided to feed the birds. I gave them crumbled old bread and they ate it all. I figured even the birds need a little help when we have so much snow.

One person told me old bread was bad for birds and another person said it was good for them. Birds usually survive on their own, but it's part of the Lord plan to use people to help satisfy the needs of some of His creatures.

The Lord uses us to help others. No matter what our occupation or role in life, we can be His arms and legs to reach out to others with His help. We cannot supply everyone's needs completely, but our vocation, our tasks, even our casual work can provide a service to people, and therefore also a service to God.

God gives us the time, abilities and resources so that we can do this. With these gifts He's also helping us. His greatest gifts to us are not wealth or health or even family. It is forgiveness of our sins so we can have life eternal with Jesus our Savior. With that most precious gift, we can live life fully here on earth and look forward to life there in heaven with God in all its joy and eternal fulfillment.

You are very important to others! We all have something to offer those in need. No matter if we think can do it or not, we should at least try. May God lead us to realize this and do our daily tasks with thanksgiving.

"The eyes of all look to You O Lord, and You give them their food at the proper time." (Psalm 145:15)

We need to help others, even if we aren't sure how.

157

JUNE 2

Johnny was visiting his grandparents on the farm. He had a slingshot and was learning to use it outside in a grove of trees. Just then one of Grandma's special ducks waddled by. Out of impulse, Johnny shot at the duck, hit it in the head and killed it! In panic, he hid the dead duck in the wood pile, only to look up and see his sister Sally watching. She had seen it all, and then walked away.

After lunch that day Grandma said, *"Sally, let's wash the dishes."* But Sally said, *"Grandma, Johnny told me he wanted to help in the kitchen."* Then she whispered to him, *"Remember the duck?"* So Johnny did the dishes and Sally went to play. Later that day Grandma said, *"I need Sally to help me make supper."* Sally smiled and said, *"Grandma, Johnny told me he wanted to help tonight."* She whispered again, *"Remember the duck?"* So Johnny stayed to help again while Sally went out to play.

After supper, Johnny's guilt finally got to him, and he confessed to Grandma that he had killed her duck. Grandma gave him a hug, and said, *"Sweetheart, I already know. I was standing at the window and saw the whole thing, and because I love you, I forgive you. I was just wondering how long you would let Sally make you her slave."*

You and I need purging of our guilt and the sins of our habits, those evil things we do *"out of sight."* Some kinds of sin enslave us. They push us into more sin and take away our resistance. Unless we ask God to intervene, forgive us and free us, we will go deeper and deeper into certain sins and may even perish because of them.

God does not wish for us to perish. He stands at the window and sees all we do, and then He cleanses us with His forgiving love. Patiently He waits for us to come to Him on our knees. Then He frees us.

Never allow a great temptation to take control. When you sense it happening, go to the Lord and He will help you.

"If any of you have **a grievance against someone, forgive as the Lord forgave you."** (Colossians 3:13)

Thanks, Lord, for freeing us from all evil.

A carpenter hired to help restore an old farmhouse had just finished a rough first day on the job. A flat tire made him lose an hour of work, his electric saw burned out and at the end of the day his old pickup truck refused to start.

The owner of the house saw this and offered to drive him home. The carpenter was silent in the car, and upon arriving home invited the owner in to meet his family. As they walked toward the front door, he paused briefly at a small tree, touching the tips of the branches with both hands. When opening the door he underwent an amazing transformation. His tanned face was wreathed in smiles and he hugged his two small children and gave his wife a kiss.

After a brief visit, the carpenter walked the owner to the car. They passed the tree again and curiosity got the better of the owner. He asked him about what he had seen him do earlier, touching that tree.

"That's my trouble tree," he replied. *"I know I can't help having troubles on the job, but I don't believe troubles belong in the house with my wife and children. So I just hang them up on that tree every night when I come home. Then in the morning I pick them up again. Funny thing is,"* he smiled, *"when I come out in the morning to pick them up, there aren't nearly as many as I remember hanging up the night before."*

Our Lord Jesus once told His disciples not to worry because God knew their needs and would provide them. Knowing that relieves our troubles. It's a great way to get them out of the way so we can be with those we love.

Jesus hung all our troubles and griefs on the tree of the cross. He left them there and no one need take them up again. His Trouble Tree results in our "trouble-free" forgiveness.

"Therefore do not worry about tomorrow, for tomorrow will worry about itself. Each day has enough trouble of its own." (Matthew 6:34)

Do you need a worry tree? Maybe it's your Bible! Touch it each day and see what happens.

JUNE 4

All of us have times in life when we doubt our worth. Difficulty at work, health problems, a shaky relationship or nasty world events may leave us feeling inconsequential or small. We may feel like a friend who jokingly told me, *"I feel so low today you could buy me for a dime and have eleven cents change."* But when we are at our lowest, God is underneath with His everlasting arms of love.

One autumn I saw a true television story about a man who had lost a leg in an auto accident and was barely able to live on his disability pay. His few possessions included a box from his parents containing an old blanket. One day while watching a television program about valuable household items, he saw an old Indian blanket appraised at over $100,000. His parents' box contained an old blanket that resembled the one on the program, so he had it appraised.

It was a Navajo *"chief's blanket"* of high quality, woven during the mid-1800s. *"It may be worth a hundred thousand dollars or more,"* the shocked young man was told. His old family heirloom was worth a fortune. After further appraisal, his blanket was sold at auction and "that old thing" brought him $1.5 million dollars!

You and I are worth more than a fortune to our Heavenly Father, and our worth is not determined by how good we are or how we feel. It is determined by God's love for us, the Creator who has given us life. Our Heavenly Father showed us our true worth when He gave us His only Son Jesus to forgive us our sins and grant us eternal life.

Jesus once told His disciples, **"Look at the birds of the air; they neither sow nor reap nor gather into barns, and yet your heavenly Father feeds them. Are you not of more value than they?" (Matthew 6:26)**

If God cares about something as small as a common sparrow, does He not far more care for us, His highest and most uncommon creation of the universe?

"Seek first the Kingdom of God and His righteousness and all the rest will be yours as well." (Matthew 6:33)

There is no pit so deep that God is not deeper still.

Grandma was visiting her son and his family, and after lunch was playing with her granddaughter. At one point, little Rachel got up from the midst of all her toys and announced she was going outside. Grandma said, *"But Rachel, you need to put away your toys first."* Without missing a beat, Rachel replied, *"I don't have time,"* and ran outside.

Rachel had just turned three! She was definitely not running on a tight schedule, so where did she learn to say that? From her parents, of course. Maybe she had even heard Grandma say it.

I wonder if God is ever surprised when He hears our responses to His requests. Jesus tells us in Matthew 11:28, **"Come to me all you who work and are tired, and I will give you rest."** We, of course, find all kinds of reasons not to. *"I'm really busy today, Lord." "This is not a good time." "I have so many important things planned, but I'm sure I'll have more time later on."*

What is your schedule like? God doesn't ask that much of us, just an hour or two to worship Him each week, and a little time during the week for prayer. All He'd like is time for us to rest with Him awhile from our busy schedules, a time to talk with us in prayer, a time to pick up our toys and give thanks that we have them.

Do you include God in your week? Are you involved in anything that's not good for you? God says, **"Be holy, because I am holy,"** but we say, *"It's more fun when I live this way!"* and then run outside to play. Later on when we get tired of our life, when the aches and pains hurt so much, or when life seems so empty and we wonder what we've accomplished, maybe then we will think of God. But too often we say, *"I don't have time right now!"*

Remember that Jesus has said, **"Come to me all you who work and feel tired and worn out, and I will give you rest."** His kind of rest is better than ours. It will last longer, make us stronger and refresh us more for the coming day. God knows than we do, so He wants us to rest. I wonder if Rachel came back inside or if she picked up her toys.

Okay, God, I have some time now. What would You like to do?

JUNE 6

It was the morning of June 6, 1944, and the decision had been made. "Operation Overlord," also known as D-Day, was set in motion. Troops and planes were deployed and ships were under way. A million soldiers were set to slam against Hitler's "Atlantic Wall" in France, and all the responsibility fell on the shoulders of one man, General Dwight D. Eisenhower.

The night before the invasion "Ike" spent time with the Screaming Eagles, soldiers of the 101st Airborne. He went from soldier to soldier encouraging men who were young enough to be his sons.

Historians say that when Eisenhower watched the C-47s take off and the ships disappear into the night, his eyes were full of tears. He went back to his quarters and wrote a note, a brief message to be delivered to the White House in the event of a defeat. Ike wrote, *"If any blame or fault attaches itself to this attempt, it is mine alone."* This great five-star general accepted blame even before it was needed.

It could be argued that of all the acts of courage and bravery that happened on D-Day, perhaps the greatest one took place at a desk where the Supreme Allied Commander took the blame for the actions of his troops, even before blame was needed.

Most of us are willing to "take the rap" for what we do, but few will take the rap for what others do. Yet our Lord Jesus did that for our sins, even before He knew what sins we would commit. He took our sins on the cross even before we committed them. With His death there, we were forgiven, even before we sinned.

In this new day God has given you, may you find a stronger faith in the One who came into this world to "take the rap" for you. He wants to do this, because He knows how it will help us eternally.

**"While we were still sinners, Christ died for us."
(Romans 5:8)**

Give thanks to God for wise and faithful leaders.

162

JUNE 7

Jesus said, **"He who has ears to hear, let him hear."** **(Matthew 11:15)** That's His way of saying we should take time to listen and understand what He is telling us. It is His way of telling us to look behind the words we hear to the real meaning of what is said.

We live in a sea of words, and that sea is too often stormy. Media, music and politicians assail us with words crafted to influence us. Preachers try to persuade us with new ideas about the Bible. Adults try to teach youth, and youth tune them out with headphones. We hear words because we have ears, but we're not always using them to hear very well.

Jesus' brother James wrote, **"Let every person be quick to hear, slow to speak and slow to anger." (James 1:19)** Good communication involves both hearing and listening. Most people with ears can hear, but listening requires discernment, wisdom and the interest to find out what is being said.

Many families suffer from poor listening. Companies have problems when workers are poor listeners. Nations require diplomats to filter words and messages spoken by leaders. Leaders may manipulate people with specially crafted messages, so their words must be carefully evaluated.

Jesus wants us to become active listeners. Rabbi Jesus of Nazareth is the best listener who ever walked the earth. He knows our hearts and hears our cries as we try to listen with ears plugged by sin. In His mercy He forgives us and helps us understand better, both in our listening as well as in our speaking.

Do you have good hearing? My hearing has gotten poorer, and I must strain to listen carefully if I am to hear the best I can. Do you use your mind to help you listen? Today, try to listen carefully to others and also to yourself, and may God bless your conversations.

Lord, help me listen today to what others say, and help me speak clearly. Amen.

What are the benefits of going to church regularly each Sunday? With summer here and vacation plans on the calendar, it will be tempting to neglect regular Sunday worship and Christian fellowship.

Once while up in the mountains I decided to make a small fire for cooking. I got the fire going, but it wasn't hot enough. I assumed more air around the little sticks would make the fire hotter so I scattered the sticks a little. Each one did burn faster but they gave off little heat. Only when I placed the sticks next to each other did they burn hot enough to cook the food. Space is necessary to get a fire going, but sticks burn hotter and more slowly when right next to each other. The heat of one stick supports the heat of the others.

You and I need to be with other Christians more than we think. Individually, we can learn and do some things, making sparks and small flames here and there. But only together can we make the most useful fire. If we stay separate from each other long enough, our own flame will go out. We need time with others and the Lord more than we need time away.

Our Christian faith does not sustain itself. For every Sunday without worship, it takes one or two Sundays in worship to make our faith stronger. Imagine what a whole summer without Sunday fellowship does. It's like lying on a bed for several weeks without walking. If we try to take a step we'll fall down, because our legs have become too weak.

If a summer Sunday finds you in your trailer, cabin, or motel room, don't leave God out. Read a few minutes from your Bible and pray whether you're alone or with loved ones. Pray and let God bless you with His presence and love.

Time away from regular routine is good for refreshment. Even Jesus took time away from the crowds. But we will have a stronger faith if we remain close to other Christians. The faith of one Christian supports the faith of the other.

"Do not give up meeting together, as some are in the habit of doing, but encourage one another." (Hebrews 10:25)

A united flame will make a great fire.

JUNE 9

In life, there is a time to follow someone's advice, and there is a time to follow your heart. Francis Ouimet grew up in Brookline, Massachusetts, living next to the seventeenth hole of "The Country Club." At a time when golf was reserved for the wealthy, Francis started caddying at age nine. Borrowing clubs and using golf balls he found on the course, he taught himself the game, eventually catching the eye of club members.

Although he became the best high school golfer in the state, his father insisted he drop out and "do something useful." Francis worked at a store, but he also kept golfing.

In 1913, young Ouimet won an amateur tournament and was invited to play in the U. S. Open which would be played that year at the course next door that he knew best. In what is considered the greatest golf match ever played, amateur golfer Francis Ouimet won the 1913 U. S. Open, besting favored British pro golfers, Ted Ray and Harry Vardon.

Francis was twenty years old and stood six feet two inches. His caddy and friend, Eddy Lowrey, was less than five feet tall and only ten years old! Their story is the basis for Mark Frost's book, The Greatest Game Ever Played.

Ouimet won several more amateur tournaments, was elected into several golf Halls of Fame and honored by his PGA friends. Since its founding, the Francis Ouimet Scholarship Fund has given twenty-five million dollars to over 5,000 young caddies, including Arnold Palmer, Jack Nicklaus and Annika Sorenstam.

Ouimet served in World War One and was married to Stella Sullivan nearly fifty years. He is the only American ever elected captain of St. Andrew's Royal Golf Club of Scotland and yet he retained his amateur status his entire life. His portrait is even on a U.S. postage stamp.

If he had followed his father's advice to "do something useful," he would have been an unknown worker. Instead, he followed his heart and became a legend in sports.

"Give thanks in all circumstances." (1 Thess. 5:18)

Give thanks that we live in a free nation to follow our dreams.

Johnny enjoyed spending time with Uncle Bill. They played catch often because Johnny loved baseball. They always had a good time together, and he even got to ride in Uncle Bill's new 1955 Chevy. One day Uncle Bill came to Johnny with a choice. *"You can either have a dime today or a dollar next week. If you get the dime today, you can buy yourself a bag of potato chips you like. But if you wait a week, you can buy yourself that baseball you've been wanting. What's your choice?"*

Johnny thought it over. He was really hungry and the chips sounded pretty good and maybe Uncle Bill would forget his promise next week about the dollar, so he said, *"I'll take the dime."* He was right - the potato chips were very good, but soon they were gone.

The next week Johnny saw the kids on his block playing with a new baseball, so he asked Uncle Bill, *"I'd really like a baseball."* But Bill replied, *"You already made your choice, Johnny, and you can't have it both ways. If you'd have waited, maybe your Mom would have bought you some chips, and then you'd have a ball, too. It's worth it to wait awhile to get what we really want."*

How true. If we're on a diet, the rewards of waiting a few months to taste ice cream is worth it. It's the same in waiting until you have the money to get that new outfit, or waiting until you're married to enjoy sexual intimacy.

We live in a world of microwave ovens, computers, cell phones, and instant cash machines. We want what we want when we want it! We're not used to waiting, and the ads entice us to "buy now and pay later."

But the best things in life come with time and patience. Whether it's completing college before starting a career, or getting in shape before running a race, or working hard on the marriage rather than diving into the pool of divorce, we often need to wait. Potato chips may sound good when we're hungry, but are they worth sacrificing something better that will come if we just wait awhile longer?

"Wait for the Lord!" **(Psalm 27:14)**

But I'm not sure I can wait that long!!

What do you do when you're stuck with a relationship or situation you don't like? How do you love someone you're having real problems with?

Joey had a wonderful puppy and he enjoyed caring for it. He loved its squirming softness and played with it every chance he could. Then it chewed on his baseball glove and began barking loudly. It had to be fed and walked, and it often made a mess on the floor and chewed on some of his CD's. Joey complained to his parents, but they said, *"He's your responsibility; you're stuck with him."*

Being stuck with a puppy is one thing, but what about an annoying neighbor, a demanding co-worker, a rebellious child or a straying spouse? What do you do when you're expected to love someone you don't even like?

We have four choices: 1) Flee, 2) Fight, 3) Forget, or 4) Forgive. Many choose to flee, to run away from a person, job or obligation and try to find something better. Some choose to fight for their rights, blame someone else or try to get their own way. Others forget the situation, ignore the person, do the minimum at work or pretend there is no problem.

Still others discover forgiveness. Jesus often must have felt that He was stuck with twelve fools rather than twelve disciples. With their arguing, complaining or bragging, He must have wanted at times to tell them all to leave.

Instead, the night before He died, Jesus washed their feet. Can you imagine what He thought as He washed Judas' feet? How could you serve someone you knew would betray you? That's why Jesus prayed so often. That's why He learned the Holy Scriptures which gave Him strength and guidance.

If you are stuck with someone you don't love, try helping or serving them in some small way. Ask God to help you love them as He would. Service and prayer will help change your heart towards a troublesome person.

"Now that I have washed your feet, you also should wash one another's feet." (John 13:14)

Then you'll understand a little of how God feels towards you.

A scorpion, unable to swim, asked a turtle to carry him on his back across the river. *"But you will sting me and I'll drown."* *"My dear turtle,"* laughed the scorpion, *"If I were to sting you, you may drown but I'd drown with you. Now where is the logic in that?"* *"You're right,"* said the turtle, *"Hop on!"* The scorpion climbed aboard and halfway across the river suddenly he gave the turtle a mighty sting. As they both began to sink, the turtle said, *"Why? You said there'd be no logic in your stinging me. Why did you do it anyway?"* The drowning scorpion sadly replied, *"Stinging you has nothing to do with logic; it's just my nature."*

"That's just the way I am. It's human nature." How often have we said or heard that? It's the logic of a person who believes there's little hope for change, or it's the one who wants to be excused for wrong actions. *"It isn't my fault - he made me do it!"* says the child, and also some adults. Whether on the playground or in the courtroom, it's our nature to point the finger of blame elsewhere. It's not my fault, because if it was, then I'd have to accept the consequences.

Early in my ministry I remember hearing an old fellow tell me, *"That's the way people are, Pastor; you'd better get used to it."* But I never have. I've always wanted to be a part of change for the better. I've always thought leading a church and preaching and teaching the Gospel would help people become better. The part I have come to accept is that I can't change anyone but myself.

People don't change people, but God does. He brings us experiences that change us. He takes away the oldness of sin and replaces it with the newness of His love. He removes our sins, but then seeks to change us to be more like Christ. St. Paul tells us in 2 Corinthians 5:17, **"If anyone is in Christ, he is a new creation; the old has gone, the new has come."**

God isn't satisfied with our old human nature. He wants to change us into something better than we are. And He can love us enough to make that change happen.

God loves us just the way we are, but He may not leave us that way for long.

I read an article that spoke of hope for Christ's return. In it, this thought stood out: *"From the human viewpoint, there is no solution for the struggles of this world. The only complete and permanent solution is found in the return of Christ to earth."*

Each generation has been certain that the world is beyond repair, that Christ must certainly come in judgment. Thus, each Christian generation has looked forward to Christ's return.

The problems today may seem extreme and complicated by rapid advancements in technology. Many problems may seem insoluble, such as illegal drugs, religious extremism, pornography, poverty, slavery, war, waste of resources, abortion, political corruption, and apathy.

Which of these do you think is possible for mankind to eradicate? Which of these will be with us a hundred years from now? What will it take to overcome these evils? What will happen to churches in the future?

This is not mere pessimism. The world really does seem on the brink of some big changes, and they don't look good. Sin brought us here, and only God can rescue us. Only faith in Jesus Christ can give us any genuine hope, for ourselves or for our children.

Since humans first rebelled against God in the Garden of Eden, history has seen evil days. It has been the hope of every Christian generation that Jesus will soon come again in glory. Meanwhile, He promises us strength for each day.

His return will change everything. Christ will not return as an earthly conqueror to vanquish our enemies. He will bring a new heaven and a new earth for His redeemed people. Christ's return will make all things new. When His judgment is complete, evil will be destroyed, and there will be no more sin. Jesus will rule a new universe, and He will make all things good and perfect. How we long for that day!

Meanwhile, we live by faith in Him, hopeful of His return. Our waiting must not be idle, for we have a message to pass on. Remember He said, **"I am with you always."** **(Matthew 28:20)**

Even so, come quickly, O Lord!

JUNE 14

After finally receiving the Building Permit for their new little church, the pastor had one contractor lined up to come in after another. If one didn't come, the rest would be delayed. So the foundation was dug, poured and backfilled. The plumber set in the sub-floor plumbing and the cement forms were all set. After negotiations the county inspector agreed to approve some of the preliminary work so the next crew could pour the concrete.

Morning came for the "floor pour" and everyone was a little late. Pouring concrete late in the day is risky in Colorado with its afternoon heat and showers, so the pastor and members prayed all weekend, asking God for good weather. *"Please, Lord, let there be no rain Monday until at 7 PM."*

The first cement truck came but the concrete the mix was wrong, so the truck went back and didn't return until 1:00 PM so the crew could begin its work. It was late in the day. Would they be able to complete the project as planned?

Rain clouds came in twice but broke up, cooling the men who worked feverishly leveling and troweling 55 yards of rapidly hardening "mud." The foreman looked at the pastor and pointed up at the sky. The Pastor folded his hands as if in prayer, and the foreman smiled.

They leveled most of it and "eyeballed" the rest, creating an incredibly flat surface despite the conditions. Finally at 6:00 PM their trucks left as rain clouds came up again. After supper the pastor returned to find a beautifully flat, hard floor that felt its first sprinkles of rain at exactly 7:00 PM! What they thought would be an "Impossible Pour" turned out just as they'd all prayed for.

God doesn't mind if we ask Him for ordinary things like good weather for building. He hears the prayers of His faithful people because of our Lord Jesus who died for us. Because of Jesus, God always hears our prayers.

"Call on me in the day of trouble; I will deliver you, and you will honor me." (Psalm 50:15)

Who says God doesn't answer prayers with just what we need when we need it?

JUNE 15

Joe tried his best to be a good Dad, but when his wife abandoned them, he doubted he could raise his children alone. At times the stress was so great Joe almost fell apart. He was bitter she had deserted them and often got angry with his kids over the smallest things. Finally he got some counseling, and after a few years married a wonderful woman who loved his children and helped raise them as her own.

Fifteen years after those dark and terrible days, Joe and his wife received a plaque, a gift from their college graduate son. This is what the plaque said:

> **TO MY CHRISTIAN PARENTS**
> *"You are my parents and I love you. Your guidance and direction have helped me more than words can express. In the struggles of life you were sensitive to my needs. When I doubted, you encouraged me. When I needed help, you were there. When I sought independence you patiently yielded, allowing me to learn from my own decisions. I saw your faith in God and learned that God loves me, too. You helped me spiritually and stressed the importance of honesty and integrity. Your love for me has been generous and yet tempered with the realities of life. For this I will be forever grateful. You are both very special to me and I will love you always."*

Teach your children well, my friends, and be sure God is in the picture. Mary and Joseph were the only parents who ever had a perfect child. Jesus was the Perfect One none of us could ever have or be. Give thanks that He forgives us when we and our children are less than perfect.

"Teach these things to your children and to your children's children." (Deuteronomy 4:9)

May God give us joy in seeing our children in heaven one day.

JUNE 16

We can't always predict the impact of our words on others. A story is told of an elderly woman had just returned to her home from an evening of worship at her church when she was startled by an intruder. She caught the man in the act of robbing her home, so she yelled, *"Stop! Acts 2:38! I said stop! Acts 2:38!"* That verse reads, **"Repent and be baptized in the name of Jesus Christ so that your sins may be forgiven."**

The burglar didn't know the words of that passage, but he still stopped dead in his tracks and dropped his weapon. The woman calmly called the police and explained what she had done. As the officer handcuffed the man to take him in, he asked the burglar, *"Why did you just stand there? All the old lady did was yell a Bible verse to you."* *"What Bible verse?"* replied the burglar. *"She said she had an axe and two 38s and I wasn't going to go against that!"*

True, we can't always predict the impact of our words on others. A stern word of warning changes one man's life and protects a woman from danger. A kind word of hope brings a person back to the Lord, but a judgmental word drives someone over the edge.

Jesus changed lives. His words gave courage to the weak and strength to the weary. They rebuked evil and spoke truth. His Holy Word continues to do the same today. We are blessed to have in our Bibles the very Word of God that shows us the way of salvation by faith in Jesus, as well as gives us guidance for Christian living.

Have you ever been robbed or had your life in danger? If so, do you remember what you were thinking? If not, what do you think might go through your mind? At such times, God's Word becomes a calming force to help us in times of danger.

"Speaking the truth in love, we will grow to become in every respect the mature body of him who is the head, that is, Christ." (Ephesians 4:15)

Be the bearer of God's Good Word to those who need to hear it, today and every day!

172

JUNE 17

Father's Day is close at hand, so today let's give thanks for all the good Dads out there, all the men doing their tasks well, loving their kids and wives, bringing home the bacon and modeling Christ's love in their life.

In my family room I have a wooden puppet my Dad made for us back in the 1940s. Seeing it always brings back good memories of him. I've used it several times to entertain my sons and grandchildren and I hope one of them will take it someday.

What is a Good Dad? Someone has described him thus:

A Good Dad is someone who wants to catch you before you fall, but instead lets you fall, picks you up, brushes you off, and encourages you to try again.

A Good Dad is someone who wants to keep you from making mistakes, but instead lets you find your own way, even though he aches in silence when you get hurt.

A Good Dad is someone who holds you when you cry, scolds you when you break the rules, shines with pride when you succeed, and has faith in you even when you fail.

A Good Dad tries his best, always forgives you, and also knows he is forgiven by his own Good Father in heaven who has given him direction for faithful living.

Our country is filled with good fathers, and most of them get little credit for the good they do. They are strong yet can be very weak, and bold yet have frail egos. They can have a big heart and a mighty laugh, yet weep tender tears they will rarely show. Not all Good Dads had good role models in life, but they have become as good as they are by God's grace.

We can't thank God enough for revealing Himself as our Heavenly Father who loves us in spite of our sins. With our Heavenly Father as our model, Christian fathers can show God's love in their homes.

"Let your light shine before others, so that they may see your good works and give glory to your Father who is in heaven." (Matthew 5:16)

Thanks be to God for Good Dads and especially for our Heavenly Father.

173

Carol and I like to "travel light," that is, we take as little with us on trips as possible. But we don't always see this in others. When some fellow travellers get their bags at the airport terminal, it looks like they'll need a small van to haul it all away.

All people carry around some baggage, things Max Lucado calls the "Luggage of Life." Odds are you already picked up a few bags of it this morning. Somewhere between the first step on the floor and the last step out the door, you stepped over to the baggage carousel and loaded up. And if you don't recall doing this, it's because your carousel wasn't the one at the airport, but the one in your mind. The bags we grabbed weren't made of leather, but of our life burdens.

We may have grabbed a suitcase of guilt, a bag of discontent or a sack of grief. We may have a duffel of weariness over one shoulder and a bag of anger over the other. Add a backpack of doubt, an overnight case of loneliness and a trunkful of fear, and pretty soon we're pulling more stuff than a skycap. Hauling needless luggage all day is exhausting.

God's Word tells us, *"Put that stuff down! You're carrying burdens you don't need to bear. Travel light!"* Jesus said it in these words, **"Come to me, all of you who are weary of carrying heavy burdens, and I will give you rest. Carry My yoke, because it's a lot lighter and easier than the loads you strap on yourselves." (Matthew 11:28, paraphrased)** In other words, travel light!

Traveling light means trusting God with the burdens we were never intended to bear. For the sake of those we love, God wants us to set aside all that unneeded luggage. He wants us to shed ourselves of whatever holds us back in loving Him or each other. He wants us to get rid of the anger and resentment that separate, the habits that strangle, and the materialism that suffocates.

Traveling light takes practice. We won't learn it in one trip, but over the course of many trips. We'll find out how to put things aside, to take what's important, and to give Jesus some of our burdens. He's our best fellow traveler.

For the sake of Jesus and all your fellow travelers, travel light!

JUNE 19

God wants us to grow up. Millions of Christians just grow older, stuck in spiritual infancy, but God wants us to grow up. Spiritual growth is not automatic. It takes intentional work and commitment. We must want to grow up, we must decide to make an effort in our growing up.

When Jesus asked Matthew to follow Him, he got up and followed. He didn't immediately understand what he was doing, nor all that the future had in store, but he got up and followed Jesus anyway. He could have thought, *"How nice that Jesus wants me to follow - I must be someone special,"* and then stayed home. Instead, he got up and followed Jesus.

Some of us are afraid to commit to important things and prefer to drift in life. Others make half-hearted commitments, which lead to mediocrity and frustration. Others commit to worldly things that disappoint and bring bitterness.

To change our life, we must change the way we think. If we are in a boat going east, and want to go west, the boat won't turn without our taking over the controls. St. Paul tells us in Romans 12:2, **"Do not conform any longer to the world, but be transformed by the renewing of your mind."** Jesus will help us in our renewal process.

God wants us to grow up, to stop thinking like children, becoming angry when we don't get our way, or being afraid of the unknown things in the dark, or nursing our hurts. We must stop thinking of ourselves only and start thinking of others, and also of Christ.

Maturity means becoming like Jesus Christ Who always thought of others first. Christianity is not a philosophy of life, it is a relationship with Christ that changes lives. When Jesus is our Lord, He makes our life new.

"When I was a child, I talked, thought, and reasoned like a child. When I grew up, I put childish things behind me." (1 Corinthians 13:11)

Part of maturity involves thinking of others.

175

JUNE 20

I have a walking staff that is remarkably beautiful. It's a gift from my brother who carved it for me from a stick of "Diamond Willow." It is lightweight, strong and has unique beauty due to a dozen or more diamond shaped notches of different sizes in its lovely rust-colored wood.

Diamond Willow is found in northern Minnesota and North Dakota, and is highly sought after for canes and walking staffs. Diamond Willow is not a species. It's a common young willow tree that's been attacked by a fungus that occurs along river banks where young willows grow.

The diamond shapes are actually enlarged notches caused by the stress of the tree trying to avoid the attacking spores. The results of the stress are rare formations of beauty not seen in any other tree. The beauty of a Diamond Willow comes from its stressed life.

A Diamond Willow staff doesn't grow looking beautiful. It is twisted and ugly in its natural state and needs to have its outer bark stripped away so its inner beauty can be seen. It needs an artist to sand it and varnish it to bring out its inner character. Without the work of the artist, people would toss the stick aside as ugly and useless.

All willows have fungi growing around them, but only certain ones are affected. Because of the stress of what the fungus does to the tree, the Diamond Willow staff is sought after and admired. Without the stress, it's just a stick.

You and I have stress in our lives that shapes us, usually in ways we'd rather not want. It can change our attitude and affect our relationships. Everyone has stress and no one can fully avoid it. The important thing lies how we react to it. Sometimes we may think stress makes us ugly, but with God's help it can make us unique and beautiful, depending on how we react to it.

Jesus has forgiven our sins by stripping away our outer ugly nature of sin. By His great love for us, He has made us beautiful so that we can **"shine like the stars" (Philippians 2:15)** as we show forth our faith in Him.

I hope you all some day can see a Diamond Willow staff.

In the early 1940's George came to the office of Dr. Smith, one of the rare physicians who treated cancer in those days. Dr. Smith told him of a new medicine he'd discovered that had some success, one that had not yet been tried on humans. George pleaded to try the new medicine.

Though his colleagues disagreed with him about giving a patient an untested medicine, Dr. Smith agreed to use it. Without it, George was a dead man, he said, so why not give him a chance at recovery? His colleagues objected and refused to cooperate. They felt that there was a right and wrong way to do things, and they insisted their way was right.

Dr. Smith administered the medicine to George and the results were amazing. He regained his appetite, gained back nearly sixty pounds and became his old cheerful self. By all accounts, his cancer had gone into remission.

Being a very busy man, Dr. Smith turned George's care over to his staff, who again refused to treat George with the untested medicine. Within a year, the cancer returned, and this time George died. The medicine would have worked, but because it was not among their list of accepted medical treatments, George did not receive it and died.

It was George Herman Ruth who died, "Babe" Ruth, the great American baseball player who died at only fifty-three years of age because a few doctors could not see past their prejudices to accept something new, something already tried and proven by a colleague.

In our Christian walk, God calls on us to take risks when the Gospel is at stake. We need to risk using our time for Him, our resources, our pride and our best efforts. May we ever be willing to do what needs to be done for the Gospel, even if it means going outside of our comfort zones.

"Be devoted to one another in love. Honor one another above yourselves." (Romans 12:10)

Take that risk for Jesus!

JUNE 22

In 1927, poet Max Ehrmann wrote the words to his "Desiderata," a word which means, "things to be desired." Though He does not identify who God is, he urges us to be at peace with Him. Today I urge you to give thanks that you know the true God, and His Son, our Lord Jesus Christ.

"DESIDERATA" (by Max Ehrmann)

Go placidly amid the noise and the haste,
And remember what peace there may be in silence.
As far as possible, without surrender, be on good terms with all persons.
Speak your truth quietly and clearly; and listen to others,
Even to the dull and the ignorant; they too have their story.
Avoid loud and aggressive persons; they are vexatious to the spirit.
If you compare yourself with others, you may become vain or bitter,
For always there will be greater and lesser persons than yourself.
Enjoy your achievements as well as your plans.
Keep interested in your own career, however humble;
It is a real possession in the changing fortunes of time.
Exercise caution in your business affairs, for the world is full of trickery,
But let this not blind you to what virtue there is.
Many persons strive for high ideals, and everywhere life is full of heroism.
Be yourself. Especially do not feign affection. Neither be cynical about love,
for in the face of all aridity and disenchantment,
It is as perennial as the grass.
Take kindly the counsel of the years, gracefully surrender the things of youth.
Nurture strength of spirit to shield you in sudden misfortune.
But do not distress yourself with dark imaginings;
Many fears are born of fatigue and loneliness.
Beyond a wholesome discipline, be gentle with yourself.
You are a child of the universe no less than the trees and the stars;
You have a right to be here. And whether or not it is clear to you,
no doubt the universe is unfolding as it should.
Therefore be at peace with God, whatever you conceive Him to be.
And whatever your labors and aspirations,
In the noisy confusion of life, keep peace in your soul.
With all its sham, drudgery, and broken dreams,
it is still a beautiful world. Be cheerful. Strive to be happy.

"Blessed are the people of whom this is true; blessed are the people whose God is the Lord." (Psalm 144:15)

Wonderful words from a fine American poet.

178

There are many facets of life, and we can learn what is important through comparisons. When your child does poorly in school, he isn't as bad as another child who has just been in a serious auto accident. The same can be true about the things of aging. What is difficult for us may pale in comparison with what is difficult for someone else.

Carol and I owned a few acres in the mountains at ten thousand feet in altitude. We were out for a walk on a mile long trail when we met Rita. She had walked to the end of her driveway and met us beautifully dressed in a red jacket and pearls. When we introduced ourselves I asked, *"Are you here for a visit?"* she responded, *"I have lived up here the past few years."* Rita told us she's lived there alone in a cabin owned by her son who came up every few weeks to stay with her for a weekend. And Rita was eighty-seven years old!

"Yes, I've walked that trail a few times, but not this year," she said. *"I drive these mountain roads almost every day, although not at night any more."* We talked some more and after saying good-bye continued on our way at a more sprightly pace. If Rita could walk this trail at her age, so could we!

Comparisons can help us see reality more clearly, but we must avoid comparing ourselves with others spiritually. *"I may have a bad habit or I may use coarse language, but at least I'm not like that fellow. I may not go to church, but at least I'm not a hypocrite."* Sounds like the Pharisee in Jesus' parable who said, *"God, I thank you I'm not as bad as that Tax Collector."*

We can never compare ourselves with God, and thankfully we don't have to. God is holy and loving. He knows our sins and still cares for us. He chose to send Jesus to be our Savior. However, having faith gives us no right to feel superior to others not so blessed. In fact, it should move us to say, *"God, be merciful to me, a sinner."* Humble faith is what God seeks, and that's what the Holy Spirit gives us.

"They will still bear fruit in old age, they will stay fresh and green." (Psalm 92:14)

What can you learn from a Rita in your life?

JUNE 24

If a little is good, a lot must be better, correct? Of course, that's not always true. In fact, it hardly ever is. With some pleasures, some foods, or some people, a little goes a long way. Any more and there will be only trouble waiting for us.

Take cashews, for instance. I can never eat just a few, and after I've eaten my fill, my stomach nearly always regrets I hadn't the sense to stop sooner. The first handful turns into many handfuls, and very soon I wish I'd not bought them. But they were so good while I was eating them!

We can know a thing is wrong but do it anyway. We can know we should stop something, but we don't. Just like Paul said in Romans 7:19, **"I do not do the good I want, but the evil I do not want is what I keep on doing."** I would say, *"The small handful I should have had, that I didn't. The many handfuls I should not have eaten, those I did!"* Paul added, **"Wretched man that I am!"** He, too, must have had too many cashews!

Living a productive life comes by knowing our limits. Too much work can be as bad as too much leisure. A little salt can be good, but too much can be a poison. Moderation and balance are needed in all things of life.

However, we cannot get too much of God's grace and mercy. His love is new to us every day because we need it every day. A handful of His grace is not enough, for we daily sin much, so we need much grace. We need His mercy by the bucketful. Rest assured, there's never a moment when we don't need Jesus.

Thanks be to God, we have all the mercy we need! When it comes to God's love for us in Jesus, a little is good, a lot is far better, and ten times the amount is never too much. The same is true of faith. Faith the size of a mustard seed is enough, but faith the size of a watermelon is even better.

I felt better later that day. Walking helped, and so did Alka Seltzer. I doubt I learned from this, however. I will always be tempted to eat too many cashews. Maybe in heaven I can have all the treats I want!

Thank you, Jesus, for forgiving us poor, miserable sinners,

Our Lord Jesus urged His followers to show love to all people, not just other Christians. Opportunities to love are all around us, especially when disaster strikes during a violent storm, and Christians respond with needed assistance.

Children of God, inspired by the Holy Spirit, want to help needy victims. We pray for them and give them money and resources. We can also support Christian agencies like the "Orphan Grain Train" which assists victims with clothing, fresh water, medicines and mobile kitchens.

Orphan Grain Train began in the 1980's through the efforts of Clayton Andrews of Nebraska who owned a trucking firm. He saw his trucks coming back from their deliveries empty too often, so he began finding things to bring back that would help people, used or new items that could be contributed to those in need.

Inspired by Jesus' words to His disciples in John 14:18, **"I will not leave you as orphans, but I will come to you,"** Andrews and other Lutheran Christians founded the "Orphan Grain Train," a highly successful ministry of procuring and sending used items to people in need.

For congregations, such as Epiphany Lutheran Church of Castle Rock, Colorado, the Orphan Grain Train has become its primary social ministry. Since 2002, its members have sorted and packed over a quarter million pounds of used clothing each year which is shipped all over the world to people in need, both inside and outside the USA. Their containers of used clothing have gone to Ukraine, the Baltic nations, Russia, India, and wherever people in need can use them.

The month of June means the summer storm season is here, but we know God will never leave us as orphans. He will bless us richly, providing our needs and giving us ways to help others. As you pray for people where storms have come, give thanks for the work of ministries like the Orphan Grain Train.

"Whatever you did for one of the least of these brothers and sisters of mine, you did for me." (Matthew 25:40)

What Christian ministries are you supporting?

A number of years ago I loaned money to a complete stranger. We were standing in line late one afternoon at a local Department of Motor Vehicles office where dozens of people were hoping the line wouldn't close before they got what they needed. I was the third person from the counter when the man in front of me became agitated. He turned around and said, *"Excuse me, sir, but I'm short of funds. Could you loan me five dollars? I promise to mail it back to you just as soon as I get home. I need to renew my driver's license, because we're taking a trip and leaving tomorrow morning."*

I recalled having forgotten money like that a time or two, and so I loaned him the five dollars. He wrote down my home address, thanked me, got his new license and left. I figured I wouldn't see the money again, but a few days later I got a letter with a nice note of thanks and a five dollar bill. It's nice to know there are some honest people around.

Most folks today would say it's a little crazy to trust a stranger, but sometimes it seems the right thing to do. Carol and I used to attend Airstream Rallies where we met lots of strangers, although at RV Rallies people are not strangers for long. Every day we ran into hundreds of people we'd never seen before, and we made many friends.

The experience at the DMV reminds me of the awesome grace of God. He loves us without any reassurance that we will return His love. He forgives us, knowing that the majority of people in the world will reject Him. He knows that His redeemed people will make promises they will not always fulfill. But still He loves and forgives us.

He sent His only Son to be our Savior. God doesn't wait until we're worthy of His grace, nor does He ask for proof of our intent or require a promissory note for the things He gives us. He just loves and gives, because He knows we need it and also because He is our Father.

"I have loved you with an everlasting love."(Jeremiah 31:3)

That's a great thought for the day, don't you think?

JUNE 27

A recent movie was made called *"The Incredible Hulk."* It was from a story about a scientist who, whenever he became angry, grew muscular and powerful and in his rage destroyed things around him. *"The Incredible Hulk"* is a good example of how anger can bring out a monster in us all.

Anger, especially uncontrolled rage, overrules common sense and reason. Angry people can impulsively and uncontrollably hurt others with their words and actions. Angry people also hurt themselves. It's been documented that thirty minutes of intense anger uses up as much energy as a full day of work. Chronically angry people suffer more illnesses, have higher blood pressure and more headaches, and can die at a younger age.

The Bible says, **"Get rid of all bitterness, rage and anger, brawling and slander, along with every form of malice."** **(Ephesians 4:31)**. It also says, **"Bear with each other and forgive as the Lord has forgiven you." (Colossians 3:13)**

Though anger itself is not a sin, it can lead to sins, including the sin of pride. Anger often comes because we believe we've not gotten what we deserve, forgetting that what we want is not always what we need. It's true our Lord Jesus became angry, but He always kept His anger in check. Sometimes when we're angry, we're not sure where to direct it. That's when we may become our own *"Incredible Hulk."*

Some people get angry at God, while others find little value in that. We know God can handle our anger, yet we must not hold onto that anger too long. After we've expressed it to God, we need to let it go. Anger continually expressed is a sign that we are stuck in a dangerous rut.

When we trust in Jesus for forgiveness and believe He died on the cross for us, He will help us let go of our anger. The Holy Spirit can teach us how to live and love as God wants, if we just ask Him. Living in the Spirit is the opposite of living in anger, for the Holy Spirit gives us, **"Love, joy, peace, patience, kindness, goodness, gentleness, faithfulness and self-control." (Galatians 5:22-23)**

Give God your anger, then take the love He gives you back.

JUNE 28

A man who lived on Long Island one day purchased for himself a fine barometer. He ordered it on the internet and was excited when it arrived. But opening the box and examining it at his home, he was disappointed to find that the indicating needle appeared to be stuck, pointing to the sector marked "HURRICANE."

After shaking the barometer vigorously several times and getting no change from the needle, the man sat down and wrote a scorching letter to the person from whom he had purchased it. He sent off the letter, and the following day a hurricane blew his house away! The barometer needle had been right, but he was certain it was broken.

You and I need to trust God in life for all we need. We need to trust His Word, and we need to trust His people, too. We live in an age of so much information and technology that we think we can figure out all things by ourselves. We're convinced if we just have enough information, we'll make correct decisions every time. But all it takes is an act of God to remind us of our limitations. He is the One in control and only He has power over this sinful and troubled world.

Our Lord tells us in Proverbs 3:5-6, **"Trust in the Lord with all your heart and lean not on your own understanding; in all your ways acknowledge Him, and he will make your paths straight."**

That sentiment is a command from God. It is His true Word, not just a wise word for mankind. The Holy Spirit urges and encourages us to trust Him each day for all things, whether at home, church, job, school or anywhere.

Trusting in the Lord means trusting His plan of salvation. The world thinks the idea of God or the need for a Savior from sin are foolishness. Paul said it's a stumbling block to those without faith, but to those who know their sin, the Savior is our good and gracious Friend in every need.

And if we trust Him, we will be blessed. That's God's promise!

184

In the 1980's, twelve year-old Amy Alden of Newfoundland, Canada, found sixteen young goslings whose mother goose had died. She brought them home and fed them and they became her pets, often staying on her front porch.

Amy wanted them to succeed in the wild. She knew if they depended on her, they would never learn to live on their own. So Amy and her father, a pilot, built an ultra-light aircraft shaped like a huge goose in flight. Her Dad taught her to fly it and somehow coaxed the young geese to follow. Amy flew the craft more than two thousand miles south until they came to the Atlantic wetlands where Canadian geese wintered. They left them there, confident they would adapt to the wild. Not surprisingly, the next summer all sixteen geese returned home to Amy's front porch. Some birds know where home is.

When you return from a long trip on the road, you're always glad to be in your own home and sit in your favorite chair again. During a road trip we took with our old travel trailer, we met several "full-timers," people whose home is on wheels, in their motor coach or "fifth wheel" trailer.

What must it be like not to have a special more permanent place where we can return, the place we call home? On that trip we worshipped at a Lutheran church, and were warmly welcomed there. As we sang hymns and worshipped with familiar liturgy, it was just almost like coming home.

Where is your permanent home? In the nineteenth century, composer Anton Dvorzak wrote his "New World Symphony" after visiting America, and incorporated into it the haunting black spiritual song, "Going Home." Its sweet and gentle melody has accompanied many a person to the cemetery. Most Christians long for their eternal home with their Lord. Thanks be to God that He provides a blessed home to all who trust in Jesus as their Lord and Savior.

"Even the sparrow has found a home, and the swallow a nest for herself, where she may have her young." (Psalm 84:3)

I'm but a stranger here; Heaven is my home!

185

JUNE 30

The passengers watched as the young woman with the white cane made her way up the bus steps. She paid her fare and walked down the aisle feeling her way until she found an empty seat. She sat down, ready for the trip.

Susan was thirty-four when she became blind. *"How could this happen to me?"* she had pleaded. Yet no matter how much she prayed, she knew she'd never be able to see again. Just getting through a day at first was an exercise in frustration. She felt all she had to cling to was her husband Mark, an Air Force officer. He'd seen her come close to despair and so was determined to help her gain back her confidence.

Susan felt ready to return to her job which she could still do without sight, but how would she get there? She formerly took the bus, but was now too frightened to do so alone. Mark drove her to work, but that couldn't be done every day. Susan wanted to take the bus again, and she wanted to do it alone.

For two weeks Mark accompanied Susan to and from her work on the bus. He taught her how to rely on her other senses to know where she was, and how to adapt to her environment. He even helped her befriend some bus drivers.

Finally, Susan decided she was ready to go on her own. She said good-bye to Mark, and for the first time in over a year, rode the bus alone. Each day that week went well, and Susan had never felt better. She was going to work by herself!

On Friday morning, the driver said, *"Lady, I sure envy you."* Susan was taken aback. *"I'm blind. Why do you say that?"* The driver said, *"Every morning for the past week, your husband has been standing across the corner watching you get off the bus. He makes sure you cross the street safely and enter your office building. Then he blows you a kiss and walks away. You're one lucky lady."*

Though she hadn't see him, Mark had been watching over her. Our loving God watches over us in just the same way. We may not know He's there or see Him, but He's there nonetheless!

"The Lord will be with you wherever you go" (Josh. 1:9)

He's there even when we're not looking for Him.

186

JULY

+ + +

JULY 1

Until Copernicus, the earth was the center of the universe. That all changed in 1534 when the scientist proved the sun was the center of the solar system. But it took fifty years and a man named Galileo to get Copernicus' findings accepted. Some authorities don't like being removed from center stage.

Today, some Americans act like we are the center of the Universe. We expect to be first in everything, and if we're not, someone is to blame. Some churches think they are the center of the Christian universe, also, with beliefs and worship more correct than all others. Some churches accuse rather than discuss and point fingers instead of shaking hands.

On July 4th, our nation will have its birthday. I am proud to be an American, but America is not the center of this planet. We have the responsible task of being the most powerful nation and an important part of the human race. But we are not superior to all others. We are strong, but still dependent. Though a secular society, we must never remove God from our nation completely. To do so would invite disaster.

I pray you all will take time in the coming days, whether in church or at home or on the road, to give thanks for the blessings of living in America, perhaps by recalling the words of Irving Berlin:

God bless America, land that I love.
Stand beside her, and guide her,
Through the night with a light from above.
From the mountains, to the prairies,
To the oceans white with foam,
God bless America, my home sweet home.

"I am the LORD your God, who has set you apart from the nations." (Leviticus 20:24)

I'm proud of the nation God has given us. I hope you are, too.

187

JULY 2

My oldest brother Edward served in the Army in the early 1950s. Later, as commander of his local American Legion Post, he often assisted with honors at the burial of veterans in the local cemetery. Once they were unable to find a bugler to play "Taps," so Edward sang the words. He had a nice voice and I am sure it was moving for those present to hear him.

Of all the melodies known in America, none is so easily recognized or more apt to render emotion, than "Taps." The twenty-four note melody is both eloquent and simple and is used at all military funerals.

"Taps" is unique to the United States military. Several stories have been circulated about how the song originated, but here are the facts:

In 1862, General Daniel A. Butterfield (1831-1901, Brigade Commander, and Medal of Honor recipient) was not pleased with "Extinguish Lights," the bugle call which ended the day in most Union brigades. With the help of the bugler Oliver W. Norton, (1839-1920), Gen. Butterfield composed the melody *"Taps"* to honor his men stationed at Harrison's Landing, Virginia, following the Seven Days battle of the Civil War.

The new bugle call was sounded on a night in July, 1862, and it soon spread to other units of the Union Army. It was reportedly also used by the Confederates. "Taps" was made an official bugle call after the war. The origin of the words to "Taps" is not known, but here are the two known verses:

Day is done. Gone the sun,
From the lake, From the hill, From the sky;
All is well, Safely rest - God is nigh.

Fading light, Dims the sight,
And a star, Gems the sky, Gleaming bright;
From afar, Drawing nigh, Falls the night.

"Dear friend, I pray that you may enjoy good health and that all may go well with you." (3 John 2)

Thank You, Lord, that all is well, for You are nigh.

Since tomorrow is Independence Day, I thought you might like to know why the flag is folded in a triangular shape. This information is from a retired Chaplain Colonel.

When folded correctly, the Flag is folded 13 times:

The 1st fold of the flag is a symbol of life.

The 2nd fold is a symbol of the belief in eternal life.

The 3rd fold is in honor of the veterans who gave all or part of their lives for the defense of our country.

The 4th fold represents our trust in God, to whom we turn in peace and in war for His divine guidance.

The 5th fold is a tribute to our country, in the words of Stephen Decatur who said, *"Our country, right or wrong."*

The 6th fold is to honor our *"Pledge of Allegiance to the Flag of the United States Of America, and the Republic for which it stands, one Nation under God, indivisible, with Liberty and Justice for all."*

The 7th fold is a tribute to its Armed Forces, as they protect their country and its flag against all enemies.

The 8th fold is a tribute to all who enter the valley of the shadow of death, that they might soon see the light of day.

The 9th fold is a tribute to women and mothers, because their faith, loyalty and devotion have molded the character of the men and women who have made this country great.

The 10th fold is a tribute to men and fathers, for they, too, have molded and shaped sons and daughters for the defense of their country.

The 11th fold represents the God of Abraham, Isaac and Jacob.

The 12th fold represents the Trinity, God the Father, the Son and the Holy Spirit.

The 13th fold leaves stars uppermost, reminding us of our nation's motto, *"In God We Trust."*

After the flag is correctly folded, it looks like a tricorn hat, reminding us of our nation in its War for Independence.

"Till you are left like a flagstaff on a mountaintop, like a banner on a hill." (Isaiah 30:7)

Happy Fourth of July (tomorrow).

JULY 4

Independence Day, July Fourth, is here again, and I think we should make it a summer Thanksgiving Day. More than one hundred years ago, the great evangelist and preacher, Dwight Moody, was preaching from the 103rd Psalm and especially the verse that says, **"Bless the Lord, O my soul, and forget not all His benefits."** Moody said with a twinkle in his eye, *"Of course, we can't remember all of God's benefits, but that doesn't mean we should forget them, either!"*

A few years ago Carol and I drove through Yellowstone, America's first and largest National Park. What marvelous handiworks of God we beheld! The grandeur of the place with its geysers and hot spring lakes, its waterfalls and mountains, is unmatched in the world.

As Old Faithful blew into the air a hundred feet or more, someone behind me said to one of his friends, *"This happens because Yellowstone is one giant caldera, one of three super volcanoes in the world, and if it ever blew, that would be the end of the United States."*

There's always someone to remind us of the possible bad in the midst of good, isn't there? We returned home to read newspaper stories of government failure, economic weakness and even a church scandal. I think we need to read and re-read Psalm 103 or Psalm 23 or Psalm 46, or any of the many passages which remind us of God's blessings. As Rev. Moody said, *"Of course, we can't remember all of God's benefits, but that doesn't mean we should forget them, either!"*

I don't know what you are planning for this July 4th, but I pray it will include a few moments of giving thanks to God for His benefits, especially to your nation. You have your list of thankfulness, just as I have. Then, having given thanks, go ahead and enjoy your food and beverage and friends, or just an easy chair in the evening.

"Bless the Lord, O my soul, and forget not all His benefits." (Psalm 103:2)

There is a whole lot more good in America than there is bad!

JULY 5

Now and then I enjoy watching a dog show on TV. This show is not about a dog who rescues a little boy, but dog competition, where the impeccably dressed dog owners parade around their polished pedigreed pooches to show off their clever canine qualities. These dogs have been trained to stand confidently with chins lifted high, with their shiny coats carefully brushed and styled, as they are poked and prodded by judges. To me, they all look like winners.

But when the audience is not around, I wonder what those dogs are really like? Do they ever relax and let their sleek fur get matted in the mud? Do they nip at each other, or even at their masters? Do they ever get "doggie breath?" Do their masters ever let them have a little fun or is life always and only more training for the next show?

A more important question is what are we like when no one sees us? Someone once said *"Integrity is what you are when no one is watching."* In Matthew 23:2-7, Jesus rebuked those who were interested in how they looked in public rather than how they were seen by God. Jesus wants us all to be obedient, faithful and committed to Him, even when nobody else is looking. The Pharisees focused on the way they were perceived by others. God's focus is on what we're like inside. His desire is for us to be like His Son.

We are not to be in competition with other Christians. God will never ask us to compete for *"Best In Show."* He measures us by the perfect standard of His Son. St. Paul wrote in Ephesians 4:13, **"Until we all reach unity in the faith and in the knowledge of the Son of God and become mature, attaining to the whole measure of the fullness of Christ."**

Because we cannot measure up to perfection, He forgives us and by the Holy Spirit's power helps us to do better. Jesus' whole life is for us. Everything He did was to make us perfect in God's eyes.

Thanks be to God who loves us in Jesus Christ.

JULY 6

You might find this story silly. Then again, you might find some truth in it. Here it is:

Joe had a dream that he'd died and gone to heaven. Peter met him at the Pearly Gate, and said, *"Here's how it works, Joe. You need 100 points to get into heaven. You tell me all the good things you've done, and I'll give you points for each item, depending on how good it was. When you reach 100 points, you're in."*

"Well," said Joe, *"I was married to the same woman for fifty years and never cheated on her once." "Wonderful!"* said St. Peter, *"That's worth three points!" "Only three points?"* Joe said. *"Well, I attended church all my life and supported its ministry with my tithe and service every chance I could."*

"Terrific!" says St. Peter. *"That's certainly worth another point." "Only one point? Look here, I started a soup kitchen in my city and worked in a shelter for homeless veterans for years and years." "Fantastic!"* said Peter, *"That's good for two more points." "Only two points?"* Joe cried. *"At this rate the only way I'll get into heaven is by the grace of God!" "Way to go!"* said Peter, *"That's worth 100 points -- come on in, friend!"*

Sometimes as we travel through life, we wonder if we're doing enough of what God wants us to do. Look at all the ways there are to help others. Am I doing enough? Should I be doing more? At those times, we need to remind ourselves that our Lord Jesus did enough in His life, and He did it all for us.

The things we do should be done in gratitude for what Jesus did for us. Those are the good and helpful things we can do for our fellow travelers. But we must never forget we can't do enough. In fact we can't do anything to get us to heaven. Jesus did that for us on the cross.

"It is by grace that you have been saved through faith. It is a gift of God, not of works, lest anyone should boast." (Ephesians 2:8-9)

And thank the Good Lord that He did!

JULY 7

If you have ever faced the unexpected tragedy of divorce, death, disease, or a demolished dream, you probably searched for answers to help you mend and heal. If so, remember these:

YOU WILL HEAL. Things will never be the way they were. After tragedy you're wounded, but you will heal. You will not be restored to exactly how you were. No one ever is. The good news is that you can carry on as a wounded survivor and face the days ahead with the hope of recovery.

LET GOD WORK. Pray for strength, but don't tell Him what to do. God knows what's best. Trust His loving, forgiving, providing, healing, and guiding ways. Lay aside expectations so you can see His answers. You may reject some of His solutions because you had in mind something different, but remember, your only hope lies in the Lord.

MAKE GOOD CHOICES. You have more control over the situation than you think. You can't turn back the clock, but you do have the choice of going under or going on. Every situation can go one of two ways; it can depress you or it can motivate you. It's up to you. Blaming God, others, or yourself will not help. It's time to learn from the hurt.

GOD WILL COME THROUGH, but you must believe He will come through for you. You will be "all right" again. Let your Heavenly Father strengthen you for the struggles.

ACKNOWLEDGE THE PAIN. God does not minimize your pain. The Lord is not in denial; neither does He expect you to be. God cares. He has not abandoned you. He is right beside you and has been there all along. He hears your cries and sees your tears.

LET THE HEALING BEGIN. God is neither handicapped nor weary in the midst of your pain. Nor is He confused or baffled. His strength will deliver you, not just barely, but mightily.

"We know that in all things God works for the good of those who love him, who have been called according to his purpose." (Romans 8:28)

In Christ our Lord, you can expect a miracle!

JULY 8

After they were married, Mary and Joe discovered they had a fundamental difference. Mary loved to move the furniture and redecorate their house. Joe was happy with a TV, refrigerator and an easy chair. Mary moved things and found ways to make their home more efficient and attractive. Joe helped her move things, but didn't see why it was needed.

But the more she decorated, the better their house looked. Soon Joe began to appreciate the changes and even offered her suggestions or made them before she asked. In her own way, Mary was helping Joe become a better person.

God loves to redecorate our lives. If you let Him live in your heart long enough, you will begin to change. Pictures of hurt will be replaced with landscapes of grace. Walls of anger are removed and shaky foundations restored. Cracks will be patched and lives redecorated. God can no more leave a life unchanged than a mother can leave her child's dirty face unwashed. God always changes us for the better.

It's not enough for God to have you for His own. He wants to change you. Suppose a father buys his little boy an ice cream cone and as he's giving it to him, notices his mouth is filled with sand. Father loves him, despite the sand, but first he washes out his mouth, and then gives him the ice cream.

God does the same for us. He loves us no less because of our dirty faces or lives. But first He cleanses us to prepare us for something better. God loves us as we are, but He'll not leave us that way for long. He wants us to be like Jesus.

The trials, sickness or struggles we have are God's way of cleansing us for something better. He loves us all, despite our sins and rebellion, and He wants to change us to be better. So let's thank God for struggles. He's preparing us for something much greater.

"He has saved us and called us to a holy life—not because of anything we have done but because of His own purpose and grace." (2 Timothy 1:9)

Like I've often said, God loves us just the way we are, but He won't leave us that way for long!

194

With all the hugs and jumping and high-fives, you'd have thought they'd won a world series game instead of ending an eleven-game losing streak. The Colorado Rockies baseball team was taking yet another chance at experiencing more pain in yet another loss. Though they played like they wanted to lose, somehow they won, and they did it at Coors Field, where winning was usually easy for them.

Scoreless through five, the Rockies finally broke out to a six to four lead, only to see it melt away with an Oakland three-run homer. Then the Rockies got two runs and the lead again. But Oakland tied it in the ninth and the game went to extra innings.

In the bottom of the tenth inning with two outs, a desperate team of apparent losers strung together enough hits and walks to get one more run to break the tie and win the game. The jubilance over their first win after eleven straight losses resembled exhausted soldiers after a terrible battle, grateful it was over, happy they'd done something positive.

Sometimes life treats us to a losing streak. The job stinks, people around us are idiots, our world looks like a circus freak show, and our bank account is a bucket with holes. Sometimes life looks like a battle field and we are the officers is charge. All we want is some relief.

The good news is that in Christ the losing streak is over. We aren't immediate champs, but at least we're no longer constant losers. In fact, we are never losers when we have faith in Christ. Because of His death on Calvary and resurrection, we win the Big One.

The prize of Heaven is the World Series of eternity. It's the Super Bowl, the Stanley Cup, the Olympic Gold medal, the Triple Crown, Wimbledon, the Master's and Final Four victory all wrapped into one. God in His mercy may see us lose here and there, but when the game is over He brings us the Grand Prize, life in His House forever.

"In all these things we are more than conquerors through Him who loved us." (Romans 8:37)

I'm looking forward one day to wearing His ring.

195

JULY 10

The moral conflict in our nation today reminds me of two famous ships, the MAYFLOWER and the TITANIC, both of which sailed from England to America. The MAYFLOWER carried pilgrims on a historic mission to establish a new society under God. Their turbulent voyage was marked by hunger, disease, storms and hardship.

The passengers on the TITANIC, however, cruised in luxury on that "unsinkable" ship. They seemed to have everything, but as they traveled, they were oblivious to the cruel sea, bad weather and an iceberg in their ship's path.

America today more closely resembles the TITANIC than the MAYFLOWER. Confident of the invincibility of our mighty nation, we seem indifferent to the danger signals of our moral direction. Too many people are concerned with physical comforts and instant gratification rather than with moral and spiritual health.

The TITANIC sank when it hit a single iceberg. The American ship of state today faces a sea full of icebergs. The iceberg of moral decadence is sinking the Ship of State more slowly, but just as surely, as the one that ripped a hole in the TITANIC's hull. Our economic prosperity is lulling us into a false sense of security. Morally, America is heading straight for a monster iceberg.

I don't like hearing unpleasant things about our nation, no matter how true. Like you, I've often ignored them rather than faced them. Perhaps that's what you'll do with this message. I hope not.

Today I want to call you to prayer, if not prayer for America to repent, then prayer for God's will to prevail and His people to accept it. His will isn't always to make things better immediately, but it's always for our good.

"Nations are in uproar, kingdoms fall; He lifts his voice, the earth melts. The Lord Almighty is with us; the God of Jacob is our fortress." (Psalm 46:6-7)

God bless America by giving more of her people a strong moral compass.

JULY 11

Living in a retirement community half of the year, one sees mostly older folks, the exception being an occasional visiting young family or grandchild. Retired folks like to laugh, even at themselves, and have their own brand of humor. Recently I saw a video of an invocation given by an older person whose message and deadpan delivery were hilarious. Near the end of her invocation she quoted a poem by Esther Mary Walker, called, "BEATITUDES FOR FRIENDS OF THE AGED".

"BLESSED are they who understand my faltering steps and shaky hand. BLESSED are they who know my ears today must strain to hear the things they say. BLESSED are they who seem to know that my eyes are dim and my thoughts are slow. BLESSED are they who looked away when coffee was spilled at dinner today. BLESSED are they with a cheery smile who take the time to chat for awhile. BLESSED are they who never say, 'You've told that story twice today.' BLESSED are they who know the way to bring back memories of yesterday. BLESSED are they who make it known I'm loved, respected and not alone. BLESSED are they who ease the days of my journey home in loving ways."

I like that poem, especially the line about hearing a story told more than once. With such healthy and active older people these days, it's easy to forget it's normal to become less able and more frail as we age.

God in His Word honors the aged person, and urges us to do the same in the Fourth Commandment. Besides telling us to respect our elders, God gives many examples of blessing the world through older people. Hannah, Elizabeth and Sarah gave the world very important children in their advanced age. Abraham, Jacob, and Simeon were old men honored by God in later life. Older people cannot demand the respect of others, but they hope to have it.

"Stand up in the presence of the aged, show respect for the elderly and revere your God." (Leviticus 19:32)

The older we grow, the more we see God's abundant blessings!

197

JULY 12

In the summer of 2001, my brother-in-law died. William Jennings Niebuhr was abandoned as a baby, left at a Nebraska orphanage nearly seventy-six years before and adopted by new parents who raised him to love the Lord and to play the piano. And play the piano he surely did, and the organ too, and he directed choir after choir, and sang like no one else.

Due to childhood illness, Bill stuttered except when he sang. He challenged his choirs to greater heights of song and played the organ masterfully, performing the established music of the masters as well as his own improvisations of hymns and melodies that thrilled all who heard him.

Bill directed Lutheran Hour Rally choirs in southern Minnesota for forty years. He was a friend to Lutheran Hour Speaker Dr. Oswald Hoffman, beginning when they were on camp staff together. And it was there he met my sister. He and Marian were parents of seven fine sons and married forty-seven years at his passing.

Just six weeks before his death and barely able to walk, he played for a chapel service presided over by the President of Minnesota South District of the Lutheran Church - Missouri Synod. It was the last time he played for a worship service.

After a two year battle with cancer, Bill fell asleep in Jesus, leaving a loving family, as well as scores of admiring relatives and friends. The hands and voice that thrilled so many are now silent, for he is in the midst of a family God has given him, an eternal family that loves him even more than we did here.

Bill was a staunch believer in Jesus Christ, a no-nonsense Lutheran man who loved the Lord. He had his weaknesses, but he relied on God's power to overcome them. He once said he didn't want any sermons at his funeral, but he can't stop a brother-in-law from going on a bit about another great servant who has gone to be with the Lord.

"Be devoted to one another in love. Honor one another above yourselves." (Romans 12:10)

We miss our loved ones who have gone before, don't we?

198

JULY 13

Martin Luther once said that, after the Gospel, music is God's greatest gift to humanity. He wasn't referring to what many try to pass off as music today (noisy, crude, random words or notes), but melodies and words that uplift the soul and turn our thoughts to God. These are the great chorales, symphonies, hymns and melodies that bless the listener. On a plaque I once saw were these words:

> **BACH** *gave us God's Word.*
> **MOZART** *gave us God's laughter.*
> **BEETHOVEN** *gave us God's fire.*
> **GOD** *gave us music so that we*
>   *could pray without words.*

What kind of music do you listen to? Does its message leave you feeling better or worse when the song is over? We sinful humans have an almost unlimited capacity to ruin a good thing, and nothing illustrates this more than the evolution of popular music. Both youth and adults now accept musical forms that neither bless nor uplift or even qualify to be called music. Today so many people have, for the most part, turned their backs on the music of the Masters. Just a few years from now most of the music composed today will be forgotten, but the "Music of the Masters" will still remain.

I hope you won't be like those who trade in that which is lasting for a brief and shallow excitement. A hymn or chorale may not seem as exciting as a new Christian praise song, but chances are good that praise song will be more quickly forgotten than that hymn. God's Word will still be there because its message is timeless.

Jesus Christ our Lord has inspired more people to write and perform great music than any other person in history. His love and forgiveness move people to greater heights of lasting joy through the useful arts.

"I will sing and make music to the Lord." (Psalm 27:6)

May your music always help you "pray without words."

JULY 14

I once wrote a Bible study called <u>The Mighty Mites,</u> a set of brief studies on the five one-chapter books of the Bible: Obadiah, Philemon, Second John, Third John and Jude.

Obadiah is the shortest book in the Old Testament. Hidden away in it is a vital question that should interest us: *"How would you respond when your enemy has misfortune?"* I recall a youth Bible study many years ago titled, *"Would you laugh if a brick fell on your enemy's head?"* I probably would. After all, it's human nature to feel glad when someone who has caused you trouble gets stopped cold. The trouble is, human nature is a result of sin.

The prophet Obadiah spoke the Word of God during a time when Jerusalem was under attack by the armies of Babylon. They were getting beaten badly, and to make matters worse, their closest neighbors, the Edomites, were cheering on the enemy armies as they destroyed and killed Israelites.

The ironic twist of this story is that the Edomites were distant blood relatives of the Israelites. They were descendants of Esau, twin brother of Jacob, the father of the Israelites. When the Edomites cheered for the Babylonians, they were cheering against their relatives, the Israelites.

Obadiah condemned them for gloating, saying, **"Do not gloat over your brother in the day of his misfortune, nor rejoice over the children of Judah in the day of their ruin."** (Obadiah 12)

If someone has been hurtful to us, or if they represent what we believe to be wrong, it is easy to be vindictive or find pleasure when they experience misfortune. But God's Word admonishes us, **"Do not rejoice when your enemy falls, nor let your heart be glad when he stumbles." (Proverbs 24:17)** Jesus gave His life on the cross for all our sins, including those we do to our enemies.

"Love your enemies and pray for those who persecute you." (Matthew 5:43)

In the Bible, as in life, mighty gifts from God often come in small packages.

JULY 15

How we deal with our stupid mistakes reveals a lot about us. In the British Open of 1999, Jean Van de Velde was six strokes and 480 yards away from his first major championship and a lot of cash. All he needed to do was score a six or less on a par four hole. It was a sure win, or so he thought.

The eighteenth hole was tricky and required a short tee shot so you didn't get into trouble. But that day Van de Velde decided to use his Driver to cross the water with one mighty swing. But he swung badly and bounced his ball off the bleachers into deep marsh grass. His next shot plopped into water, and the next one into a sand trap.

Van de Velde got a seven just to tie the match, and then he lost the play-off, the tournament and the prize. All he needed was a Five Iron lay-up on his first shot and he'd have won it easily, but he had to go and use his Driver.

What Van De Velde did on that eighteenth hole should remind us a lot of ourselves. For example, all we need to do is apologize, but instead we argue. Or all we need to do is listen, but instead we open our mouth and stick our foot in. Or all we need to do is be patient, but instead we rush too quickly. Or all we need to do is give a problem to God, but instead we try fixing it ourselves and mess it up completely.

Each of the above examples ended up with more trouble instead of a solution. How we deal with our foolish mistakes reveals a lot about us.

Our Lord Jesus will fix those problem areas of life if we just let Him. He died for our sins and rose again because He did all things right. He will help us do them right, too. The next time you're tempted to take a short-cut with something important, make sure it's worth being wrong.

"Forgive Your people, who have sinned against You, O Lord." (1 Kings 8:50)

When you shank your shot into the crowd, may the Good Lord help make it right again!

JULY 16

While attending the Seminary, I worked for three months at the St. Louis Juvenile Detention Center, a warehouse for troubled youth on their way back to their own house or else to the "Big House." These tough, street-wise boys survived by their wits and their fists. Yet after being there some weeks, I had the feeling those youth were in a prison bigger than the JDC. It was a prison with more inmates than beds, more prisoners than plates, a place few of them leave. It's a place Max Lucado calls the "Prison of Want".

What is the "Prison of Want?" You may know one of the inmates. He's "In Want." He wants something - something bigger, nicer, faster, prettier. He doesn't want much, mind you, just one thing: one new job, one new car, one new spouse or one new house. He wants just one thing, and when he has it, he's sure he'll be "happy." When he finally gets his one thing, he'll leave the prison, at least that's what he thinks. But then the new car smell is gone, the new job gets old, a bigger TV is invented, or a new spouse has bad habits. The new gets old and soon another ex-con returns to the "Prison of Want."

Are you in that prison? You are if you feel better when you have more or feel worse when you have less. You're in the "Prison of Want" if your joy is just one delivery away, one transfer away, one makeover away. If your contentment comes from something you deposit, drive, drink or digest, then you're in the "Prison of Want." That's the bad news.

The Good News is that you have visitors and they can get you paroled. Come on out to the Visitation Room and meet David and Paul. They have a secret to tell you, and it's called "CONTENTMENT."

Paul said: **"I have learned the secret of being content in any and every situation, whether well fed or hungry, whether living in plenty or in WANT. I can do everything through Christ who gives me strength." (Philipp. 4:12-13)**

David said: **"The Lord is my Shepherd, I shall not be in WANT." (Psalm 23:1)**

Are you staying out of the "Prison of Want?"

202

JULY 17

A story is told of a man on an African safari deep in the jungle. The guide before him was whacking at vines with a machete to make a path. The traveler, hot and frustrated, said, *"Where are we? Do you know where you're taking me? Where is this path we're supposed to be on?"* The guide kept chopping and said, *"It's not important for you to know the exact point on a map, but it's important for you to do your part. Keep chopping."*

The traveler was now worried and a bit angry. *"But I want to know! Where is this path taking us?"* The guide raised up and said, *"Mister, it's enough for you to know that I am the path. Now stick with me and keep chopping."*

We ask the same questions of God, don't we? We ask Him, *"Where are You taking me? Why am I here? Where am I going?"* But He doesn't tell us the exact answer we want to hear. We want to know location, but God tells us, *"It's enough for you to know I am the path."*

It's most difficult to hear God's answers, because His answers are not always clear. We want more specifics, more clarity. We'd like Him to give us a list, and especially we'd like Him to clear the path for us.

So when we ask God, does He remove the jungle? No, the vegetation remains. Does He kill the wild animals? No, danger still lurks. Does He answer all our questions? No, He says it's enough that He knows them.

We all need that reminder, and we all need that hope. Some of us may not need it right now. Our jungle is a gentle meadow and our journey a delight. Few of us know what tomorrow will bring or where the road will lead. We may be one bend away from the thickest jungle we can imagine. If so, remember that Jesus walks the road with us. He knows the way out, and He knows the way home, because He is "The Way."

"I am with you always, to the end of the world." **(Matthew 28:20)**

Have a blessed Journey!

203

JULY 18

Two people can see the exact same thing and have an opposite perspective. The late author, Tony Hillerman, wrote about the people and cultures of the American southwest. He was once riding the Santa Fe Chief railroad towards California, watching as the Zuni Buttes and Mount Taylor came into view. The spectacular country with its colors and shapes thrilled him. The golds and tans of the mesas contrasted with the blue sky and its billowing white clouds. The unfolding landscape and colors filled his heart with joy.

Next to him were three businessmen in suits, presumably from somewhere back east, and as they looked at the majestic views, one of them said to the others, *"My God, why would anyone want to live out here?"* In the following moments of silence, Hillerman recalled thinking, *"My God, why wouldn't everyone want to live out here?"* (Reader's Digest, July/August 2012, p. 146)

People can see the exact same thing but come up with a totally different perspective. Consider the Church's history. One sees the saving Gospel, universities, hospitals, music and the arts, orphanages, education and scientific discovery. Looking at the same evidence, another sees the Crusades, dogmatism, the Inquisition, immorality and oppression. The second asks, *"Why in the world would anyone want to be a Christian?"* while the first asks, *"Why wouldn't everyone want to be a Christian?"*

Both views may seem equally valid but both are not. Humanism says, *"My viewpoint is just as good as yours,"* but Christianity says, *"God's viewpoint is better than all of ours."* Our holy God gives us minds so we can learn, analyze and decide. But because there is sin in the world, our minds are selfish, myopic and greedy. God is replaced by opinion, love is replaced with lust, and wisdom with foolishness. Thanks be to God that we have forgiveness of sins through Jesus Christ.

"As the heavens are higher than the earth, so are my ways higher than your ways and my thoughts than your thoughts, declares the Lord." (Isaiah 55:9)

Despite what people may think, God has the last Word.

204

JULY 19

One summer our son, his wife and their three precious children spent a week visiting us. When they left, our house suddenly became very quiet. No more soft little feet pattering the floor at night, no more quiet, expectant voices in the morning, or squeals of delight outside, or toys under foot. Their presence was a sweet blessing that can't be duplicated. Carol and I missed them the moment they headed down the jet way and we headed home.

We drove away from the airport with empty car seats and full hearts, a little sad but also glad. Sad they must leave, but glad they are healthy, loving, happy, and growing. That night we recalled how their father, our son, grew up so quickly and now knows a parent's love. He and his wife are wonderful parents and more patient, playful and attentive than we were. We thank God for that.

But they won't have loved their children more than we loved him and his brother. Being a parent is among the greatest of God's blessings.

Parenting is never over. It's not like making the final touchdown, spiking the ball and going home after the game. Being a parent is a thing for life, an unending relationship. When it's good, it's the best experience one can know in life. When it's not, the remorse and regret can be overwhelming.

Psalm 68:6 says, **"God sets the lonely into families."** Families can be large or small, nearby or far away, emotionally close or distant. Whatever the case, they are still family, and we need them.

Carol and I look forward to more grandchildren visits in the future, and I'm already mentally planning activities for when they come. I wonder if God feels this way when His children visit Him on Sunday but then go home. I wonder if He awaits their next visit like we do.

A tidy house is nice, but a messy one with love and laughter beats it any day.

In recent years we've heard a lot about angels, some of it true, but most of it not. Here's a true story that shows my belief on the topic.

She was a student, a single mother alone with her baby, struggling to make ends meet. She and her child rode the bus between campus and day-care, her baby's twenty smiling pounds tucked snugly into a front carrier while she had a book pack on her back.

One afternoon, two elderly women befriended them. The four of them met a few times, sharing brief but enjoyable conversations on the bus. The young mother never told them she didn't have much, but they knew. One day, they asked for her address. Weeks later, a handmade baby quilt was delivered to her door.

About a year later, a woman with whom she had chatted a few times stopped the mother on campus, pressed an envelope with money into her hand and said, *"Please accept this. You don't need to say anything. A stranger helped me once when I needed help."* That act of generosity helped heal the young mother's wounded spirit that day.

On the eve of her daughter's second Christmas the doorbell rang. There, bow trimmed and radiant in the snowy front porch, were presents. The anonymous card read, *"Wishing you and Rachel happiness and peace always. You are noticed. You are valued. You are not alone."*

Angels do live among us, and they come in the form of neighbors, friends, co-workers, or even strangers on a bus. They help us, but seek no fanfare, no sainthood, no reward. In spite of the sorrow in this world, their gifts move us to a gentler place, a reminder that God is caring for us. With small hands that still the chaos and gentle voices that move the world, there are angels among us, one loving gesture at a time.

"I will send an angel before you." (Exodus 33:2)

Be an angel to someone today!

JULY 21

Little Ed lived in Columbia, South Carolina, on a dirt road. Across the road from his place were some woods, and in the middle of the woods was a small lake. One evening Ed and his Daddy walked down a path to the bank of that little lake to watch the sunset.

Out of the blue, Daddy asked, *"Son, do you want to see a big water moccasin?"* *"Yes, sir, I do,"* said Ed. Sure enough, right on the bank was a five foot long water moccasin. *"That's a big snake,"* little Ed said. *"Is that another one?"* Daddy looked and said, *"I believe it is. That's interesting, son, we've seen two big snakes in thirty seconds. Wow!"*

Little Ed asked again, *"Dad, is that another one?"* And suddenly they saw a dozen or more water moccasins, there on the bank, just into the water, some moving towards their feet! Ed was frightened and wondered if they were in danger.

Then Ed heard his father say something he never forgot. *"Son, jump on my back."* The boy didn't need a running start. He hopped onto his Dad's back and grabbed him and buried his face in his Dad's shirt. He clung to his father's strong back as he shone the tiny flashlight on the winding path as together they negotiated a safe exit home past all those dangerous snakes. Ed wasn't afraid because he knew his father was in control of the situation.

Are you living in fear? Are turmoil, apprehension, and anxiety making you feel trapped, like there's no way out? If so, listen for your Heavenly Father who is saying right now, *"Jump on My back. Don't worry. I'm in control. I will shine My light on your situation and help you through it. I will walk with you and show you the path. I will take you home, but first you must jump on my back."*

"Always giving thanks to God the Father for everything, in the name of our Lord Jesus Christ." (Ephesians 5:20)

Hold still, Daddy, because here I come!

JULY 22

Problems do not always mean trouble, and trouble is not always a bad thing. It depends on how you view the problems or troubles. Are they roadblocks or are they opportunities? Are the "bad things" really bad, or are they ways for us to start our life on a different and better path?

In 1849 when Nathaniel Hawthorne was dismissed from his government job in the Department of Customs, he went home in despair. His wife listened to his tale of woe, then set pen and ink on the table, lit the lamp, put her arms around his shoulders and said, *"Now you will be able to write your novel."* Fortunately, Hawthorne did not waste much time despairing because soon the literary world was enriched with the first of several fine novels, The Scarlet Letter.

There are countless other historical stories that tell the same thing. A hopelessly bad situation is turned into something of amazing goodness. A seeming tragedy is turned into a minor triumph. Perhaps right now you are feeling there is little good or little to hope for in your life. Maybe you feel locked in one of those valleys where the sun never seems to shine. If so, have faith! Pray to Jesus and see how God will help you make life better.

If all the doors seem closed right now, God will open a window. All you need to do is trust Him. Pray to Him and place yourself into His hands. Each day open your eyes to see what God will show you.

He who gave the life of His only Son so that you might have eternal life will not let you down. He will be with you through the small things and lead you into the greatness of your future. Trust God to provide the future opportunities you will need. He will not disappoint you.

"God has never forsaken those who seek Him." (Psalm 9:10)

Trust Him for each day and watch how He provides your many needs.

JULY 23

We rarely know the long-term affects of some of our actions, whether right or wrong. In the 1950's twelve year-old Harold had a paper route in a small town in South Carolina. One day as he rode his bike, he heard a sound coming from one of the houses on his route. Under a rickety porch he saw some chicken wire, and as he approached it, small dirty fingers poked out. Someone was being kept under there, a boy perhaps his age, probably mentally handicapped. Harold kept that paper route for two more years, but he never went back to that house. He always wondered if he should have.

In the 1970's Harold became a successful High School football coach. One day during practice he noticed a young black man standing behind a fence watching them. After practice he took him some water and realized the young man was mentally handicapped.

Over the next few weeks Harold took the man under his wing, giving him small jobs, food, and a radio. Soon the young man, James Robert Kennedy, learned to talk a few words, and he responded with love and kindness to all he met. James attended high school and slowly began to learn, but he never left his Hanna, South Carolina, High School.

Over the years, limited though he was, James affected the lives of thousands of young people at T. L. Hanna High School in a positive way. His story was told in the movie, "Radio."

Today, Coach Harold has retired and been inducted in the South Carolina Athletic Hall of Fame. James is still at T. L. Hanna, a "permanent student" at school and an "assistant coach" in their High School football program. But it all started with a young boy's failure to do something about a little boy being kept under a porch behind chicken wire.

You and I rarely know the affects of our actions. With the help of God, even our mistakes and failures of yesterday can be helpful if they prompt us to do the right thing today. God can even use our mistakes for something good.

"Love one another, as I have loved you." (John 13:34)

I hope I have learned from mine.

JULY 24

In 1992, a Los Angeles County parking control officer came upon a new Cadillac illegally parked in a tow-away zone. The officer dutifully wrote out a ticket, ignoring the man seated at the driver's wheel. He reached inside the open window, placed the $30 citation on the dashboard and drove away.

The driver of the car made no excuses, voiced no complaint, and for good reason. He was dead! He'd had a fatal heart attack shortly before, but was still sitting up in the car seat. The officer, bent on his work, didn't notice. He just did his job and went on his way.

It seems to me that many in our society today are making it their job to slap labels on others without seeing the people themselves. Tell someone they are wrong and that's enough; they've done their job. Point out this wrong or that error, but don't offer any solutions. Show them the Law, but neglect to show them the Gospel. Sometimes preachers are the worst offenders at this.

It is obvious that millions of people around us are dead in their transgressions and sins, living without Christ. But so are we all! Everyone is dead because of sin – that's God's Law! Unless we get help, we are doomed! Every single one of us should be "ticketed" by God because, **"All have sinned and fallen short of the glory of God." (Romans 3:23)**

The glory of the Gospel is that it gives us a solution, an alternative to the problems of life. It shows us a person (Jesus) not just a problem (Sin). The Gospel is God's love, not a list of our mistakes. Jesus saw people around Him, not only what they were doing wrong. Even on the cross He saw the thief, He saw those who accused Him, and He saw His mother. And for one and all, He forgave them.

"God so loved the world that He gave His only Son. Whosoever believes in Him will not perish, but have everlasting life." (John 3:16)

We don't need a citation; we need a Savior.

When I was a small boy I was afraid of the dark. Now and then at night my Dad would tell me to go outside to turn off the pump or check on the chickens or some such thing. Since it was night time out there, I dreaded having to walk across our dark farmyard. We had a yard light on a high pole, but it cast big shadows around the farm buildings. Who knew what dangers lurked in those shadows?

One particular moonless summer night I had to go out to the barn to retrieve something, and I paused in a big shadow behind our granary. I knew Dad had parked a piece of machinery near there and didn't want to run into it and break a leg. Then I felt something there in the shadows and I couldn't see it! I waited a moment for my eyes to adjust and just then something cold and slimy touched my hand!

Yikes! My heart jumped, pumping its adrenalin. I jerked my hand away and ran like the wind, letting out a frightful yell. I ran the forty yard dash back to the house in record time, but not before our old dog Zeke got there ahead of me. You see, it was his wet nose I'd felt and I'd probably scared him more than he scared me. Old Zeke was a scary monster and didn't know it! The next morning Zeke was by the front door wagging his tail harmlessly, and the yard was sunny, and there was no monster, and I felt foolish at being so frightened. It was a new day and everything was okay.

Every now and then we may feel something cold and slimy touch us in the dark. It's a disease, or it's a bad relationship, or it's the ugliness of politics, or it's the fear of the unknown. Part of the problem is real, but part is imagined because we can't see into the shadows.

God is with us in both the night and day so we need to realize life is not as bad as we think it is. God who is with us in the sunny daylight, is also with us in the dark shadows. He's the same Lord, same Jesus, same caring God. He who brings us through the day will also get us through the night.

"I trust in You, Lord; I say, 'You are my God'." (Psalm 31:14)

We just need to trust Him and not be afraid.

JULY 26

One year, Carol and I spent two weeks in Wittenberg, Germany, where I preached English services for residents and tourists. Living there gives a far different perspective than a one day stopover on a tour. Bus tours are good to see many things quickly, but staying in one place has its special blessings.

You get to know a few of the people and hear the sounds, such as church bells tolling quietly at night, footsteps on the sidewalk below, bicycles whizzing by, and even horse hooves on cobblestone streets. Picturesque cafés become your dining room, and historic churches energize you as you sing "A Mighty Fortress" with pipe organ power and Lutheran gusto!

Meeting people from all over the world is great. One Saturday afternoon after leading worship at St. Mary's Church, Luther's parish for twenty-two years, I met with a group of Hawaiians. As Americans, they joined Christians I had met from twenty or more nations around the world. God's people come there in all colors, sizes and languages, and it's humbling to know God loves them all.

Most come there, weary and amazed at being where God did His wonders through the Reformers. One night we beheld an unexpected fireworks display outside our hotel window, ignited in the Castle Church plaza and lighting up the sky.

One of our last places to visit there was Schmetterling Park, a butterfly pavilion where dozens of lovely, brilliant butterflies live in a jungle atmosphere, with caterpillars and cocoons awaiting their brief life as God's delicate creatures.

I had been reading Lee Stroebel's book, The Case for Faith, where he speaks of the hand of the Almighty Creator around us. In one chapter he speaks of the wonder of God's creating a caterpillar that can change into a moth. As a trained and investigative reporter, Stroebel cited scientist after scientist as coming to believe that an Intelligent Creator made the universe. I'm glad such authors are able to share their faith.

"O Lord, our Lord, how excellent is Your name in all the earth!" (Psalm 8:1)

Do you see the hand of the creator around you each day?

212

I read an article in which the writer encouraged people to accept and even promote sexual behavior among young people, so long as they use protective devices. The author believed young people were going to be sexually active anyway, so it's up to adults to teach them how to do it safely. It reminded me of the parents a few decades ago who said, *"Underage kids are going to drink, so why not have them drink at home where we can make sure they're safe?"*

People today often cite "others" as reasons for their own poor conduct or choices. *"Others are doing it, so why can't I?"* they say. This attitude shows weakness, not strength. Excusing bad behavior, or asking others to condone what you're doing because "others" are doing it, are all signs of weakness. Blaming "others" for your mistakes, or joining with those who do wrong because it sounds fun or it is easier than doing what is right, is a sign of failure, not success.

Most people, especially Christians, know the essentials of what is wrong, but they don't always have the courage to stand up for what is right. Encouraging others to assist them in doing wrong only doubles their troubles. It is always best to do the right thing, no matter the consequences, for this is the way Jesus would take, and it is the way He will bless us.

Our Lord came into the world to grant us salvation. By faith in Him, we are forgiven. We have been released from our bondage to sin. Because we are forgiven, we are freed to follow Him in doing the right thing. The Holy Spirit even helps us, both in believing Christ and in following Him.

No amount of human reason can justify doing what is unwise or wrong. God wants us to be true to our faith in Him, and to show that faith to others. When people know what's right, we must not let someone else lead us into actions we know are wrong.

"Receive instruction in prudent behavior, doing what is right and just and fair." (Proverbs 1:3)

Thank you, Lord, for forgiving us!

JULY 28

Children can teach us more and in better ways than we might expect. A father wanted to read his new magazine but was continuously interrupted by his little girl's questions. *"Daddy,"* she asked, *"what does America look like?"* He knew he'd better answer her or he'd have no peace.

There happened to be a map of the United States in the magazine he was reading, so he tore it out carefully and then tore the map into several smaller pieces, and gave it all to his daughter. *"See if you can put this together."* he said with a father's knowing smile. *"When you are done it will show you what America looks like. Use some tape to put it together."*

He had only a few minutes of peace when she came back with the map correctly fitted and taped together correctly. *"How did you do that so fast, honey?"* he asked. She replied, *"It was easy. On the other side of the page is a picture of Jesus. When I got Jesus put back where he belonged, then America came together just right, too."*

"From the lips of children You have ordained praise," said Jesus in Matthew 21:16. I hope that father learned something from his daughter, because she said it more correctly than she realized. When Jesus is put back where He belongs, the rest of life comes together right also, in our own life, and even in the life of a whole country.

Our Lord Jesus gave His life that we might live our lives in a way far better than we could without Him. He gave Himself unto death on the cross that we might be forgiven, and that we might also forgive others and give hope to them as we do. Jesus poured Himself out on the cross of Calvary that we might have hope. Now we can share that hope we have with those who may be feeling hopeless.

"Make me to know Your ways, O Lord; teach me Your paths." (Psalm 25:4)

Life is always better when we have Jesus put back where He belongs.

214

JULY 29

During the building of the Golden Gate Bridge over San Francisco Bay in the 1930's, construction fell behind schedule because several workers accidentally fell from the scaffolding and were killed. Administrators were frustrated by the costly delays until someone suggested a gigantic net be hung under the construction area of the bridge to catch any worker who might fall.

Despite its enormous cost, engineers built the safety net, and the result worked well. After it was installed, a worker or two fell, but their lives were saved by the net. Ultimately, all the time lost to fear was regained by replacing fear with faith in a net that saved lives.

God's grace in Jesus Christ is the net. The umbrella of His mercy is above us, and the net of His grace is below us. We have their combined safety because of faith in what Christ did for us on the cross. But if we intentionally stand outside the umbrella, or if we go to where there is no net, we no longer will have its protection. If we choose to push away God's grace, His net will not catch us.

Grace is not a birthright, but a gift of God that comes through faith in Christ. The costly grace of God is for all people, but it can be rejected. In Jesus' story of the Pharisee and Tax Collector, it was the repentant Tax Collector who went home from the Temple forgiven. But the unrepentant Pharisee saw no need to change his prideful life.

The person who lives life on his own terms receives nothing that truly lasts. Grace does nothing for the one who thinks of self as being good enough that the cross of Jesus Christ is not needed. All people are sinful, and therefore all people need Jesus.

"For the message of the cross is foolishness to those who are perishing, but to us who are being saved it is the power of God." (1 Corinthians 1:18)

Thanks be to God for His grace!

JULY 30

"I wish I could have met him," she said as we left the old house. Have you ever known or met someone famous, a celebrity everyone knows? I guess it depends on what one would consider "famous." We all at some time have met a "name dropper," someone who likes to tell others of the famous people he knows. A man once regaled us such with an array of important people he knew that we found him far more boring than amazing.

Years ago Carol and I visited Winterset, Iowa, the Madison County seat and site of the book, <u>Bridges of Madison County</u>. It is also the birthplace of Marion Robert Morrison, also known as the actor John Wayne. We slipped into a tour of the tiny house on the corner of Second and South Streets where he was born and lived three years. The rooms were filled with photos and memorabilia of "Duke's" life. The guide said as we left, *"I wish I could have met him, but he died in 1979."*

Most of us would like to know someone famous. I must be one of those, as I've even had dreams about meeting an actor or a president. It felt good in the dream, even after I woke up. But I've never personally met anyone truly famous.

Yet I am a close friend of the most important person who ever lived. This Person knows me at my worst and still likes me! He is Jesus of Nazareth, the King of kings and Lord of lords. He is the Son of the Living God and offers eternal life to me and everyone who trusts in Him. I know Him personally, and I try to talk to Him every day.

Though He lived two thousand years ago, all believers have met Him, and today He lives in their hearts. There are millions of "little Christs" in the world who strive to live according to His will and ways.

"I wish I could have met him," said our guide. The Good News is that we can all meet the Lord of heaven and earth, through His Holy Word which gives us life forever.

"May I never boast except in the cross of our Lord Jesus Christ." (Galatians 6:14)

Some day we'll be with Him forever!

JULY 31

We all have things around our houses that we don't use, but we don't want to get rid of them, either. Our exercise equipment is a good example. A few years ago I bought a used exercise bike and took it home with great plans. It would help my legs, breathing and strength, and maybe even bring back those "six-pack abs" I thought I once had. And all for the garage sale price of five dollars!

I used it that first day for about 10 minutes, and admired it as it sat there on my deck. The next day I was too busy to use it, and also the next. In the coming months, I used it less, but always kept it there in sight, ready for use.

Though I rarely used it, it was good just having it there. I was sure one day I'd use it regularly, maybe when I retired. A month into retirement, I put it in storage and later sold it in my own garage sale. It was getting in the way! Even now I can picture just where it was on my deck, gathering dust.

Sometimes we treat our Bibles that way. We all have one, maybe several, and they look nice as they sit on our shelves or coffee tables. They may be a bit dusty and unused, but they are there, ready for when we need them! We feel better just having our Bible near at hand.

Perhaps one of these days we're going to read it, maybe even regularly. When that day comes, it will be right there to strengthen our faith, increase our knowledge, brace up our morals, and make us a better person. But right now we're a busy. Of course, we will never get rid of it just because we don't use it. We feel better just knowing our Bible is close by. We just don't have the time right now.

Today will be different. When I get done with my tasks, I'm going to get that exercise bike out again. I just know this time I will use it regularly. Oh, I sold it! Now, where is that Bible I am planning to read?

"Blessed are those who hear the word of God and obey it." (Luke 11:28)

Will you join me in exercising our faith through the Word?

DAILY WALK WITH JESUS in...

AUGUST

+ + +

AUGUST 1

Tony Snow, Christian journalist and former White House Press Secretary, died of cancer in 2008. His positive and godly perspective is what kept this husband and youthful father going amid his health crises that covered several years. Today I hope you will find something helpful in his words:

> *"Through such trials, God bids us to choose: Do we believe, or do we not? Will we be bold enough to love, daring enough to serve, humble enough to submit, and strong enough to acknowledge our limitations? Can we surrender our concern in things that don't matter so that we might devote our remaining days to things that do?*
>
> *"When our faith flags, He throws reminders in our way. Think of the prayer warriors in our midst. They change things, and those of us who have been on the receiving end of their petitions and intercessions know it. It is hard to describe, but there are times when suddenly the hairs on the back of your neck stand up, and you feel a surge of the Spirit. Somehow you just know: Others have chosen, when talking to the Author of creation, to lift us up, to speak of us!*
>
> *"This is love of a very special order. But so is the ability to sit back and appreciate the wonder of every created thing. The mere thought of death somehow makes every blessing vivid, every happiness more luminous and intense. We may not know how our contest with sickness will end, but we have felt the true touch of God.*
>
> *"What is man that Thou art mindful of him? We don't know much, but we know this: No matter where we are, no matter what we do, no matter how bleak or frightening our prospects, each and every one of us who believe, each and every day, lies in the same safe and impregnable place, in the hollow of God's hand."*

"Let your light shine before others, that they may see your good deeds and glorify your Father in heaven." (Matthew 5:16)

May God give us many such shining lights in the public arena.

219

AUGUST 2

The little things in life can often cause big trouble. Many years ago my car wouldn't run right. The engine would run a few minutes, and then quit. A mechanic attempted several solutions before discovering there was fine, nearly invisible, dirt particles in the gas tank. The dirt would settle out, allowing the motor to start, but when the gas was stirred up, it plugged the intake filter, and the motor would stop. The mechanic finally drained the tank, put in clean gas and my car ran great again!

Interesting, isn't it? Tiny, unseen particles of dirt stopping a powerful motor. It made me think of the problems we have from the buildup of dirt in our lives, or dust in our lungs, or garbage that quietly settles into our lives causing us to do things God never intended us to do. We need our spiritual tanks drained and filled with God's pure Word of power.

Perhaps it is the dirt of "acceptable" wrongdoing, or the dust of hatred or the unseen sins that creep into our life. If the source of the bad stuff is not removed, our life will get "out of kilter" as my father used to say. A life absent of a moral center and fueled by secret sin can lead to unbalanced behavior that will cause a person to do terrible things.

Having a moral compass can bring back a Godly balance. Hearing the saving Word of Jesus or seeing it lived out in the lives of those around us can help us avoid evil. Turning from sin and accepting the forgiveness of Jesus will align an imbalanced life.

A terrible incident of shooting and death occurred at a movie theater one night in the Denver area near us. Our hearts went out to the individuals and families involved. May such evils never occur again, in Colorado, the United States, or anywhere in the world.

"Seek the Lord while He may be found; Call upon Him while He is near. Let the wicked forsake his way, and the unrighteous man his thoughts; let him return to the Lord, that he may have compassion on him, and to our God, for he will abundantly pardon." (Isaiah 55:6-7)

Is your life out of kilter? Depending on Jesus can make it better.

AUGUST 3

Learning to speak can take several years when we are very young. Our parents treasure the first words we speak, no matter how badly we may say them.

Learning to speak properly and truthfully may take a lifetime. There has always been a trend to use language to bend and twist the truth to accomplish their purposes. The apostle Paul spoke and wrote carefully and truthfully. He knew his words needed to be correctly chosen. Here is some of what he said that is memorable:

"If I speak in tongues of men and of angels but have not love, I am a noisy gong or a clanging cymbal." (1 Corinthians 13:1) We tend to think this chapter is only for weddings, but it's really about speaking the truth in love.

"Speaking the truth in Love" says St. Paul. **(Ephesians 4:15)** How hard this can be! People today, both young and old, think it's okay to skirt the truth, tell half-truths, bend and twist the truth, or simply deny it.

St. Paul continued, **"Speaking the truth in love, we are to grow up in every way into Him who is the head, into Christ."** This involves growth in our Christian faith. Growing in faith means learning practical things such as hearing without blaming, assuming the best rather than the worst, and not judging before we have all the facts.

I only hope truth will come back into vogue among today's leaders, especially those governing our nation. Truth has always been a victim in war and politics. However, the truth must always be present among Christians.

Perhaps today we might consider what **"speaking the truth in love"** means in our home, our work place, our churches and schools, or among our acquaintances.

What does speaking untruth lead to in a society? It may seem painful, but it will always be helpful. Let's honor God and each other by practicing our faith and speaking God's truth in love by we do and say. As followers of Jesus Christ, we should do no other than what He would have us do.

Practicing what we preach – now there's a grand idea!

AUGUST 4

What does it mean to have "faith?" I have "faith" that the sun will rise tomorrow, or that my paycheck will come on payday, or that my wife will do my laundry. I have faith that my sons will succeed at what they do, and I have faith that Christian people will honor God in most of what they do and say each day. I even have faith I will wake up tomorrow.

Any one of these things may or may not happen, but yet I continue to have faith in things that may ultimately fail my expectations. I may not be concerned with the technical aspects of how those things may happen, but I believe they will. I don't ask for proof or evidence prior to believing. I just believe they will happen.

So why is it that I, and probably you as well, find it hard to have faith in God, or that our Heavenly Father will live up to His promises? Has He ever failed you? Has He been true to His promises? If so, why then do we demand to know the details of how He will answer our prayers? Why demand proof that He can do it? Why do we need evidence? I don't need evidence about my kids or paycheck or waking up in the morning, yet I seek evidence of God in my life all the time.

The very definition of faith is to believe without seeing. You and I can always depend on Him who never ceases to love us. He is the source of true faith. Ask Him for more faith, and He will give it. Ask Him to take away your need for unanswered questions and replace it with ever stronger faith. We need to do this every day.

I have faith that God will send us all the things we need. God uses people to answer our prayers. Will you perhaps be among those who are an answer to someone else's prayers today? Will you be willing to be God's answers to someone in need?

"Now faith is confidence in what we hope for and assurance about what we do not see." (Hebrews 11:1)

I have faith God will provide those who are in need. I know He will, perhaps through you.

AUGUST 5

On my home office wall I have a small plaque from my mother. It reads (in German), *"Das Leben ist am schwersten drei Tage vor dem Ersten,"* which means, *"Life seems most difficult three days before it happens."* It's a statement about worry.

Worry affects us all, doesn't it? Surprisingly, I've found I struggle as much with worry now that I'm retired as I did before when I had less time to do it. Worry is concern without faith. Everyone should be concerned about what might happen and plan or prepare for it, but when we think it all depends on us, we get bogged down with worry.

Jesus once said, **"Who of you by worrying can add a single hour to his life? And why do you worry about clothes or food or drink? The pagans run after these things, and your heavenly Father knows you need them."**

Then Jesus gets to the heart of things: **"But seek first His kingdom and His righteousness, and all these things will be given to you as well." (Matthew 6:31-33)**

I usually do some fall house cleaning (wash windows, dust, clean garage). One fall I discovered that I'd put my Bible up high on a shelf. The saying, *"A place for everything and everything in its place"* may be good, but my Bible was doing me no good up there. So I put it by my favorite chair where I can easily reach it.

If we put God first in our lives (like getting Him off the shelf), worry becomes less of a problem. But it doesn't disappear. Worry is like dust. You'll always have it around, but you can take steps to get rid of it now and then. We can pray more often. Or worship God each week. Or read the Bible more. Or encourage someone. Or volunteer at church.

As sinners we will never be completely rid of worry, and we do have legitimate concerns about self or family or the world. But Jesus came to forgive our worrying, and to help us trust Him. In His Word God reminds us that He always provides. So first seek the Lord, His kingdom and His righteousness, and that other stuff will take care of itself. It's His promise, and Jesus always keeps His promises.

I think I have more dusting to do!

AUGUST 6

There once was a little boy who wanted to meet God. He knew it was a long trip to where God lived, so he packed a sack with some Twinkies and root beer and started his journey. When he had gone about three blocks, he met an old woman who was sitting in the park staring at some pigeons. The boy sat next to her and opened his sack.

He was about to take a drink from his root beer when he thought that the lady might be hungry, so he offered her a Twinkie. She accepted it and smiled at him. Her smile was so pretty that the boy wanted to see it again, so he offered her a root beer. Once again, she smiled at him. The boy was delighted! They sat there all afternoon eating and smiling, and hardly speaking a word to each other.

As it grew dark, the boy realized how tired he was and got up to leave. But before he had gone more than a few steps, he turned around, ran back to the old woman, and gave her a hug. She gave him her biggest smile ever.

When the boy opened the door to his own house a short time later, his mother was surprised by the look of joy on his face. She asked him, *"What did you do today that made you so happy?"* He replied, *"I had lunch with God."* And before his mother could respond he added, *"You know what? She's got the most beautiful smile I've ever seen!"*

Meanwhile, the old woman, almost radiant with joy, returned to her home. Her son was stunned by the look of peace on her face, so he asked, *"Mother, what did you do today that made you so happy?"* She replied, *"I ate Twinkies in the park with God."* Before he could respond she added, *"You know, he's much younger than I expected."*

Too often we underestimate the power of a touch, a smile, a kind word, a listening ear, a compliment, or a small act of caring, all of which have the potential to turn a life around. People come into our lives for a reason, a moment, a season, or a lifetime. Give thanks Jesus came to stay forever.

"Let the light of Your face shine on us." (Psalm 4:6)

May we see God in someone's smile today.

AUGUST 7

Some of us come from a rural background, and someone recently told me he appreciates my "rural humor." I take that as a compliment, since so much of life today requires a sense of humor to keep things in balance.

There is much we can learn from farmers. James Bender, in his book, How to Talk Well (McGraw-Hill, 1994), relates the story of a farmer who grew award-winning corn. Each year he entered his corn in the state fair where it won a blue ribbon. One year a newspaper reporter interviewed him and learned something interesting about how he grew it.

The reporter discovered the farmer shared his seed corn with his neighbors. *"How can you afford to share your best seed corn with your neighbors when they are entering corn in competition with yours each year?"* the reporter asked.

"Why sir," said the farmer, *"didn't you know? The wind picks up pollen from the ripening corn and swirls it from field to field. If my neighbors grow inferior corn, cross-pollination will steadily degrade the quality of my corn seed. If I am to grow good seed, I must help my neighbors grow good corn."* That farmer was aware of the connectedness of life. His own corn wouldn't improve unless his neighbors' also did.

Those who choose to be at peace in life must help their neighbors be at peace. Those who choose to live well must help others live well. The value of one life is not measured by its wealth, but by the lives it touches. Those who choose to be happy can help others to find happiness, because the welfare of each of us is bound up with the welfare of all. If you want good corn, you have to help your neighbor grow good corn, also.

Jesus once said this to His disciples using the axiom we have called, "The Golden Rule." It is a rule that helps us get along well in many areas of life.

"In everything, do to others what you would have them do to you, for this sums up the Law and the Prophets." (Matthew 7:12)

That sums it up pretty well!

AUGUST 8

Did you ever feel worthless? Or have you felt you are not worth much? A well-known speaker started off his seminar by holding up a $20 bill. In the room of two hundred, he asked, *"Who would like this $20 bill?"* Hands went up all over. He said, *"I am going to give this $20 to one of you, but first let me do this."* He proceeded to crumple the dollar bill up.

He then asked, *"Who still wants it?"* The hands went up in the air again. *"Well,"* he replied, *"what if I do this?"* and he dropped it on the floor and ground it with his heel. He picked it up, now all crumpled and dirty. *"Now who still wants it?"* Still the hands went into the air. *"My friends,"* he said, *"you have all learned a valuable lesson. You still want this $20 because no matter what I did to it, it did not decrease in value. Brand new or all smashed up, it is still worth $20."*

There are times in our lives when we feel as if we are being dropped, crumpled, and ground into the dirt by people around us, or by the decisions we make, or by the nasty circumstances that happen in life. In such times we may feel as though we are worthless.

But no matter what has happened or what will happen, we will never lose our value in God's eyes. To our loving Lord, whether we are dirty or clean, crumpled or smooth, we are still priceless. Psalm 17:8 states that God will keep us, **"As the apple of His eye."**

The worth of our lives comes not in what we do or who we are, but in whose we are! Today is the birthday of my wife. She is the *"apple of my eye,"* a valuable part of my life and I love her dearly. God has shown His love for us both in bringing us together. He has given us a family of which we are proud. We know we are loved by Him and by each other.

"For this reason I bow my knees before the Father, from whom every family in heaven and on earth is named." **(Ephesians 3:14-15)**

You are a child of the Family of God. Don't ever forget it!

AUGUST 9

A boy was sitting on a park bench with an open Bible, loudly praising God. *"Hallelujah! Hallelujah! God is great!"* he shouted, not caring whether anyone heard him or not. As he did this, along came a young man from the local university. Feeling himself very enlightened in the ways of truth and eager to share his enlightenment, he asked the boy what the source of his joy was. *"Hey!"* said the boy with a bright laugh, *"Don't you realize how great God is? I just read that He opened up the waves of the Red Sea and led the whole nation of Israel through the middle safely to the other side."*

The "enlightened" man chuckled lightly, sat down and began to explain his knowledge of the "miracles" of the Bible. *"That can all be very easily explained,"* he said. *"Modern scholarship has shown that the Red Sea in that area was only 10-inches deep at that time. It was no problem for the Israelites to wade across it."*

The boy's face fell, and his eyes wandered from the man back to the open Bible in his lap. The learned man, content that he had enlightened a poor, naive boy to the finer points of scientific insight, turned to go. Scarcely had he taken a step when the boy shouted, *"Hallelujah! Hallelujah! God is really great!"* The man turned and asked why. *"Wow!"* exclaimed the boy, *"God is greater than I thought! Not only did He lead the whole nation of Israel through the Red Sea, He drowned the whole Egyptian army in just ten inches of water!"*

We live in an age when modern scholarship is trying its best to discount the Bible. We might wonder why? If it's such a harmless book, why do people work so hard to disprove it? Perhaps they are afraid it might really be true.

The central point of the Bible is that God sent His Savior to redeem the world from sin and Satan. All who trust in Jesus as Lord are granted eternal life. That's great news!

"Where is the wise man? Where is the scholar? Where is the philosopher of this age? Has not God made foolish the wisdom of the world?" (1 Corinthians 1:20)

That young boy was wise beyond his years.

Maybe you've seen the photo of an old woman sitting in an alley near an overturned garbage can. She is eating some food she'd found in the garbage, and she is smiling. Most of us won't eat food we accidentally drop on the floor, but this hungry woman didn't care who touched it last. She was happy she had found food. News stories warn us of obesity and urge us to diet, and yet this woman seemed satisfied with her few mouthfuls of "food."

There is much talk about our struggling economy and the cost of living going steadily higher. Many people are anxious about their livelihood. Jobs, even the most humble ones, are causing hundreds of people to line up to apply. Economists cite statistics on foreclosures and bankruptcies, and predictably the politicians promise to fix it all.

Is it possible, in the midst of gloomy times, to heed the words of our Lord in Matthew 6:25, **"Do not worry about your life, what you will eat or what you will drink; nor about your body, what you will put on?"** Our Lord is not telling us we don't need to work, nor should we be unconcerned with what we will eat or wear. He is warning against letting money or possessions rule us instead of trusting Him for our needs.

Jesus tells us, **"Seek first the Kingdom of God and His righteousness, and all these things shall be added unto you." (Matthew 6:33)** This urges us to recognize that no matter how much effort we expend to make a better life for ourselves and our families, that true contentment comes from knowing it is the Lord who provides our needs.

Since God is our Heavenly Father who truly does love us, we believe we will have enough for our life. He promises to provide for us, and He is faithful to all His promises.

"Lord, I believe - help my unbelief!" (Mark 9:24)

Have you ever been so hungry that you had to eat from a garbage can? Have you thanked God for that?

Do you remember the "good old days" when we played hide and seek, ate warm bread and butter or caramel rolls, and we didn't feel guilty? Remember when nearly everyone's Mom was there when the kids got home, a quarter was a decent allowance, and "gay" just meant having fun? Remember when you had your gas pumped, windshield cleaned and oil checked by an attendant without asking, and they even gave you green stamps?

Remember when mother bought flour in fifty pound bags, and large boxes of detergent came with a free dish or towel inside? Remember when it was considered a privilege to go to a restaurant, and being sent to the principal's office was nothing compared to what awaited you when you got home?

But do you also remember when kids and adults were crippled by polio, your kitchen had flies, or you had to haul drinking water from the pump? Remember using that smelly outhouse even in the wintertime, fearing the atomic bomb, being drafted into the Army or getting smallpox? Remember when smoking was cool and work places were not air conditioned, and hardly anyone had health insurance?

Were the "Good Old Days" really that good? Things long ago may seem better looking back, but those days had big problems, too. Too many young men died in World War Two, Korea and Viet Nam. Youth had terrible auto accidents due to no seat belts, farm accidents left adults or children lame, and people of color were tormented.

Sometimes we see the past only through rose-colored glasses and forget the hard work, risks, danger and prejudice that we accepted. Life, no matter what the era, can be good or bad. It all depends on our perspective and relationships, especially with God, families, and friends. Today can be just as good. It all depends on how we trust God and how much effort we put into loving and helping each other.

"In times of disaster the believers will not wither; in days of famine they will enjoy plenty." (Psalm 37:19)

Let's all try being really thankful today!

229

AUGUST 12

We're all afraid of something. Usually our fears center around what's valuable to us, our family and loved ones, that we might lose them or they might suffer. We can also fear loss of job or health or even reputation. Most of our fears are about loss of people or things that give us purpose and stability.

Here are six major kinds of loss in life:

1. *Material Loss - Loss of objects very important to us*
2. *Relationship Loss - Loss of having a certain person with us*
3. *Intra-psychic Loss – Loss of self-respect, dreams or plans*
4. *Functional Loss – Loss of ability to do certain things*
5. *Role Loss – Loss of your place in a social network or activity*
6. *Systemic Loss - Loss of being valued in a relationship*

There are other minor kinds of losses. Almost any loss we experience involves more than one kind. If you lose your job, you're also losing work friends, an income and perhaps even self-respect. If you are divorced, you lose not only a spouse, but also your role in the family, or your self-image, or an income provider. A divorced man once said he discovered twelve distinctive kinds of loss he had suffered. *"No wonder I feel so rotten,"* he told me.

God doesn't want us to be driven by fear. Paul told young Timothy, **"God did not give us a spirit of fear, but of power and of love and of sound mind." (2 Timothy 1:7)** In times of loss we may feel helpless, angry or out of control. In severe loss, we may even feel we're losing our mind.

Jesus once told His disciples He was going to leave them, so He said, **"Let not your hearts be troubled. Trust in God; trust also in me." (John 14:1)** He encouraged them not to be afraid or lose heart, but to trust in their Heavenly Father who would never leave them.

It's easy to spend time fearing what might happen. But as long as we trust Jesus, He will make sure life is okay. He is always with us and loves us, no matter what.

"Commit your way to the Lord, trust in Him, and He will bring it to pass." (Psalm 37:5)

Have a fine day trusting in the Lord.

AUGUST 13

A boy was visiting his Grandma and he told her how everything was going wrong for him. School was hard, his parents had grounded him, he had a miserable cold, and even his best friend hadn't played with him all week. As she listened, Grandma was working at her kitchen counter.

She suddenly asked him if he would like a snack. *"You bet!"* he said. *"Here, have a sip of cooking oil." "Yuck, Grandma!"* said the boy, *"I can't drink that." "Then how about a couple eggs. They're raw but fresh!"* said Grandma. *"That's gross, Grandma, who eats raw eggs?" "How about a handful of flour?"* she asked, *"Or a mouthful of baking soda? Here's a cup of sugar!" "Grandma, those are all yucky!"* the boy said. *"Don't you have something better?"*

She smiled and took his hands in hers and said, *"Yes, all those things are pretty bad by themselves. But when they're put together in the right way, they make a chocolate cake that tastes pretty good. Would you like some cake?" "You bet!"* the boy said.

She continued, *"Life often happens to us the same way, one thing at a time. We wonder why God lets us get sick or go through hard times or get pushed around by people. But God knows that when He gives us all those things in the right way, they can make something very good in our life. They can help us trust Him and see the good things He wants for us."* Then she read to him a poem posted on her refrigerator.

THE WEAVER

My life is but a weaving, between my God and me;
I only choose the colors; He weaveth steadily.
Sometimes He weaveth sorrow, and I, in foolish pride,
Forget He sees the upper, but I, the underside.

Not till the loom is silent and the shuttles cease to fly
Will God unroll the canvas, and explain the reasons why
The dark threads are as useful in the Weaver's skillful hand
As the threads of gold and silver, in the pattern He has planned.
(by Grant Colfax Tuller, 1869-1950)

"My days are swifter than a weaver's shuttle." (Job 7:6)

I hope you get some chocolate cake today.

231

AUGUST 14

Henry was a disabled child, and his father once said, *"Everything God does is done with perfection even though my child cannot understand or do things as other children do. When God brings a child like this into the world, I believe the perfection He seeks is in the way other people react to him."*

One afternoon he and Henry were walking past a park where some boys Henry knew were playing baseball. Henry asked, *"Do you think they will let me play?"* The father asked a boy if Henry could join them and he said, *"We're losing by six runs and the game is almost over. It's okay if he plays for us."*

Henry smiled as he put on a glove and walked out to play center field. Henry's team scored a few more runs but was still behind by three. In the last inning, Henry's team scored again and now with two outs and the bases loaded, Henry was up to bat. But would his team let him bat?

Surprisingly, they did. Everyone knew he couldn't hit, but as he stepped to the plate, the pitcher moved a few steps closer to toss the ball slowly so he could perhaps make contact. On the first pitch Henry swung and missed. One of his teammates came up to help and together they held the bat for the next pitch. The ball was thrown softly and together they swung and hit a slow grounder to the pitcher. The pitcher picked it up to end the game, but instead threw it far into right field.

Everyone yelled, *"Henry, run to first,"* so he scampered down the baseline all wide-eyed. The right fielder threw the ball far over the third baseman's head and under the stands, and everyone yelled, *"Run to second, Henry, run to second."*

As he ran towards second, the runners ahead of him crossed home plate, and the second baseman said, *"Run to third."* As Henry rounded third, the boys from both teams shouted, *"Home, Henry, run home!"* As he crossed home plate, all the boys lifted him on their shoulders because he'd hit a "grand slam" and won the game for his team. *"That day,"* said Henry's father, *"those 18 boys reached a level of God's perfection."*

"Run so that you may win the prize." (1 Corinthians 9:24)

May we all reach such a level!
232

A group of frogs were hopping through the woods when two of them fell into a deep pit. All the other frogs gathered around to help, but when they saw how deep the pit was, they told the unfortunate frogs things looked really bad - they'd probably never get out.

But the two frogs ignored their comments and tried jumping out anyway. As they tried, the frogs up above shouted that they'd never make it out and were as good as dead. After a long time of trying, one of the frogs gave up trying and died of exhaustion.

But the other frog kept jumping as hard as he could. The others yelled at him to stop since he'd never get out. But the more they shouted, the harder he tried until finally, in one mighty jump, he grabbed a ledge and made it out. The other frogs asked, *"We're glad you're out, but why did you keep jumping? Didn't you hear us?"* It was then they realized he was deaf. He thought all their shouts of discouragement were cheers of encouragement, so he tried harder!

"Sticks and stones may break my bones, but words can never hurt me," we learned as a child. How wrong we were! Our words can have the power of life and death in them. A good word to someone who is down and out can encourage, lift up and help a person make it through the day. On the other hand, a destructive word can discourage and even destroy. Words, indeed, are powerful and can hurt or help us.

Give those you meet today a word of hope. Our world has enough pessimists and cynics. Be an optimist, an encourager of people. Blessed is the person who takes the time to build up and encourage others with words.

Jesus encouraged everyone with His words, even the harsh ones spoken to the proud. He wants us to trust Him and what He says, for His words give life to our souls.

"Each of us should please his neighbor for his good, to build him up." (Romans 15:2)

May you share your good words with someone in need today.

233

AUGUST 16

Have you ever tried running away from God? Most of us don't run, we shuffle or slide away from Him, a step at a time, and quite often do it in the summertime. Then one day we look around and wonder why God seems so far away. Running from God is a part of our sinful human nature that will never leave us this side of heaven.

But once in awhile we find God has moved away from us. He's wanted us to come with Him, but we haven't been listening, so God moves. If we want to live by God's will, we can't stay in one place.

God is always working among people and He invites us to join what He's doing. God speaks to us through His Word in the Church, through events, and in our hearts to reveal His will. His invitation to follow may lead us to a crisis of faith that requires us to step out of our comfort zones. But if we make some adjustments to follow Him, we will be blessed.

After eleven great years at a fine church, I had become restless and resigned, wondering what God had next for me. The result was my starting a new mission church in a nearby town, one that grew strong in the eight years I pastored it.

Every now and then I wonder what life would have been like had I stayed at my former church with its wonderful people and ministries. Staying there would have been easier, but God was doing something great in that town nearby, and I sensed He wanted me to join in what He was doing.

Life is like climbing a mountain. The most important thing is to concentrate on where you are and the next step you have to take, rather than what you've done, or all that's left to do. If you look ahead too often, the mountain top will look too high. If you look back down the mountain, you may become frightened at how high you've come. But if you trust God for each step that's coming, you'll continue on your climb safely.

Keep focused on where you are and what your next step will be. Then your climb won't look as difficult.

"Seek the Lord while He may be found; call on Him while He is near." (Isaiah 55:6)

Blessings to all you fellow climbers!

234

AUGUST 17

One winter I read in my hometown local newspaper that a man named Clarence Jones had died. I had a School classmate named Allen Jones with whom I've kept in touch, so I emailed him asking if Clarence was a relative. He wrote back:

"Clarence Jones was my second cousin and also a good friend. He also had a son named Allen, so that gave us lots of confusion over the years. His son Allen died a little over four years ago from diabetes complications. Some friends of ours in Nebraska heard about it, but they didn't know there were two Allen Joneses.

They thought it was me who'd died, so they sent my wife a very nice sympathy card and message. She said that she almost cried at first when she read it (I guess they must have said nice things about me). I called them later on the phone to tell what really happened. They had caller ID and knew the call was from me. Their first question was, 'Where are you calling from?' I guess they wondered if it was heaven or perdition!"

That's a great story. Sometimes we get confused over names, and other times we're confused from what's going on in our own lives. Sometimes I wonder what it would be like if we could hear what people would say at our own funeral.

My wife tells the story about three guys discussing what they would like people to say about them at their funeral. One said, *"I'd like it said that I was a fine father and husband."* Another said, *"I'd like it said that I was a good Christian man."* The third man said, *"I'd like someone to say, 'Look! He's still breathing!'"*

What would you like others to say about you at your funeral? I suppose I'd want to be like the third man, hoping I had a little more time on earth. Yet, life with God – how much better can it get than that?

Wise King Solomon wrote, **"A good name is better than precious perfume, and the day of death is better than the day of birth."** (Ecclesiastes 7:1)

How do you react to that verse? What does it tell you?

When God is ready for you, you'd better be ready for Him.

235

AUGUST 18

Next to a small church building in my town stands a ponderosa pine tree, a smaller version of a larger fallen tree lying a dozen or more feet away, rotting on the ground. For a hundred years that fallen tree used to stand forty or more feet tall, a giant among the scrub oak bushes next to it. It could be seen for miles around.

Across the highway from that church property is a hill that looks like a volcano because it had its top removed by a rock quarry that provided material for roads and other projects.

Local legend tells us that in 1895, a worker in that rock quarry was found to be stealing. His fellow workers caught him and meted out the swift and harsh justice of the day. They took him down and hanged him from a limb of that big pine tree until he was dead. It was on a tree that stood a short distance from where a church building now stands.

Think of it. Right near a building where people worship God was an old hanging tree. Some have said they think this is unfortunate, but I don't think so. Maybe it has a special purpose. During the construction phase of that church building, I told each of the sub-contractors about the thief who was hanged there, and not a single item was stolen during our building process!

More importantly, each one of us need to be reminded that our Lord Jesus died on a tree. He was hanged on the tree of Calvary's cross, an innocent man who died between two thieves. Because He was so punished, you and I won't receive the punishment we deserve for our sins.

Because of Jesus, we are set free to live as God's people, all of us men, women, and children. We are all given a second chance at life because our Savior was crucified on a tree. Think about it, and then praise God for it!

"Abraham planted a tamarisk tree in Beersheba, and there he called on the name of the Lord." (Genesis 21:33)

Thank the Lord for the tree of the cross!

AUGUST 19

Carol and I enjoy watching documentaries about different countries. With today's amazing photography, it's almost as good as being there. We once watched "Wild China," a fine series live-streamed into our home through our laptop. There we can see many television series about our amazing world.

It's so easy to do. Just punch a button or two on a small remote control, wait a few moments, and you're in another country. Watch it on a "High Def" TV while sitting on recliners in a comfortable home. Travel has never been so easy!

How fortunate we are to be living in a free country with good food and water during this amazing time of history. We could have been born a hundred years ago on the barren Steppes of China, or from a mother who wears a burka, or in a drug-ridden town in South America.

We can now take a non-stop flight to Iceland for about the price of a good set of tires. If I don't feel well, there are a dozen places to get excellent medical care within a half hour of our home. If you have a few million dollars, in a few years you might even be to able take a flight into space.

We have no control where, when or to whom we are born. But the fact that we have been born at this time, in this country, with these privileges and blessings ought to move us to give God thanks. Instead, we'll probably get angry at politicians, or worry about our loved ones or grumble about our pains.

Every one of us ought to consider writing God a long letter of thanks that we are alive today. Our life may not be exactly what we wanted it to be, but we are alive, and we are richly blessed. People who lived just a century ago would have given all they had to live the life we have lived. They would also have been happy to be reading a book like this.

Instead of disappointment over what we don't have, let's be grateful for what we have. The poorest American is richer than three-fourths of the rest of the world. A Christian child has more blessings than a Buddhist, Hindu or Moslem child.

"O give thanks to the Lord for He is good. His love endures forever." (Psalm 136:1)

For what would you give thanks to God?

237

No matter how long something has been done a certain way, a succeeding generation may change it. Every idea or activity must be measured by God's truth in Jesus Christ. Even the best idea must change if it no longer has merit.

I grew up loving my mother's fresh bread. She made it once a week in big mixing bowls on the kitchen table. She'd mix the ingredients and knead the dough. At bedtime, she'd knead it again and cover it with damp towels. The next morning she'd knead the dough once more, shape it into loaves or rolls, put it into pans and bake it. Freshly baked bread in the morning is a delicious, wonderful treat. No other bread is better! I recall eating five loaves of fresh bread with two friends one afternoon. It was a memorable feast!

But we don't make bread that way any more, not because we found a better way, but because we needed a faster way. Look at all the steps my mother had to do: mixing, kneading, waiting, kneading again, waiting overnight, kneading again, shaping and baking. Then wash all the pots and pans!

Today the few folks who make their own bread toss the ingredients into a $200 bread machine, punch a button and come back two hours later when the loaf is done. Even the best of diets must change, especially when we gain weight.

Like yeast in bread, the Word of the Lord grows, changing people and churches, fermenting and moving all it touches. Of course, not all the change is good. We must filter change through the unchangeable Gospel of Jesus, and what He did for us on the cross. When the Lord brings needed change into the church, we'd best stand back and let Him do His work.

This is not "our church," nor is it Luther's or Calvin's church. It is the Lord's church. Yes, it may be Reformed or Lutheran in character, but it is still the Lord's church, and He will build His church His way.

"I am the bread of life. Whoever comes to Me will never go hungry, and whoever believes in Me will never be thirsty." (John 6:35)

We are servants in the Vineyard, not owners of the field.

AUGUST 21

A number of years ago I received a stinging commentary on a particular Sunday sermon I'd preached when a parishioner told me on her way out, *"You ought to practice what you preach, Pastor!"* Ouch! That hurt, especially since she said it loudly enough for others to hear.

I'm not even sure what I spoke about that day, but someone saw a weakness. Shortly thereafter, though, an older woman who had heard this comment tried to console me, *"Don't worry, Pastor. If you spoke only on subjects where you were good enough, you'd have little or nothing to say."* I thought that over and wasn't sure that was a kind remark or not.

The messenger of the Gospel should speak to himself as well as to his listeners. He knows that neither he nor any of his listeners can measure up to the perfection God requires. We must all rely on the perfection of Jesus Christ for our salvation. He lived a perfect life in order to forgive us weak humans who can never be perfect.

God is faithful despite our unfaithfulness. Jesus loves us despite our lovelessness. How He does it, I don't know. God's unfailing love does the impossible. It covers all our sins and gives us eternal life. His love continues to do the improbable. It empowers us to be faithful to Him and to each other.

Faithfulness is a gift from God, a treasure to cherish, a gift to live by. Every pastor or teacher knows he or she must take care to mirror the teachings of Christ in their life as much as possible.

When a pastor falls into the disgrace of public sin, it affects the whole congregation. Even though God forgives the worst of sinners, the sins of the disgraced leader greatly harm the Body of Christ. He or she needs God's unquestioned mercy and our special understanding and forgiveness.

"Well done, good and faithful servant!" (Matthew 25:21)

Thank You, God, for honest people!

On a trip to the Midwest, we were at my brother's farm on a Sunday afternoon and decided to go to an auction in the neighboring town. A hundred or more folks were looking over the items of the sale when Carol brought to my attention several men dressed in bib overalls. Even though she grew up on a farm, seeing heavy men standing around in tee shirts, seed corn caps and bib overalls still gives her the giggles.

Those big guys stood around with hands in pockets, chewing tobacco, looking plain and even homely. My brother told me later to be careful what I thought of them, because they were some of the wealthiest farmers in the area.

The prophet Amos was a farmer from the south of Israel sent to preach to the well-dressed, wealthy folks in the north. Because of this, he was not well received. Israel had achieved things we Americans can relate to: full social calendars but hollow hearts, money and military security, and an easy life with plenty of leisure time. But they were neglecting the important thing in life, their relationship with God.

One wonders how the prophet Amos would respond to our culture today. Ours is a world that always has enough money to build a new stadium or casino, but never enough to cure diseases, feed the hungry, or even educate our children in lasting and God-pleasing truths.

Sometimes we modern people can get too big for our britches. We're educated beyond our intelligence. We think our own ideas are superior to God's. Sometimes it takes a "hayseed" in bib overalls like Amos to remind us of God's truths.

My prayer is that if you or I ever get too big for our britches, someone will come along and tell us. It's happened before, and God can send us another prophet again.

"The Lord, the Lord Almighty, He touches the earth and it melts, and all who live in it shall mourn." (Amos 9:5)

I pray that person who comes to us will make God's truth so plain and simple that we can understand it.

AUGUST 23

Today was my brother Bill's birthday and he has now gone to eternal glory. He was a talented artist and career school teacher, and I think he would have enjoyed this true story.

Rose was eighty-seven and enrolled in college. She loved life and it showed. Rose quickly became a campus icon and easily made friends wherever she went. She loved to dress up and reveled in the attention from the other students. She was living it up. *"I always dreamed of having a college education and now I'm getting one!"* she said.

Because of her popularity, at the end of one semester Rose was invited to speak at the college football banquet. She was introduced and this is what she said:

"We do not stop playing because we are old; we grow old because we stop playing. There are only a few secrets to staying young, being happy, and achieving success. You have to laugh and find humor every day. You've got to have a dream. When you lose your dreams, you die. We have so many people walking around who are dead and don't even know it!

There is a huge difference between growing older and growing up. If you are nineteen years old and lie in bed for one full year and don't do one productive thing, you will still turn twenty years old. Anybody can grow older. That doesn't take any talent or ability. The idea is to grow up by always finding the opportunity in change and having no regrets.

The elderly usually don't have regrets for what they did, but rather for things they did not do. The only people who fear death are those with regrets."

Three years later, a week after graduating with her college degree, Rose died peacefully in her sleep. Over two thousand young college students attended her funeral in tribute to a wonderful woman who taught by example that it's never too late to be all you can possibly be. When God gives us a life to live, let's make the best of it, and honor Him in all we do, no matter how old we are.

"A wise son brings joy to his father, but a foolish man despises his mother." (Proverbs 15:20)

Growing old is mandatory, but growing up is optional.

241

AUGUST 24

Chang Shen was a terrible man, known among his people as Wu So Pu Wei Te, meaning, "one without a particle of good in him." As a gambler, womanizer, addict and thief, he had driven away his family, and later when he was stricken with blindness, people said it was surely judgment on him for his evil ways.

In 1886, Chang heard of a missionary hospital where blind people were healed, so he traveled hundreds of miles there, and was given a bed. When Chang's eyesight was partially restored, he heard about Jesus for the first time. *"Never had we a patient who received the Gospel with such joy,"* they said.

When blind Chang asked to be baptized, a man told him, *"Go home and tell your neighbors that you have changed. I will visit you, and if you are still following Jesus, then I will baptize you."* Five months later, the man came and found hundreds of people learning of Jesus, so he baptized Chang with great joy.

Although totally blind, Chang traveled from village to village, witnessing about Jesus, praising God even when cursed and spat upon. He learned most of the Bible by memory and quoted entire chapters to people. Missionaries followed him, baptizing converts and organizing churches.

When the Boxer Rebellion arose in the 1890's, Christians were rounded up for execution. Someone said, *"You're fools to kill all these. For every one you kill, ten will spring up while that man Chang Shen lives."* The Boxers then came to kill Chang. When told of this, he said, *"I'll gladly die for Jesus."*

When he arrived, he was told he must worship Buddha. *"I can only worship the One Living and True God,"* he declared. So they put him in an open cart and drove him to the cemetery for execution. As he went, he sang this song:

"Jesus loves me, He who died, Heaven's gate to open wide;
He will wash away my sin, Let His little child come in."

At the cemetery, Chang was beheaded, and the fearful Boxers fled the village. By the year's end, hundreds more missionaries and families were martyred, but Blind Chang's witness led to the conversion of thousands more.

Would we be able to do what blind Chang did for His Lord?

AUGUST 25

God's will is not complicated. It is important that His people trust Him, live in His love and get along with each other. Of course, there is more to God's will than these few thoughts, but these can help us understand the following:

God wants His people with Him in heaven, and to help get them there, He brings us together into the Church. God wants His church united. However, we cannot achieve unity, let alone publicly declare it, when true unity is not present. To have unity, we must look to Jesus Christ, to Him only. We must make Him the center of our unity. Any other reason for unity, such as public opinion or following current trends, are empty and false.

For awhile I tried my hand at tuning pianos. I didn't do very well, but I did well enough for me to play the pianos I tuned. One day it occurred to me that a hundred pianos all tuned to the same pitch are automatically tuned to each other. They are not tuned to each other to begin with, but they can be turned to a standard pitch which would make them all tuned the same. Being tuned to the same standard pitch makes all the pianos tuned to each other.

When a hundred worshipers meet together, and each one looks up to their Lord Jesus Christ in faith, they are nearer to each other in heart and mind than they could possibly be if they sought unity only to each other.

Our unity can only be achieved through our dependence upon Jesus Christ, the Divine Standard to which we all must look for salvation. When all trust in Him, they are united with each other.

God wants us united with Himself by faith in Christ, and then united with each other, in word and in deed. He wants us to be, "One in the Spirit, One in the Lord."

"My goal is that they may be encouraged in heart and united in love." (Colossians 2:2)

May Jesus give us that unity in Himself!

AUGUST 26

Jim and Jack were neighbors and became friends in elementary school. Both boys were brought up in the same church, made friends easily and were enjoyable to be around. But as time went on, Jack saw Jim growing callous towards religion. He went to church less and eventually stopped going all together. Jack told Jim that he worried about this and urged him to worship God again. But Jim told him to back off, that he'd make up his own mind. So Jack prayed for Jim.

Jim and Jack remained friends. They both married, lived not far apart, had families and became successful in their careers. Jim encouraged his wife and daughters to attend church, but he stayed home. Jack tried witnessing to Jim, but it created a wall between them, so he quit mentioning it. He also kept praying God would somehow get through to Jim.

Then came the bad news - Jim got cancer, a form that resisted treatment. His health declined rapidly, and it was evident his life was in peril. Jack visited him one day and talked about trusting God and His will, but Jim said nothing. A few weeks later Jim died. Jack was shocked! Not only was his friend gone, he wasn't sure about his salvation.

At the funeral there was joy despite the young man's death. One of his friends said he had often talked to Jim about Jesus and Jim assured him that he believed, and they even prayed together. Jack was shocked and moved to tears. God answered his prayers through a man he'd never met.

God-fearing men and women may struggle with how to relate to a friend or relative who seems to have lost faith. Our efforts and prayers may seem in vain. But you and I don't always know how God will answer us. It may be through a friend, a child, or even a stranger who delivers the Gospel message that finally strikes home. When that happens, there will be joy that only God can give us.

"There is joy before the angels of God over one sinner who repents." (Luke 15:10)

Give thanks for those who witness to our loved ones!

244

Recently I was packing a new carry-on suitcase for a trip I was taking. Packing for a trip is easier if you have everything in its place and do not take along too much or too little. You need to make sure all the space is used effectively.

Our days are like a suitcase. They're only a certain size, but sometimes we pack more into them than they can hold. Sometimes, when we're under pressure, our careful packing goes out the window and we stuff everything in, folded or not, jamming everything we can into each day. Then when the day is over, we find we did too many needless things and not enough of what we should have done.

My wife and I often start packing days ahead of a trip. Packing early helps us look forward to the trip, mentally plan activities, and see what we want to take along. Then we don't have to do all our packing at the last minute and we won't forget the essentials.

I have another practice. On most nights I lay out my next day's clothing. I believe I can choose color and style better at night than in the morning. Some may think this silly, but it also helps me relax and sleep better.

How do you pack the daily suitcase of your life? What activities do you lay out for yourself for the coming day? What happens to your day when unexpected pressures arise and your life is all work and no play? Do you make time for prayer? Does your daily suitcase have good priorities, or is stuff just jammed in here and there?

Start your day packing with prayer, even if you do it the night before. Ask God for His counsel. Set your priorities using His Word as your Guide, and ask Him to help you make wise decisions. Make sure you have the essentials, including faith and forgiveness. Then you'll have what you need, a well-packed suitcase for your daily journey.

"Large crowds were traveling with Jesus, and He preached to them." (Luke 14:25)

Travel light! Too much stuff weighs you down.

AUGUST 28

On July 26, 2005, Mark Hickethier took his family out for a special dinner. His son, Matt, had joined the Marines, and this would be one of their last meals together before he shipped out for a year in Iraq. They decided to go to "The Fort," one of Denver's nicest restaurants.

Matt had decided to wear his Dress Blue uniform. His mother, sister, and father also dressed nicely for the occasion. They ordered whatever they desired, including champagne, appetizers, and dessert. It was a grand evening meal and all were having a fine dinner.

But when it came time for the bill, they found it was already paid. A gentleman sitting at another table during their meal realized what was happening and decided to pick up their tab. He'd even left his credit card tab open to cover anything else they wanted, and then discreetly left the restaurant, stipulating that the management not reveal his identity. Channel Nine News reported the story of the man's generosity, but his identity was never revealed.

While this story shows us a fine way to honor those who serve us in the military, it also reminds us of what Christ did for us. He paid the debt we owe. He went into harm's way for each one of us, that all who trust in Him might live without fear. He gave His life that we might live.

There is also a spiritual war, and for this we need faithful soldiers willing to lay their lives on the line so that the enemy will not overtake us. *"Onward Christian soldiers, marching as to war"* is a hymn that ought to have a special meaning for Christians today.

May God give us all insight to see the enemy and the courage always to remain faithful to God, no matter what. The spiritual war is as real in our world as the physical one. God calls on us to defend our faith and all the faithful.

"Put on the full armor of God, so that you can take your stand against the devil's schemes." (Ephesians 6:11)

Semper Fi!

AUGUST 29

When I was young, before there were huge amusement parks, the County Fair was the annual big attraction, especially the midway carnival with its amazing rides such as the Ferris wheel which took you "way up high" above the rest of the world below. Looking down on everyone else as the wheel turned around helped me see the "big picture" of our little town. Sometimes it made me think of how God must view everything from His perspective and know how it all fits together. His view of the world must be incredibly complex.

Carol and I once took a hot air balloon ride, and it was a wonderful trip. Ironically, we flew right over our house on the morning breeze. During some of the trip we were a thousand feet up, and at other times we barely skimmed over the trees. The pilot had many years of experience, so he knew what he was doing. Those who fear heights might find a hot air balloon ride safer and better than they think. We felt secure with our pilot, and seeing the world from such heights was amazing.

From high in the sky you can't see faces, just houses, highways, trains and cars, and they all look like toys. Down below everyone was busy living and planning their day and what they wanted to do, but up there we were thinking of how it all fit together.

I once saw a huge stained glass window in a cathedral. As the crowd forced me to stand against the back wall, I felt a light behind my head. It was the sun shining through a piece of stained glass in a large mosaic. Up close it was red glass, but from farther away I saw it was part of an apostle's toe! Only by standing farther back could we see what the big picture was.

We all look at life from a close angle. We see ourselves and our struggles, our pains and our problems as the center of life. But God sees us as part of a larger picture. We see only today, but He sees how today fits into tomorrow and a lifetime. Since He is the artist, He has something good in mind for us.

"Seek first His kingdom and His righteousness, and all these things will be given to you as well." (Matthew 6:33)

One day we will see how God fits all the pieces together.

247

AUGUST 30

Myrtie Howell was a devoted Christian woman who lived a hard life. Because her family was poor, she quit school at age ten and worked in a steel mill for ten cents a day. She married at age seventeen, but when we was in her thirties her husband died. She lost her house, so she moved to an apartment and went back to work to support her three children. Health problems forced her into early retirement and a nursing home. When her youngest son died, she fell into a depression. *"Why me,"* Lord, she prayed, *"I've lost everything and now I'm stuck in this prison of a nursing home."*

One night she awoke, believing God had spoken to her in a dream. *"Write to prisoners,"* she heard in the night and she was certain God had spoken to her. So she wrote a letter to "Any Prisoner" at the Atlanta State Penitentiary near where she lived. Her letter was given to a chaplain who gave her the names of eight prisoners to write. Soon Myrtie Howel was writing forty inmates every day. *"I thought my life was over,"* she said looking back, *"but those years were the most fulfilling of my life."*

Some days we may feel like nothing is going right. We may feel like we are trapped in a prison, wondering what's left in life for us. But God has not left us, nor has He been ignoring us. We just need to listen for His voice. May the Lord speak to you today, through His Word, a person or even a dream, and tell you what He wants you to do.

There are many people who need a visit or a letter to help them with their burdens in life. Whether we are a prisoner in jail, or a prisoner to illness, or even we feel we are in the "prison" of a nursing home, there are people to whom we can be loving and helpful.

In Matthew 25, Jesus said, **"I was a stranger, and you ministered to Me... Whatever you did to the least of these, you also did it to Me. "** We can have no better person to help than Jesus Himself.

"I was in prison and you visited Me." (Matthew 25:36)

May we all heed what He tells us.

AUGUST 31

A group of university alumni, highly established in their careers, got together one afternoon to visit a favorite retired professor. Conversation in the group soon turned to the stress in their work and life. All of them had good jobs, but most of them found something they didn't like about theirs.

Offering his guests coffee, the old professor went to the kitchen and returned with a large pot of coffee and an assortment of cups, porcelain, plastic, glass and crystal, some plain, some expensive, some quite exquisite and others chipped. He told them to take one and help themselves to the coffee. When all his students had a cup of coffee in hand, the professor asked for their attention and said the following:

"I noticed that most of you chose the nicer and more expensive cups first, leaving behind the plainer and cheaper ones. While it is normal for you to want only the best for yourselves, that may be the source of some of your stress. The cup itself adds no quality to the coffee. The cup is just a cup and its value can distract us from what we are drinking. What all of you really wanted was coffee, not the cup, but most of you consciously went for the best cups. And I even saw some of you eyeing each other's cup."

"Life is the coffee," he continued. *"Our jobs, money, possessions and position are the cups. They're just tools that help hold and contain our life. The cup does not define us, nor does it change the quality of life we live. Yet by concentrating only on the cup, we may fail to enjoy the coffee God has provided us."*

The professor was still teaching them, wasn't he? And hopefully all the people there went home having learned a good lesson. God provides us with so much in life. It's good that we also learn not to concentrate so hard on the kind of vessel that we miss what is in it.

"Give thanks to the Lord, for He is good; His love endures forever." (1 Chronicles 16:34)

God brews the coffee, not the cups!

249

SEPTEMBER

+ + +

SEPTEMBER 1

Peter McGuire was an Irish-American cabinet maker who in 1882 proposed a day dedicated to honor all who labor. He was a red-headed, fiery leader of the Brotherhood of Carpenters and Joiners and said, *"Let us have a festive day during which a parade through the streets would permit a public tribute to American Industry,"*

The following years, this holiday moved across the country. In 1884, Detroit workers celebrated their first Labor Day, and in 1894, President Grover Cleveland signed a bill making it a national observance. The timing was ironic since earlier that year he had called up federal troops to stop a strike.

God gives human labor dignity and value, yet He also gives us a day of rest. Sunday is the Christian "Sabbath," the day when people can rest from their labors and take time for worship. Worshipping each week in God's house to receive His Word and Sacrament is more valuable than any money we can earn during that time. It is refreshment for our souls.

After retiring, we joined a small mission church not far from our home and volunteered to update their membership directory. After we published it, we gave the project to another member. Church membership should be active, not passive.

Give thanks to God on this Labor Day for the privilege of work. Most people no longer engage in the kind of heavy physical labor once common to all, but we still labor to earn a living and to help others in some way.

"Take my yoke upon you and learn from me, for I am gentle and humble in heart, and you will find rest for your souls." (Matthew 11:29)

May your Labor Day be a good one!

251

SEPTEMBER 2

How do we get rid of our burdens? When they get so heavy that we can't carry them, what do we do with them? Most of us want to unload them somewhere, and the best place would seem to be at the feet of the Lord, who said, **"Come unto me all you who are tired and weary and I will give you rest."** (Matthew 11:28) St. Peter also said, **"Cast all your cares on Him, for He cares for you."** (1 Peter 5:7) With such advice, it is good to lay our cares at the feet of Jesus.

Sometimes the Lord's way is not to take away our burdens, but to give us stronger backs. That may not be what we want at the time, but it will be the best way. It can be a hard pill to swallow, but it's medicine we need.

Consider the man who prays his wife's cancer will be healed, but the disease continues. Or the woman who prays that her husband will stop drinking, and endures years of struggle, loving a man who won't stop. Or the man who dislikes his job but endures it because it's the best he can find.

"Come unto me all you who are tired and weary and I will give you rest." The key is the "rest." Rest does not mean life is over, but that life is renewed. Rest is strength regained to shoulder the task again. Rest is learning to carry a load differently, making the back stronger.

Rest is always needed. The best kind of rest Jesus offers will come at the end of our life journey, our eternal rest. When we have faith that He is our Savior, He will give us eternal joy in our rest with Him. Then there will be no more burdens, only peaceful rest in His presence.

We need to take time now and then to rest on our journey. Jesus got away from the crowds to rest. He prayed often, getting His rest through communicating with His Father. In these busy days of work, paying bills and meeting deadlines, take time for Godly rest for your body and for your soul.

May you find your rest in Jesus today, no matter how heavy your burden or how difficult your journey. One day it will be over, and the rest we long for will be ours.

"Cast your cares on Him; He cares for you." (1 Peter 5:7)

Be sure to get your rest today!

I was working on a Bible Study one warm afternoon and I took off my hearing aids and set them down. (It is never good to get a hearing aid sweaty.) Hours later when it was nearly dark, I went to put them away and could find only one. I looked and looked, using my little bright detective flashlight.

I finally found it on the floor under a chair, right next to its roller wheel. If I'd have moved that chair an inch to the right, the tiny earpiece would have been smashed, and I'd have had to pay a thousand bucks for a replacement.

I was quite happy when I found it and told Carol, *"Guess what? I found the hearing aid I lost."* It reminded me of Jesus' parable about the woman who lost a coin and swept her house until she found it and then invited the neighbors over for coffee and cookies **(Luke 15)**. Jesus' parable had the woman finding only a coin, and my economy model hearing aid cost many, many coins. So Carol and I celebrated with a frozen fudge bar!

My wife says we're matched for each other: I have a gift to find things, and she has a gift to lose them. I always feel better when I find something that's been lost. Have you ever lost something really valuable and never found it? I once found a woman's two-carat diamond that had fallen out of her ring while she was attending a funeral at my church. It was lying just inches from a floor drain!

Whenever Carol or I lose something, we usually find it just about where we think it should be. Does that happen to you, too? When our Good shepherd loses one of His lambs, or a lamb loses its way, He goes looking till He finds it. Jesus doesn't give up easily, and we should be glad of that.

Perhaps you have lost something really important, like a relationship or a good paying job or a large investment or even your health? Are you still hoping to find it? If you haven't found it yet, I pray God will soon help you find something even better.

"Rejoice with me, for I have found my sheep that was lost." (Luke 15:16)

If you find it, I it will probably be in the last place you look.

253

SEPTEMBER 4

Do you ever wonder how people view Christians on Sunday morning? And then compare that with how they view them during the rest of the week? Have you considered that Christians are more "visible" to others than they might think they are?

One Sunday a man went to visit a church. He arrived early, parked his car, and got out. But another car pulled up near him, and the driver told him, *"I always park there. You took my place!"* So the visitor found another place to park his car.

The visitor went inside for Sunday School, found an empty seat, and sat down. A young lady from the church approached him and stated, *"I'm sorry but that's my seat! You took my place!"* The visitor was somewhat disheartened by this rude welcome, but still said, *"Good morning!"* and found another seat.

After Sunday School, the visitor went into the sanctuary and sat down. Again someone said to him, *"That's where I always sit. You took my place!"* The visitor was troubled by this comment, but said nothing and found another.

Later, as the congregation was praying for Christ to come and dwell among them, the visitor stood, and all the people saw him, as if for the first time. He had scars on His hands, His side and His feet. Someone from the congregation noticed his scars and asked, *"What happened to you?"* The visitor replied, *"I took your place."*

We will never encounter a living, walking, breathing Jesus in our church, but many who visit there are wondering what He is like. When they see and hear us, it is the only way they will see and hear Jesus. Keep this in mind as you greet people and interact with them in church on Sunday or any day of the week.

"Dear friends, let us love one another, for love comes from God. Everyone who loves has been born of God and knows God. Whoever does not love does not know God, because God is love." (1 John 4:7-8)

Thank You, Lord, that You took our place! Help us reflect You.

SEPTEMBER 5

Years ago in the early 1930's, a man and his wife entered a small hotel in Philadelphia, hoping to get shelter on a rainy night. *"Could you possibly give us a room?"* the husband asked. The clerk, a friendly man with a winning smile, explained that there were three conventions in town. *"All of our rooms are taken,"* the clerk said. *"But I can't send you out into the rain so late. Would you be willing to sleep in my room? It's not large, but it will be good enough to make you comfortable for the night."*

When the couple declined because they didn't want to take his room, the young man insisted, *"Don't worry, I'll be just fine."* So they took his room. As he paid his bill the next morning, the man said, *"You should manage a fine hotel. Maybe someday I'll build one for you."*

The clerk thanked them, and they drove away. Two years passed and the clerk had forgotten the incident when a letter came from that same man. It recalled that rainy night and enclosed a round-trip ticket to New York, asking him to visit.

The gentleman met the clerk in New York, and took him to Fifth Avenue and Thirty-Fourth Street. He pointed to a new hotel with its reddish stone turrets and towers thrusting up to the sky. *"That,"* said the older man, *"is the hotel I have built for you to manage."* *"You must be joking,"* the young man said. *"I can assure you I am not,"* said the man, smiling.

The elderly man's name was William Waldorf Astor, and the magnificent structure was the original Waldorf-Astoria Hotel. The young clerk who became its first manager was George C. Boldt who never could have foreseen the turn of events that would lead him to become the manager of one of the world's finest hotels.

Mary and Joseph were turned away from the Inn. Think of the blessing that came to the world when they were given a place to stay for the birth of Mary's child. I wonder if the Innkeeper ever wished he had given them a better room.

"Do not forget to entertain strangers, for by so doing some people have entertained angels without knowing it." **(Hebrews 13:2)**

Integrity is who we are when no one is looking.

255

SEPTEMBER 6

People will usually live up, or down, to the value you place on them. Johnny Lingo, the richest man on his South Pacific island, came seeking a wife. In that culture, wives were purchased with the exchange of one or two cows, and a good wife required three cows. Only rarely was one so valued that she fetched four cows. But a five-cow wife? It had never happened.

Near Johnny Lingo's village lived a man with a daughter who complained much and rarely came out of her house. Women made fun of her and her father despaired of ever finding anyone to marry her. When Johnny came calling on his daughter the father was ecstatic. He perhaps would get one cow for her. That would be great!

You can imagine how dumbfounded he was when Johnny Lingo offered him ten cows for the hand of his daughter. The village was in an uproar. Had Johnny Lingo lost his mind? Was he was making fun of the man? His daughter was ugly and skinny! Other daughters were worth much more. Her father quickly called the tribal chief who performed the marriage before Johnny could change his mind!

In those days a honeymoon lasted one month, but when you have a ten-cow wife, it must last longer. Johnny and his wife were gone a full year! When the day arrived for them to return, the whole village came out to watch.

The villagers recognized Johnny but not the woman. She was beautiful, self-assured, graceful, smiling and confident, and yes, she was the old man's daughter! Because Johnny valued her highly, she came to act like a woman of great value.

If you want a ten-cow wife, or friend, or son, daughter, employee or church member, start treating them like it. People will live up or down to the value we place upon them. God loves us lowly sinners in Jesus, and has made us His children. What a great blessing that is for us!

"A good name is more desirable than great riches; to be esteemed is better than silver or gold." (Proverbs 22:1)

God values us, for we are worth the life of His only son!

256

SEPTEMBER 7

Six year old Brandon decided one Saturday morning to make breakfast for his parents. He found a big bowl and a spoon, pulled a chair to the counter, opened the cupboard and pulled out the heavy flour canister, spilling some on the floor. He scooped some of the flour into the bowl with his hands, splashed in a cup of milk and added some sugar, leaving a floury, milky trail on the floor which also included tracks left by his kitten and some crunchy egg shells.

Brandon was covered with flour and getting frustrated. He wanted this to be something good for Mom and Dad, but it was turning out bad. He didn't know what to do next, whether to put it all into the oven or on the stove, and he didn't know how the stove worked. Suddenly he saw his kitten licking from the bowl of "pancake mix" and pushed her away, knocking the egg carton to the floor with a crash. He tried to clean up the mess but slipped on the eggs, getting his pajamas white and sticky. Just then he saw his Dad standing at the door watching him.

Big tears welled up in Brandon's eyes. All he'd wanted to do was something good, but he'd made a mess. He was sure he'd be scolded, maybe even spanked, so he started to cry. But his father didn't scold or spank him. Walking through the mess, he picked his crying boy up, hugged him and loved him, getting his own pajamas all sticky in the process.

That's how God deals with us. We try to do something good in life, but it turns into a mess. Our marriage gets all sticky or we insult a friend or our job becomes really bad or our health fails. Sometimes we just stand there in tears because we can't think of anything else to do. That's when God picks us up and loves us and forgives us, even though some of our mess gets all over Him.

Just because we might mess up, we can't stop trying to "make pancakes" for God or for others. Sooner or later we'll get it right, and then we will be very glad we tried.

"Take delight in the Lord, and He will give you the desires of your heart." (Psalm 37:4)

Pancakes made by loving hands are a real treasure.

257

SEPTEMBER 8

The only survivor of a shipwreck was washed up on a small, uninhabited island. He prayed feverishly for God to rescue him, and week after week scanned the horizon for help, but none came. He built a small hut from driftwood and palm branches to protect himself from the elements and store his few possessions. He prayed night and day for help, but was becoming exhausted from lack of proper nourishment. Worst of all, he began to lose hope.

Then one afternoon as he returned from scavenging for food, he found his little hut in flames, black smoke rolling up to the sky. He'd left his cook fire burning and now all was lost. His food and the few useful things that had washed up from the shipwreck were all gone. He was stunned with grief and anger. *"God, how could you do this to me!"* he cried out in misery, and he lay down and wept until he fell asleep.

Late in the evening, just as the sun was going down, he was awakened by the sound of a ship's horn. A ship's boat was approaching his island. He was saved! *"How did you know I was here?"* the weary man asked as his rescuers brought him on board. *"We saw your smoke signal,"* they replied. His burning hut, the thing he felt was a tragedy, had drawn their attention and saved his life.

It is easy to get discouraged by unfortunate events. But no matter how bad life may appear, we must not lose heart. God is at work in our lives, even in the midst of pain, loss and apparent meaningless events.

The next time you see your little hut burning to the ground, don't give up! It just may be the smoke signal that summons the grace of God and rescues you from your island of despair. Our loving God will not abandon us, even if we abandon Him. He will come to us when we most need Him and rescue us with His forgiveness and love.

"Trust in him at all times, you people; pour out your hearts to Him, for God is our refuge." (Psalm 62:8)

"No man is an island; no man stands alone." (John Donne)

SEPTEMBER 9

I have a love-hate relationship with the Olympics. I enjoy some parts, but not all. My wife, however, loves them all, so during the Summer Olympics our television is going day and night, tuned to whatever event is happening. For me, it's a time to find another place to go where I can avoid "Olympic overdose."

During week one of the Sidney Olympics, Eric Mosambrini was one of four athletes from the tiny country of Equitorial Guinea in West Africa. He was admitted to the swimming competition without qualifying, as part of a program that encourages emerging nations to train athletes in sports that are relatively unknown in their homeland.

Eric, a fine athlete, was in the "slow heat," one of three who were last to swim the Hundred Meter Freestyle. When the other two swimmers false started and were disqualified, Eric had to swim his race alone.

As the horn sounded, he dove in, furiously stroked to get to the other end, and it was apparent he had never swam a hundred meter race before. Though he had carried his nation's flag in the opening ceremonies, he had no coach and had only practiced a few weeks in a shallow hotel pool.

At first the spectators laughed at this inept swimmer, barely moving and keeping his head above water. But then they began to cheer. Here was a man who had come thousands of miles to compete in his first Olympics, wanting only to do his best and finish his race. When he finally reached the finish, a full minute behind qualifying time, the applause was so great Eric thought he'd won a medal.

If the best you can do might only make people laugh, don't let that stop you from doing it. Great things have been done while others scorned. Athletes competed at the Sidney Olympics and records were broken, and no one finished farther off the pace than this brave man. Yet for many who watched, Eric Mosambrini is the only one they remember.

"Let us run with perseverance the race marked out for us." (Hebrews 12:1)

Give thanks for athletes who make life enjoyable.

259

SEPTEMBER 10

Charles Plumb was a jet pilot in Vietnam. After seventy-five combat missions, his plane was destroyed by a surface-to-air missile. Plumb ejected safely but parachuted into enemy hands. He was captured and spent six years in a communist Vietnamese prison. After his release, Plumb made a tour speaking on the lessons he learned from that experience.

One day, when Plumb and his wife were sitting in a restaurant, a man at another table came up and said, *"You're Captain Plumb! You flew jet fighters in Vietnam from the Kitty Hawk. You were shot down!"* "How did you know that?" asked Plumb. "I packed your parachute," the man said. He shook Plumb's hand and said, "I guess it worked!" Plumb said, "If your chute hadn't worked, I wouldn't be here today."

Plumb couldn't sleep that night, thinking about that man. He later said, *"I kept wondering what he might have looked like in a Navy uniform with his white hat, a bib in the back, and bell-bottom trousers. I wonder how many times I might have seen him and not even said, 'Good morning,' Because, you see, I was an important fighter pilot and he was just a sailor."*

Plumb thought of the many hours that sailor had spent on a long wooden table, carefully weaving the shrouds and folding the silks of each parachute, each time holding in his hands the fate of someone he didn't even know.

Who is packing your parachute? Every one of us has people who provide what we need to make it through the day. We have many kinds of parachutes, a physical parachute, or a mental one. We need an emotional parachute, and also a spiritual one. We use these supports in our lives each day.

Sometimes in the daily challenges that life gives us, we miss what is really important. As you go through this day, think of the people who pack your parachute. And if you get the chance, tell one of them you appreciate them. Call them by name and smile as you do.

"Let them give thanks to the Lord for His unfailing love and His wonderful deeds for mankind." (Psalm 107:8)

Who is packing your parachute these days?

SEPTEMBER 11

"Don't be afraid!" The Bible is filled with this phrase, beginning with God's word of comfort to Abraham as he traveled to a new land which he did not yet know. God said, "Don't be afraid!" to Joshua, the leader after Moses died. He said, "Don't be afraid!" to Mary and Joseph and also the shepherds, as they heard of a Savior born into the world.

Today is my brother Fritz's birthday. The day he died, I was a little frightened. He wasn't supposed to die that young. The thought occurred that maybe I would, too.

"Don't be afraid!" God has always spoken words of comfort to generations of people who are fearful of their enemies, fearful of death or fearful of any number of different things that are unknown. On this day Americans understand fear differently than they did since the year 2001 when the World Trade Center was bombed by Muslim radicals.

Sometimes on the anniversary of a tragedy, Americans will stop to ponder what they have to fear. The memory of those tragic events is still fresh, still smoldering, still strong enough to bring the taste of fear to our mouths.

A son sat next to his dying mother's bedside, holding her hand tightly, tears in his eyes and fear on his face. His mother opened her weary eyes and said, *"Son, what are you holding on to? Let me go and you can hold on to God."*

What are we afraid of, and what are we holding on to in this life? An old friend of mine died and was found lying next to his open Bible. He'd been reading God's Word in his final moments on this earth. After years of struggle with heart failure and cancer, Bernie was holding fast to God's Word, the only thing in this world that lasts. **"Heaven and earth shall pass away, but my words shall never pass away,"** said our Lord Jesus. (Luke 21:33)

"Don't be afraid!" says Jesus, don't fear enemies, or cancer, or failure or death. Let go of the things of the world, and hold on to God. Place your hand in His, let Him walk beside and lead you. He will bring you safely home.

"Don't be afraid!" (Luke 2:10)

What are you holding onto?

261

SEPTEMBER 12

Perhaps you are struggling, as I am, with feelings of frustration and anger, over the double standard faced each day in this "Christian vs. Muslim" tension. It seems acceptable for the world to demean Christianity, but any negative comments towards Islam are met with anger or even threats. So many Christian people openly side with Muslims, yet will not stand up for their own faith. It doesn't seem fair, but not everyone's concept of fairness is the same.

Some people would like to strike back, but they don't know how or to whom. That, of course, would be playing the enemy's game. Some people think Christians deserve what they're getting because of the Crusades, Inquisition or other mistakes of Christian history. Whatever may be your point of view, you may need a dose of antacid to deal with the indigestion this tension produces.

What would Jesus do? He faced a double standard from His own people. He and His followers were condemned for their beliefs that followed God's Word, but they were forbidden from pointing out inconsistencies among those who condemned them. Jesus Himself exposed the truth to the local hypocrites. He exposed them for what they were, but their ears were plugged so they did not hear. Those who refuse to heed the truth will pay God's ultimate penalty.

The truth often hurts, and people strike out at what hurts them. That's not what followers of Jesus Christ must do. Let others threaten or kill or point the finger of blame. Christians must forgive their persecutors. Christians are to be compassionate to their enemies and do good to those who abuse them. Christians know Christ's love conquers all. His love is for all people, His enemies as well as His followers.

Ask Jesus for a compassionate heart. Stand up for Him, but do it with love and forgiveness. Dwell on things that build up, not tear down. Pray for soldiers and their families, too.

"Pray for your enemies," (Matthew 5:44)

Prayer helps ease the heartburn!

Who can forgive sins, and how is it done? I saw a film called, "The Last Sin Eater," about the ancient Welsh practice of trying to cleanse the sins of a deceased person. At the funeral, an outcast of the community "the sin eater" was given food and drink by the villagers which he consumed, and with it took away the sins of the deceased person so he or she could rest in peace. The sin eater is then shunned, for in him the villagers see their sins and evil deeds.

This practice came from the need to have our sins forgiven. The ancient Israelites used a "scapegoat," a live goat over whose head the high priest confessed all the sins of the people. The goat was sent into the wilderness on the Day of Atonement (Yom Kippur), to die there, symbolizing the removal of sins. It foreshadowed the work of Jesus.

In the movie, the 1850's Appalachian community finally stopped using this practice after being reminded of the Gospel in which Jesus was the final sin eater and the last scapegoat. Today we know that His words on Calvary, **"It is finished!"** **(John 19:30)** signaled the end of the need for human attempts to remove sin. You and I can't do it. God has removed our sin and no human ritual can do again what He has already done.

On September 11, 2001, nearly 3,000 innocent people died at the hands of our enemies. Each year we remember those who were lost, but we also need to remember forgiveness. Forgiveness does not mean excusing sin, making friends of our enemies or letting our guard down. Forgiveness is laying aside our right of retribution or striking back. It is our decision not to pursue punishment that is justly ours, but to give it to God who balances the scales. Forgiveness is what God did for us in Jesus. He made Him the scapegoat, and in the cross He absorbed our sins.

As much as we might like to, we cannot make Muslims our scapegoat. When we trust in the merits of our Lord Jesus, our sins are forgiven and we can forgive others. We all need Jesus Christ and the blessings which He alone can give.

"He said, 'Your sins are forgiven you.'" (Luke 7:48)

Today I hope you will forgive someone.

263

SEPTEMBER 14

Never underestimate the power of being faithful to God. In the 1924 Olympics, a man did a remarkable thing. Eric Liddell of Scotland refused to run in the One Hundred Yard Dash at the Paris Games because the race was scheduled on a Sunday, which his faith taught him would violate the Sabbath. As we know from the film, "Chariots of Fire," Liddell managed to negotiate a switch from the One Hundred Yard Dash he had been scheduled to run, to the Four Hundred Yard Race for which he had not trained.

On July 11, 1924, Liddell won that race and was showered with Olympic glory. But instead of cashing in, Liddell turned his back on fame and fortune and followed in his parents' footsteps. He became a missionary in China, where he made his most powerful contributions to God and his fellow people. Olympic champion Eric Liddell died there in defense of his faith. He was a martyr and also a champion.

In this day of "me-first" mentality and uncertainty about our beliefs, Eric Liddell's example continues to stand out. A fanatical religious adherent might have demanded that others not run on Sunday, either. Or perhaps other followers would have organized a protest or enacted legislation to conform society to their point of view.

Not Eric Liddell. He just followed his faith and didn't run. Some newspapers denounced him as a traitor to king and country. How quickly they changed their tune, though, when he won a gold medal.

Had Eric Liddell yielded to temptation and compromised his beliefs, we might never have heard of him again. Instead, he's been an inspiration to generations of people of Scotland, of Great Britain and of the world.

Our Lord Jesus could have given up when He considered what was to come. But He remained faithful to God and to us.

"I press on toward the goal to win the prize for which God has called me heavenward in Christ Jesus." (Philippians 3:14)

Keep running toward the goal!

SEPTEMBER 15

Some children are playing on an ocean beach. They're near the edge of the water, giggling and building sand castles. They are intent on their project, carefully building corners, towers and tiny windows. The look on their faces as they work in earnest concentration is priceless.

Just then a big wave starts to close in! But the kids don't panic. They jump to their feet, scream with excitement, and watch with wide eyes as the waves wash away their creations.

There's no hysteria, no sadness, no bitterness with these "little builders." Children have learned to know the fate that awaits their sand castles, so they are neither shocked nor angry when the big wave comes in. They just start over, building another castle with delight.

We can take a lesson from these children. The possessions we gather up in this world are as permanent as sand castles, yet we keep trying to get them, defending them, insuring them, and even getting depressed when we lose them.

God didn't say our possessions would be permanent. All the physical stuff around us will pass away. Only in heaven will we have a permanent place. There we will give God glory and live with Him forever by faith in Jesus Christ.

Everything about this life is transient. The incoming wave of mortality is going to sweep us all away. Like sand castles on the beach, nothing we do for the sake of this world will survive. Only what comes to us in Jesus Christ will last. Only the treasures given by faith in Jesus Christ will escape the waves of time.

Like the plaque on my bedroom wall that read, *"Only One Life, 'Twill Soon Be Past. Only What's Done For Christ Will Last."* I don't know who gave it to me, but I always remember what it said.

"For this world in its present form is passing away." (1 Corinthians 7:31)

Enjoy making your castles in the sand, but don't get too attached to them.

265

SEPTEMBER 16

I always find lessons to learn at home. An incident one day while preparing to mow my lawn provided a good one. I had planned to mow my lawn in about a half hour, the usual time, but my lawn mower had other ideas. It wouldn't start!

The trusty old Craftsman had been fickle before, but it always worked, except that day. It would start, then stop. Start, stop. So I pushed it to the garage and got out some tools. The tank was nearly empty, but after more gas, it still wouldn't start, no matter what.

I knew enough about small motors to realize it was a fuel problem, so I took apart the carburetor, cleaned it and put it together. It still wouldn't start. Took it apart again, cleaned it more, put it together, but still wouldn't run. I took it apart a third time, this time blowing out the lines and openings with compressed air. Put it together and it started on the first pull!

What did I learn? 1) A person can't always fix a problem on a first try, 2) A little dirt can create a big problem, and, 3) Problems don't fix themselves; you have to help.

I usually try to follow "Occam's Razor." William of Occam (d. 1347) said that when there are many solutions to a problem, the simplest one is usually the best. Example: if your printer won't print, check your cables before buying a new printer. Or, blow out a fuel line before re-assembling a motor.

Dirt can clog our lives too. We know it's there, but we may not believe it's a problem. Something or someone else is the problem, but not us. Rather than first getting rid of our own dirt, we blame others for their dirt, or we say dirt is good for us, or we ignore it and hope it will disappear. But dirt stays, and life may not run well again until it's gone.

That's why Jesus is so important. He died on Calvary to get rid of our dirt. First we must admit we are dirty, and then believe He's the one who can clean us up. Trusting Jesus is the best solution, and William of Occam would agree.

"If we confess our sins, He is faithful and will forgive our sins, and cleanse us from unrighteousness." (1 John 1:9)

Where's your dirt that needs cleaning?

SEPTEMBER 17

When I was twelve and allowed to plow with a tractor, my dad taught me first how to "open a field" that was to be plowed. The goal was to plow the first furrow in as straight a line as possible so that the rest of the field would be plowed straight and well.

If you plowed the first furrow on a new field crooked, the whole field would be crooked. He told me to pick a fence post or a tree at the other end of the field and to plow straight towards it. *"Fix your eyes on that mark and don't look away,"* he said. *"Look straight ahead and don't look back or to the side or you'll go crooked."*

The first time I tried it was pretty bad, because I kept looking back to see how good I was doing. The more I checked by looking back, the worse the line was. *"It's not so bad,"* I said, *"No one can see it from the road."* *"But you can see it and I can see it,"* Dad said, *"You know you could have done better, and that's what really counts."* The next time I tried it was better, but I never could open a field as well as he could. He could make a straighter line with his eyes shut than I could with mine open.

If our eyes of faith are not wide open and fixed on Jesus every day, our life will get crooked. If we keep looking at other things instead of Jesus the Important One, things in our life will get out of line. Tilt this way or that way in one part of life, and the rest will be crooked too.

Thanks be to God that His death and resurrection has straightened out all the crooked parts of life. Without His divine corrections, we'd all fail.

"Fix your eyes on Jesus, the pioneer and perfecter of faith." (Hebrews 12:2)

Dear God, help us all keep our eyes fixed on Jesus, and if we go crooked, straighten out our lives. Amen!

SEPTEMBER 18

In 1914, Irish explorer Ernest Shackleton set out to cross the frozen continent of Antarctica, traveling fifteen hundred miles across the South Pole, using thirty-nine sled dogs to transport his men and their supplies. Once there, they did not set foot on land for a year and a half.

In the process, their ship, the "Endurance," was crushed by the ice floes, and for months they survived by eating their dogs. They endured frostbite, isolation and hardships we can only imagine. When the ice began to melt and crack, they boarded the three life rafts they'd made from salvaged shipboards and sailed eight hundred miles to Easter Island where they were rescued.

How did Shackleton get men to volunteer for such a hazardous voyage? History tells us they had signed up in response to an ad he placed in the London Times that read, *"Men wanted for hazardous journey. Small wages, bitter cold, long months of complete darkness, constant danger. Safe return doubtful."* Despite this frank warning, many brave men came from all over to sign up for this historic journey.

Shackleton pledged that no man would die on this voyage, saying to his crew, *"Follow as I lead, do what I say, and I'll get you home."* Incredibly, two years later, what he said came true. Not a single one of his men was lost.

Isn't it amazing that people will sign up to follow a man for a questionable cause under such dangerous conditions? Yet, so many people are reluctant to leave their homes for a few hours for Sunday worship or Sunday School! Where are the courageous men and women willing to sign up for the Big Trip, the eternal one led by our Lord Jesus?

Following Jesus can be dangerous for those who live in societies that hate Christians. There have been millions die for the faith in the past century. But they know their Lord's death on the cross will atone for their sins. Take the big step, in faith, to follow Jesus and worship Him regularly.

"Come, follow me," Jesus said. (Matthew 14:19)

May God move us all to sign on with the Lord as our Captain.

268

SEPTEMBER 19

Once upon a time, two brothers who lived on adjoining farms fell into conflict, their first serious rift in forty years. It began with a small misunderstanding, grew into a major argument, and exploded into bitter words followed by a long period of silence.

One morning, there was a knock on the older brother's door. He opened it to find a man with a carpenter's toolbox. *"I'm looking for a few days' work,"* he said. *"Perhaps you would have a few small jobs here and there that I could help with?"*

"Yes," said the older brother. *"I do have a job for you. Look across the creek at that farm. That's my brother's place! Last week, there was a meadow between us, but he took his bulldozer and dug a small river between us. Well, I'm going to fix that. I want you to build a twenty foot high fence between us. Then I won't need to see his place anymore."* The carpenter said, *"Show me the materials, and I will begin."*

The older brother went to town for the day. When he returned, he saw no fence built at all. Instead, there was a bridge from one side of the river to the other, even equipped with handrails! And as he looked at it, he saw his brother coming towards them. *"You're quite the guy,"* the brother said, *"building a bridge after all I've said and done."*

The two brothers met on the bridge and shook hands. They turned to see the carpenter leaving. *"Wait! Stay a few days. I've a lot of other projects for you,"* said the older brother. *"I'd like to,"* the carpenter said, *"but I have other bridges to build."*

When you and I come to the end of our days, God won't ask how many fences we've made, but He may ask how many bridges we have built.

Our Lord Jesus is God's eternal "Bridge Over Troubled Waters." He has laid down His life that we might be able to cross over to the Other Side when the time comes for our life in eternity. Trust Him, and all will be fine.

"Love your neighbor as yourself." (Luke 10:27)

Are you ready to build a bridge?

269

Years ago a farmer bought land along the Atlantic seacoast, but he had trouble hiring help to work it. This was because men were reluctant to work on the ocean side where storms blew in so violently and unpredictably. Finally, a thin little man came to him seeking the job. *"Are you a good farm hand?"* the farmer asked. *"Well, I can always sleep when the wind blows,"* he answered. Though puzzled by the answer, the farmer hired him anyway.

The hired man proved to be a good worker, busy from dawn to dusk, and he did his work well. One night a loud gale wind came up. Jumping out of bed, the farmer rushed to the hired hand's quarters. *"Get up and get a lantern!"* he shouted, *"Tie things down before the wind blows them away!"* The hired man sat up in bed and said, *"No sir. As I told you, I can sleep when the wind blows."*

Though tempted to fire him on the spot, the farmer hurried outside, and to his amazement, he discovered all things were in order. The cows were in the barn, chickens were in the coop, and all the doors were barred. All window shutters were closed, and even the haystacks were covered with tarps. Amazed, the farmer returned to bed. He, too, was then able to sleep while the wind blew.

Can you sleep when the wind blows in your life? Besides physical and mental preparation, we will need spiritual preparation, securing ourselves against the storms of life by grounding ourselves in the Word of God. To have peace during the storms of life, we don't need to understand God. We just need to trust Him. We need to do as He says and hold firmly to His Word.

"Jesus said to them, 'It is I, don't be afraid.'" (John 6:20)

I pray the hurricane winds of life will not harm you today.

SEPTEMBER 21

As part of the "Beatles Generation," I recall words of a song they made popular fifty years ago, *"Will you still love me, will you still need me, when I'm sixty four?"* My wife and I are past that age now, but our grandchildren are very young. Will they still need us as they grow?

Today is our grandson's birthday. When we celebrated his first birthday, the outpouring of love and joy was awesome. Parents, grandparents, aunts and uncles, cousins, baptismal sponsors and friends all joined in showering him with gifts, cake, a home-made pizza feast and lots of love.

It was doubly special because our grandson is adopted. Born nearly two months early and weighing just over two and a half pounds, he still had drugs in his bloodstream from his birthmother and an uphill battle to face in life. But despite all that was against him at birth, today he is a vibrant, active, happy boy who is growing up normally in every way.

He has two younger sisters now, also adopted, and the three are all wonderful children. We credit it all to our loving God, but also to my son and his wife who are dedicated and faithful Christian parents.

All three of our grandchildren were adopted on "National Adoption Day," on three separate Saturdays before Thanksgiving. As Christians, we are all adopted by our loving God. By our birth and sinful nature we were born enemies of God and children of wrath, but God in His mercy has adopted us into His family.

By the merits of our Lord Jesus who gave His life on Calvary's cross, we are now children of God by faith in Christ Jesus. His unconditional love for us lasts forever, for all our earthly life and into eternal life. Whether four or sixty-four, we are surrounded by His love.

"You are all children of God by faith in Christ Jesus." (Galatians 3:26)

How old are you now? When were you adopted into God's family?

SEPTEMBER 22

It is the mid 1700's. Pilgrims had been in America a hundred years, George the First was King of England, and it would be sixty years until the Revolutionary War. Sometime that year an acorn was dropped by a bird or a Native American on the treeless plains of what would later become the boundary between North and South Dakota.

The acorn fell into good soil and sprouted because its roots found water from a small natural spring. As the oak tree grew tall and stately, the natives regarded it as sacred, and honored it by laying their dead to rest on its branches. Birds used it for shelter, this great tree growing on the plains, giving shade from the summer sun and acorns to birds and animals.

In the early 1900's, a family of immigrants built a homestead in its shade near a tiny prairie town. By this time the great oak was ninety feet tall, its trunk many feet in diameter, its girth large and strong. The great oak tree was visible from the tiny settlement miles away.

A few years later the family sold their homestead and moved on. That autumn one of the townsmen looked to the west on a clear day, hoping to see the mighty tree, but he saw none. Where had it gone? The terrible truth was soon made known - it had been cut down! Preparing for winter, the new owner had cut down the magnificent tree for firewood! The people were outraged at his destroying a wonderful tree. The foolish man was nearly lynched and soon left the area.

The townspeople removed the stump and brought it to town. The oak stump now rests in the town park, a monument to the greatness of creation and the foolishness of man.

But it does show that when your roots are in the right soil, you can grow strong and tall on an otherwise treeless plain. Sink your roots in the Lord and you may feel the wind blow or the lightning strike or the woodcutter's axe. But when you're rooted in Christ, you will still stand strong.

"He is like a tree planted by streams, which yields its fruit in season and whose leaf does not wither." (Psalm 1:3)

Be rooted in Jesus!

School has started, and nearly every year at this time I have a dream or two about going back to school as a student. Carol often does too, but she dreams she is teaching again.

I recently attended the funeral of a retired Lutheran School Teacher. In the sermon, the pastor said, *"Never underestimate what God has done through your life."* How true this is! Never think God can't do something wonderful through your acts, teaching or witness. He does so every day.

Sometimes we think that wonderful things are only done by the talented, the trained or the clever. But God speaks wonderful words, does fine deeds, and instills lasting values in people through the lives of His men, women and children who faithfully live their Christian Faith.

I attended Country School for Grades One through Six. My school had one main room for up to thirty students, plus cloak rooms, a library and a big basement where we played when it was too cold to go outside. It had no indoor plumbing and drinking water was carried from the farm across the road. Their telephone was our only connection with our homes.

It wasn't the one-room building that made Country School important; it was our teachers. They imparted the knowledge we needed and opened young minds to history, arithmetic, reading, writing, spelling and science.

Believe it or not, I still hear from my Second Grade teacher! After all these years, she still sends me a card for birthday or Christmas, and when she does, I often sit down and write her a short letter telling her what I am doing now. And I always tell her, *"Thank you for being my teacher!"*

Teachers help nurture a lifetime of learning. When I was in the fifth and sixth grades, I helped the younger students learn spelling or arithmetic. Perhaps others who are reading this also learned in a one-room school. As my pastor said, *"Never underestimate what God has done through your life."*

"Show me Your ways, O Lord, and teach me Your paths." (Psalm 25:4)

If you can read and understand this, thank a teacher!

SEPTEMBER 24

One year our neighbors of twelve years moved. After days of packing, touch-up and moving things, their house was empty. The realtor placed a "For Sale" sign on the lawn, and the home was sold the first day it was on the market.

A home is more than a building. So many homes today seem too large for the amount of people in them. Carol and I have lived in our present home the longest we've lived in any one place. That means we've moved a few times, but also that we like it here now.

Making a home is a blessing, but losing a home can be devastating. One summer five hundred homes were lost in a huge fire forty miles south of us. To lose a home through fire is difficult, and to lose one through divorce or financial reversal can be devastating.

How many rooms do you have in your house? How many of those rooms do you live in? It's estimated that regardless of size, people usually live in about one thousand square feet of their house. I'm sure our former neighbor's family of seven occupied every square inch of their home. They were good neighbors and we miss them, but we enjoy our new neighbors also.

I was born and grew up in a house that was probably purchased as a kit. It was there when Mom and Dad bought the farm in 1937 and is the exact replica of one we saw in a 1909 Sears Roebuck catalog. Mom and Dad lived there forty years, and it is still standing today.

More important than how many rooms we have is whether or not we will be in our Father's House when our time of departure comes. Believers will be there, not because of the goodness of their lives, but because of Christ's perfect life and death and His promise that all who trust and have faith in Him will have eternal life in our Father's House.

"In my Father's house are many rooms, and I am going there to prepare a place for you." (John 14:2)

What a houseful of children our Father will have then!

274

One day after a rainstorm I went out to see if my downspouts were plugged, and I stayed mostly dry under my big umbrella. I like a big umbrella. It reminds me of God's grace. Grace is God's umbrella of love covering all who believe Jesus is their Savior. His grace covers all believers, and it doesn't matter where you are under the umbrella, whether on the left side or the right side, in the very center, or on the edge with your big toe sticking out. Just being under the umbrella of God's grace is enough for eternity. No matter where we are located under that holy umbrella, grace covers us entirely, because God loves us completely, no matter what.

Back in my High School days I once received a tongue lashing from a teacher who accused me of talking during shop class. He'd grabbed me by the shoulders and was scolding me when someone next to me said, *"But, teacher, Bobby wasn't talking; it was someone else."* My teacher looked at him, then back at me and said, *"Okay, but remember this, because the next time you got it coming, you won't get it!"* That's grace! When you have it coming (punishment for sin), you won't get it.

Jacob's ten sons had it coming. They'd been resentful and hateful toward their brother Joseph and finally sold him as a slave in Egypt. But what looked at first like a terrible thing turned out good, for Joseph and his whole family.

J.R.R. Tolkein once wrote of *"good catastrophes,"* those sudden joyous turns in the face of horrific events. He said that when joy is snatched from the jaws of tragedy, it points to the compassion of God. He called Christ's death and resurrection the *"best catastrophe."* Good Friday looked like Satan won, but he hadn't. Jesus' resurrection brought life to all believers.

Tolkein's Lord of the Rings books are based on the idea of good coming from evil, and that's the theme of the story of Joseph. When evil should have prevailed, it lost out. That's grace! When Joseph's brothers should have gotten their due, they didn't get it. That's grace!

"By grace you are saved, through faith." (Ephesians 2:8)

What act of grace from God can you be thankful for today?

SEPTEMBER 26

Anyone who has driven in the summer probably has a "detour story." When your trip is all planned out, road detours can be irritating and inconvenient. They slow us down, disrupt our schedule, and may even ruin our plans. Detours make us wonder *"Why?"* or, *"Why now?"*

When we're forced to take a detour, it helps if we will try to find a reason beyond the obvious which is usually road construction or an accident. Are we being taught patience? Will our detour show us a part of God's creation we would otherwise have missed? Have we avoided something worse by not staying on our planned path?

Detours in life can prevent us from doing what we'd planned or hoped for. Illness, bad experience or some kind of loss may cause us to question God. Why can't we get to our goal? What can we learn from this? Why couldn't God have taught us some other way?

We may discover the "detour" is a better way for us, but at the time we may not be looking for it. We may even try to take a different route than the detour signs direct us. I once took a "better way" and ended up in a field of mud. Detours are there for a reason, and we are usually better off if we stay on the recommended road.

We people can make sinful detours away from God, into fields of mud and sin that can sink us. That's why Jesus had to take a detour from His eternal glory road to live a few years in this world. He did it so He could help us get back on the right road to God.

His detour led Him to the cross. He went there so we wouldn't have to. Calvary consumed Him for a short time so that we could spend an eternity in heaven, but it didn't keep Him. Praise God!

"He is not here. He has risen!" (Mark 16:6)

Trust the Lord for what He has done, and follow those road signs!

SEPTEMBER 27

During a phone call to a friend back in Minnesota I told him how bad our mosquitoes had been here in Colorado one summer. Normally our summer has few of those pesky bugs. My friend said something surprising for a Minnesotan: *"Be thankful you have mosquitoes!"*

I thought I'd heard it all, but not that line. I've tried to give God thanks for all kinds of blessings and circumstances in life, but thankful for mosquitoes? I believe I'll pass on that one, and I told him so.

However, he responded, *"If you've had mosquitoes, it means you've had rain. It's been so dry here we haven't had mosquitoes all summer. Right now I'd give anything if we'd have had mosquitoes like in a normal summer. There is almost no crop at all, and with grain prices being so high, it's doubly hard. So be grateful you have mosquitoes."*

I couldn't argue with him on that. If they come with rain for the crops, even mosquitoes can be a blessing.

I once sang in a chorus to a Monty Python song with the chorus line, *"Always Look on the Bright Side of Life."* Its lyrics mock all kinds of things, but that line still has a good thought. If we look for some good things in life rather than just the bad, we stand a better chance of being content.

With ugly national politics, a shaky economy, family problems and growing world tensions, it is tempting only to look on the dark side of life. But St. Paul wrote in Philippians 4:11, **"I have learned in whatever situation I am to be content."** He wrote those words from prison, not the brightest place in life to be! Yet that was where he found contentment through trusting in Jesus. Problems need not control us if we look for blessings, even in mosquitoes!

Our Lord Jesus came to this earth to give us eternal life. Until we experience His precious gift fully in heaven, He has given us an earthly life of blessings. Here even problems can be a blessing if we look at the bigger picture.

"I can do all things through Christ who gives me strength." (Philippians 4:13)

Can you give thanks for mosquitoes?
277

SEPTEMBER 28

In our ever-changing and disposable world, some things continue to endure. Consider the King James Version of the Bible, now over four hundred years old, written in 1611. When King James I set up a committee of translators to work on a new Bible translation, England was in religious turmoil.

Seventy years before, King Henry VIII had detached England from the yoke of Catholicism, and succeeding monarchs adopted new articles of faith which were rapidly changed, resulting in leaders being in good standing one year and sent to the gallows the next. The King James Bible of 1611 was produced at a tumultuous moment in history

The KJV was not the first English translation. The Tyndale Bible was completed in the 1530's, although William Tyndale was martyred in 1536 before he could complete an entire English translation. He had consulted with Luther in Wittenberg, and, like Luther, translated the New Testament from a new Greek version recently published by Erasmus of Rotterdam.

The KJV today is still revered by some church bodies as the best English translation. Since 1611, many other English translations have been published. Amazingly, the KJV was able to escape the heated church arguments of the Renaissance period, which was no small feat.

The language used in the KJV was already slightly outdated in its own day, with "thee" and "thou" already passing out of everyday usage. Modern translations keep being published because the English language is changing. Also, more ancient manuscripts are being discovered, helping Bible scholars to write more accurate translations.

The King James Version endures. There is even a "King-James-Only" movement which considers the KJV the biblical foundation of the Christian faith. Some Christians must believe our Lord spoke only the King's English.

"Heaven and earth shall pass away, but My words shall not pass away." (Matthew 24:35)

The true and everlasting Word of God, Jesus Christ, will always survive translation!

278

SEPTEMBER 29

A man in China had two large pots which he hung by short ropes on the ends of a yoke, and carried them across his shoulders. One pot was perfect and always delivered a full portion of water. The other was cracked and lost water on every trip, dripping water along the path. At the end of the long walk from the stream to the house, the perfect pot was full, but the cracked pot arrived only half full. The cracked pot was ashamed of its imperfection, sad that it was able to do only half of what it was made for.

Finally the cracked pot spoke to the water bearer, *"I am ashamed of myself because my cracks cause water to leak out on the way to your home. I am not able to do what I should."* But the man said to the pot, *"I have always known of your flaws. Did you notice the flowers on your side of the path, but not on the other? I planted flower seeds on your side of the path, and every day while we walked, you watered them. Because of that, I have had beautiful flowers to decorate my table. Without your flaws, I would not have beauty to grace my home."*

Each of us has our own unique flaws, but we are still useful to God and to others. God knows we are all cracked pots, but He uses our flaws to make life interesting and rewarding, both to ourselves and to others.

God loves each one of us as we are, but He may not always keep us that way. As we try to do His will, we need to accept His grace, and also ourselves for what we are, seeking to find the good in each one, even in our flaws.

Our cracks need not be a sign of our flaws. They can become ways to bless others. A blind man named Ray Charles thrilled people with his music, and a deaf man named Beethoven composed great music. Joni Erikson Tada, a paralyzed woman, paints pictures with a pen held in her mouth. Our cracks can produce blessings for others.

"He is the Rock, His works are perfect, and all His ways are just." (Deuteronomy 32:4)

Thank You, God, for planting the flowers.

279

SEPTEMBER 30

God provides for our needs, often in surprising ways. One sultry morning I was walking toward a Dallas Airport. I'd flown in the day before to help friends renew their wedding vows, and they'd left me at my motel so I could take my early morning flight. There was no shuttle and my shoes were not good for walking, but I started walking anyway.

After I'd walked about two blocks, a car pulled over and a woman driver said, *"Can I take you somewhere?"* *"Excuse me?"* I replied. *"Can I give you a lift?"* she asked. She was neatly dressed, about fifty years old, probably on her way to work, and she was offering me a ride in the heat. So I accepted!

"Were you at my motel, the Red Roof Inn back there?" I asked as I got in. *"No,"* she replied, *"but I used to work there. They gave me a job when I needed one."* *"Why did you offer me a ride?"* I asked. *"You remind me of my father,"* she said wistfully. *"He left us long ago, but I often think of him. Maybe he is like you now."*

I thanked her for a cool ride in the humidity and offered her five dollars for the ride but she said, *"No, no, I do this for you! I'm a Christian woman. My friends tell me, 'Carmen, stop doing that, somebody's going to hurt you one day,' and I say, 'I'm going to die anyway, so I might as well be doing something good.' This I want to do."* She dropped me off at the front gate and left me standing there amazed. Why had she offered and why had I accepted her kind gesture?

"She was looking for a pickup," a cynic might say. But at 8:30 AM? A friend told me I was unwise accepting a ride from a stranger. *"Next time call a cab!"* he said. *"Think what could have happened."* Her actions certainly improved my attitude about a hot, muggy Dallas!

Maybe Carmen is searching for her father, or maybe I looked like a pathetic old man who needed help. Whatever the case, I appreciated it. Often God moves people to do surprising things, to take chances, even in this uncertain world.

"Do not forget to entertain strangers." (Hebrews 13:5)

Thank you, Carmen, and thank You, Lord.

DAILY WALK WITH JESUS in...
OCTOBER

+ + +

OCTOBER 1

One autumn we returned from a two week cruise to the Mediterranean with souvenirs, memories and a nasty cold. We'd stopped at Spain, France, Italy, Greece and Turkey. We walked a lot, ate too much, and stayed with thirty two hundred passengers and fifteen hundred crew members on a ship larger than most aircraft carriers.

The most memorable part was visiting the ruins of Rome, Pompeii, Ephesus and Corinth. The artwork of Florence, the Vatican and Venice is amazing, but there's something impressive about ancient ruins. Perhaps it's that they represent what is past and gone. In my travels I've seen ancient places, especially in Israel, sites of cities that lie abandoned today, and I wonder, *"Why did this place fall into ruin?"*

Archaeological digs also make me wonder if other people, centuries from now, will dig up our ruins. What will they find? That leads one to the larger question of how long this world will last. World economic and political problems can make us pause and wonder about things like that.

"Jesus Christ is the Same Yesterday, Today and Forever." (Hebrews 13:8) Those words have always been a comfort to Christians. In Jesus Christ who is our constant life source, life is never just a pile of rubble. We may ruin some things, but He rebuilds and makes them new again. Our ruins may seem deserted, but our Lord never deserts us. **"Never will I leave you, never will I forsake you." (Hebrews 13:5)**

God doesn't live in cathedrals or temples, but in our hearts. He doesn't need sculptures or paintings or tapestries or mosaics to represent Him. His Holy Word shows us who He is, our Savior who rescues us from the world's sin.

Jesus is all we need at any time in history.

281

OCTOBER 2

A man bought a house in a good neighborhood where the soil was rich and there was a small area in back good for a garden. But when he began spading his garden, he struck rock! He soon discovered his entire garden had a rock layer a few inches under the surface, so the soil could grow little.

The man was disappointed. *"Why me?"* he said. Yes, the house was nice and the lawn mostly green, but even when he hauled in more soil, his garden grew hardly a thing. Then he discovered below the rock was a vein of coal on which little could grow. He had no garden, so he was sad.

When bad things come our way, our first response usually is, *"Why me?"* But when good things come our way, do we ever ask, *"Why me?"* We like to believe good things should be the norm, and bad things should be the exception. Most people expect life should be most always good

We humans are very adept at labeling events either "good" or "bad." But are those labels correct? For instance, we call business success "good," but don't consider that it can lead to excessively long work hours, separated families, exhausted people, or the temptation to love money. We call disease or trouble "bad," but forget that such events can teach us perseverance, strength, or even draw us closer to God.

God has a larger view of life than we do. He has promised that all things will work together for the good of those who trust Him. He can make "good" come out of "bad." Disease, disappointment, troubles and even death can touch each of us. But when we trust Jesus, He can make it all turn out good.

I could finish the story by saying the man made a fortune from that vein of coal, but that would miss the point. In the midst of our troubles we can see God smoothing the rough edges, maybe even making a diamond out of our lump of coal.

"We know that in all things God works for the good of those who love Him, who have been called according to His purpose." (Romans 8:28)

What bad things in your life has God made good for you?

OCTOBER 3

Autumn in rural areas brings the harvest. Harvest time in biblical days was joyful, for in it the people saw God's blessings for them through food and animals. Having more than enough food and animals was a sign of wealth and the knowledge that they would be safe and well fed until the next harvest.

In both Old and New Testament times, "Firstfruits" was the act of giving back to God the first portion of what one had received from the Lord in the harvest. It was done as an act of worship, and we can still do this today.

In "Firstfruits" giving, Christians return a portion to God of what they've been given, trusting He will give them the rest of their needs, according to His plan. If you and I choose to use all of God's gifts for ourselves only, we risk missing His blessings entirely. "Firstfruits" giving is a great way to show one's faith in action.

We hear much these days about the wisdom and need for good planning. *"Plan your work and work your plan,"* we are told. But a thought occurs: Rather than asking God to bless the plans we make, perhaps we should look for where He is working and then join our plans with His.

However, if we want to join Him, we must first give ourselves to Him in faith for His use according to His plans. You and I do not belong to ourselves alone. Our gifts from God, including our life, time, talents, treasures and plans, are all intended for use in His Kingdom.

We can never "out-give" God. Whatever we give Him will always come back to us, and usually increased. Whatever you and I give to God will always come back to us and will be blessed with increase according to His promise.

"Give and it shall be given unto you, pressed down, shaken and running over." (Luke 6:38)

Meanwhile, it will bless those to whom you have given it.

OCTOBER 4

Bill, a bright graduate student, decided to go to church. He had missed worshipping the past year or so because of his studies, and had grown careless about his appearance, letting his hair and beard grow.

One spring Sunday morning Bill walked to a large congregation a few blocks from his dormitory dressed in his usual jeans, t-shirt and flip-flops. The service was packed and had already begun, so he had a hard time finding a seat. Some of the people scowled as he came in, staring at his hair wildly askew from the windy morning. No one spoke to him.

The sermon was about to begin as Bill walked towards the front. Realizing there were no seats, he sat down cross-legged on the carpet right in front of the pulpit. Someone then offered him a place, but he shook his head, quite content to sit on the floor, something clearly not done in that church.

As the pastor prepared to speak, an elderly Deacon arose and began walking towards Bill. The old man was impeccably dressed in a suit and tie, and tension arose as the people wondered what he would do. So did the pastor, who took his time beginning his sermon.

When the silver-haired Deacon reached the young man, he looked down at him, then slowly lowered himself to the carpet next to him. The two men smiled, shook hands and then looked up expectantly for the pastor to begin his sermon.

The pastor's first words were, *"What I am about to preach you will never remember, but what you have just seen, you will probably never forget."*

One never knows these days what people will wear to church. I've wished at times worshippers would dress more thoughtfully, but perhaps just being there is better than one's appearance. I wonder if I would have sat down on the floor next to that young college student in my Van Heusen shirt, Brooks Brothers coat and Florscheims. Would you? Do you think the people remembered the pastor's sermon?

"You are the light of the world." (Matthew 5:14)

What is the best sermon you've heard? Or seen?

OCTOBER 5

Why should we forgive? What is the point of forgiveness? Is it for God or for us, for our benefit or the benefit of the other person? We understand our need for forgiveness from God. Did God have to forgive us? If so, where is "choice" in all this? If not, then why did He require us to forgive, when He said, **"If you do not forgive your brother his sins, neither will God forgive your sins"?** (Matthew 6:24-25)

In her book, Left to Tell, Immaculee Ilibagiza survived the 1994 Rwanda genocide by hiding ninety days in a small bathroom with seven other women. Immaculee's "sin" was that she was a Tutsi, one of Rwanda's educated minority, and she was hunted by the majority Hutu people in the Rwandan rebellion. Immaculee's parents and brothers were among the nine hundred thousand people killed in just three months during that brutal tribal war.

Amazingly, it was a Hutu pastor who hid the eight Tutsi women in his home, and his own adult children did not know they were there. Immaculee survived those terrible days by prayer and faith. Emerging from her tiny cell, she weighed only sixty-five pounds. When brought face-to-face with the Hutus who killed her family, she forgave them. The officer was angry she did not curse them or spit on them. She said no, she would forgive them because she did not want them to hinder her from living the rest of her life.

It was Immaculee's trust in her Savior that gave her the ability to forgive and move forward in life. Actually, it was not her faith that allowed her to forgive, but rather God. Her prayers led her to see Him at work in her life. Immaculee was a sinful person as we all are, but God showed her the value of forgiveness. The Holy Spirit can also help us triumph over our enemies and forgive them as we have been forgiven.

Forgiveness releases us from the pain of the past. Forgiveness is not so much for other people as it is for ourselves. God has forgiven us for our benefit. When we forgive others, it helps both them and us. God's gifts go to both sides, because both sides need His blessings.

Could you have forgiven as Immaculee did?

OCTOBER 6

Grandpa walked into his daughter's family room and found his little grandson, Jeffy, standing up in his playpen, crying. He looked pitiful, standing there in his little baseball T-shirt and droopy diaper. When Jeffy saw his grandpa, his face lit up. He held up his arms and said, *"Out Papa, out!"* Grandpa was just about to lift him out when his mother came into the room. *"No, Jeffy!"* she said, *"You are being punished. You must stay in bed. Just leave him there, Dad."* Then Mom left the room with the two of them still standing there.

Now what's a Grandpa to do? His grandson is reaching out little hands that tug his heart one way, but he doesn't want to interfere with a mother's discipline. Yet he can't just stand there looking at the little boy, nor could he turn around and walk out the door. What could he do?

Grandpa's love found a way. He climbed into the playpen with the little fellow. *"If you're in there, Buddy, I'm in with you."* he said. *"What's your sentence? How long are you in for?"* And finding a big, warm grandpa next to him, little Jeffy found comfort even in his "captivity."

Mom later found the two of them sleeping, snuggled together in the playpen. We can only hope she appreciated the significance of her father's loving act.

That's what God has done for us through His Son. He crawled into the prison of our world, lived with us for a time and took our punishment upon Himself through His Son Jesus. And He remains with us now all the way through this life and into the life which is yet to come.

How can you help someone in need this way? Jesus says we're to visit the prisoners and the sick. Is there a way you can do this today?

"When the set time had fully come, God sent his Son, born of a woman, born under the law, to redeem those under the law." (Galatians 4:4-5)

Jesus became human, so He could be with us always.

286

OCTOBER 7

In a novel I once read (which name escapes me), four men were confessing their sins to one another. On hearing the vile nature of their sins, one of the men exclaims, *"How can God let us live? Why doesn't He just kill us to purify His creation?"* Another man said, *"Because God is a potter. He works in mud."*

This is literally what God did in Genesis when He formed the first human being from the dust of the earth. Like a potter, He molded and fashioned the first human from the clay of the earth into a vessel useful to Himself.

I wonder how many times God looked at what He'd made and considered starting over before He finally breathed His breath of life into Adam. I also wonder if any of the people reading this devotion think He quit too soon and should have tried one more time!

God continues to work with dust and mud still today, fashioning us, changing us and molding us through hard times and difficult experiences, shaping us into the people He wants us to be. He wants us to serve Him and love others, and that usually takes major changes before we can become those useful people.

Most of the time, you and I are difficult "projects." Our sin makes any goodness elusive and self-serving. We want to be like God, but God wants us our fellowship with Him. He wants humble servants who can make the world He created a better place, and we aren't very good at doing that.

After Adam and Eve sinned, God continued working with our mud, fixing, re-developing and changing us. Finally He decided to send His Son into the world to do it right. Jesus died in the mud and muck of Sin on Calvary's cross so that He could straighten out the mess we have made in this world.

Today let's be grateful we are alive on this amazing planet, not to be perfect (Jesus already did that), nor to save the planet (one Savior is enough). Rather, let us serve and love Him the best we can, knowing He accepts us and forgives us.

"I am fearfully and wonderfully made." (Psalm 139:14)

Here's mud in your eye!

OCTOBER 8

Driving rural North Dakota roads can be an experience. Many roads are still made of gravel, connected to occasional stretches of pavement near the larger cities. After winter thaws and spring rains, a car can easily get stuck on a muddy road. Country roads can be an adventure. Overshoes are still helpful, because the mud can get deep.

A young man and his family, dressed in good clothes and going somewhere important, got onto a road where a large mud hole had appeared overnight. The father had driven that road the day before, but today he could not make it through. So the drill began: Mom got behind the wheel and let the clutch out slowly while the Dad and the boys pushed, and the car moved forward through the mud hole. *"Take it easy,"* shouted Dad to Mom. Then for some reason, just as the car cleared the mud hole, Mom floored it. The car fishtailed out of the mud, but all her men's pants were sprayed with mud, and they were wearing their good clothes!

"Let them dry and I'll brush you off when we get there," was Mom's advice. When they arrived it was obvious they were not the only ones who'd had to push a car through the mud. Some of the other men had mud even on their coat sleeves. However, all the women were quite clean and tidy. The men were proud that they had enabled their ladies to arrive so clean, even if it cost them a trip to the cleaners. Without a word you could tell who were drivers and who were pushers.

It's a great example of Jesus' love for us. By His grace, we arrive at Heaven's Gate all clean and forgiven, pushed through the sinful mud of this world by our Lord who was dirtied by His innocent death on the cross. The Dirty One cleanses us from the mire of our sin and presents us, spotless and pure, to the Heavenly Father.

"Though your sins are like scarlet, they shall be as white as snow; though they are red as crimson, they shall be like wool." (Isaiah 1:18)

Jesus is our eternal cleaning agency, and He works for free!

288

OCTOBER 9

Mrs. Smith, Sally's teacher, was known for her elaborate object lessons. One day Sally walked into class and on the wall she saw a big target hanging above a table with many darts. As class began, Mrs. Smith told the students to draw a picture of someone they disliked, because she would allow them to throw darts at that person's picture.

Sally's best friend drew a picture of a girl who had stolen her boyfriend. Another classmate drew a picture of his pesky little brother, and another drew a picture of her father. Sally drew a picture of Mrs. Smith, drawing her picture so all would know who it was. Sally was very pleased with her picture and the effect it would have on the class.

The class lined up and began throwing darts, with much laughter and hilarity. Some of the students threw their darts so hard their targets ripped. Sally looked forward to her turn, and was disappointed when Mrs. Smith, because of time limits, asked the students to return to their seats.

As Sally sat there, angry that she didn't have a chance to throw her darts, Mrs. Smith removed their pictures and the large target from the wall. Underneath the target for all their drawings was a picture of Jesus!

A hush fell over the room as each student viewed the mangled picture of Jesus. Holes and jagged marks covered His face and nose, and one of His eyes was punctured. After a few moments, Mrs. Smith said these words, *"The Bible says, 'If you have done it unto the least of these my brethren, you have done it unto Me.'" (Matthew 25:40)*

We may not throw actual darts, but our words can hurt just as much and often as quickly. A kind word takes no more effort to say than an angry one, but its benefits will last longer. Jesus urges us to speak kind words to all, for that is what He would do.

"So whatever you wish that others would do to you, do also to them, for this is the Law and the Prophets." (Matthew 7:12, the "Golden Rule")

Choose your words carefully today.

OCTOBER 10

Have you noticed that the other line always seems to move faster than yours? Whether you're waiting to check out items at the store or driving the city streets during rush hour, the other line always seems to move faster. It's easy to envy those others moving along while you're standing still. If only you could be in that other line!

But some days we may find ourselves in the fast lane. Do you recall what it felt like moving along smoothly while the other side of the highway was at a standstill? Do you think those poor people over there were envying you?

Back in a small town North Dakota sheriff's office where we often had morning coffee, there was a framed picture of two horses, one black and one white, each leaning over the same fence to nibble grass from the other side. We joked about that picture often. Life always seems better on the other side, doesn't it? If we could just get to that other side, our life would be great. People on each side of the fence think the same.

But the apostle Paul said, **"I have learned the secret of being content in any and every situation. I can do everything through Him who gives me strength."** (Philippians 4:11-13)

Americans seem to live with continual discontent. The "Ad Men" of Madison Avenue want us discontented so we'll buy their products. But instead of coveting what we don't have, perhaps a long walk on a warm autumn day is what we really need. It can make us realize the beauty of the world our Lord has given us.

"Good enough!" Now that's a concept modern people tend to scorn. We're told to seek the best, be the fastest and get the most. *"'Good enough' is for losers!"* we hear. But "good enough" is looking better to me every day. I know that by sin I am not good enough. Yet because of Jesus I am good enough. Not that I am that good enough by myself,. It is Christ who makes me good enough. All it takes is faith in Him and His love. "Good enough" for God is "good enough" for me.

"By grace you are saved through faith." (Ephesians 2:8)

Enjoy a "good enough" day.

OCTOBER 11

Did you know the only animal a Grizzly Bear will share its food with is a skunk? It isn't that the Grizzly wants to share its food, but rather that he chooses to, for he could easily crush the skunk with a swipe of his paw. So why does this powerful creature allow the lowly skunk to eat with him? Because a smart bear knows the high cost of having a skunk angry with him. He knows this from experience.

Why is it that we humans aren't as smart? So often we'd rather carry grudges around, always hurting ourselves more than the objects of our grudge, failing to see how damaging an unforgiving spirit can be. Like a doctor once told his patient, *"If you don't cut out your resentment, one of these days I'll have to cut out your intestines."* Nursing hard feelings hurts everyone, but reconciliation is sweet to body and soul.

Reconciliation can also mean letting something alone and letting a hurt heal. I once hurt my leg while ice skating on a frozen pond. I fell down and cut a large gash in my shin. My Mom cleaned it, bandaged it and told me to leave it alone, but I wouldn't. Several times I took the bandage off and picked at the wound, thinking that would help. If I had left it alone, it would have healed much faster. Today I can still see a scar on that leg because I kept picking at the scab.

You and I will never get over a wound if we don't let it heal. The more we rehearse our hurts, the more we risk the scars of never getting over them. It's better that we should give our hurts to the Lord who has removed them on the cross. There's no point in carrying around unhealthy resentment and anger when Jesus has already forgiven it.

"Do not worry about tomorrow, for tomorrow will worry about itself. Each day has enough trouble of its own." (Matthew 6:34)

Forgive and forget. Let those nasty feelings go and discover the peace of forgiveness.

OCTOBER 12

She sat in the lobby of the nursing home, ninety-two years old, poised and handsomely dressed. Legally blind and no longer able to live alone, she was waiting to be moved to a room. Her husband of seventy years had recently passed away, making the move necessary.

After many hours of waiting patiently, she smiled sweetly when told her room was ready. As she maneuvered her walker to the elevator, a worker gave her a visual description of her tiny room, including the window curtains. *"Oh, I love it already,"* she stated with the enthusiasm of a child just given a new puppy.

"But Mrs. Jones, you haven't seen the room yet," said the worker. *"That doesn't have anything to do with it, my dear,"* Mrs. Jones replied. *"You see, happiness is something I decide on ahead of time. Whether I like my room or not doesn't depend on how I arrange the furniture. It's how I arrange my mind, and I've already decided to love it."*

"You see," she continued, *"It's a decision I make every morning when I wake up. I have a choice. I can spend the day in bed recounting the difficulty I have with the parts of my body that no longer work well, or I can get out of bed and be thankful for the ones that do. Each day is a gift from God, and for the rest of my days I have decided to focus on each new day and all the happy memories I've stored away for just this time of my life."*

What a wonderful attitude! Whether or not we are happy truly does depend on our frame of mind. Happiness is usually a by-product of other things, especially our relationships, those with each other, with God, or with ourselves. When we give the Lord first place in our lives, the rest of life will be better. Happiness can be ours, not as a goal in itself, but as a by-product of a greater goal.

"Godliness with contentment is great gain." (1 Timothy 6:6)

I hope today you will find some small happiness.

OCTOBER 13

Ever wonder why maps of the whole world have funny shaped edges, or why they make some countries bigger than they are on a Globe? Cartographers have found there's no perfect way to draw a round surface on a flat map, so they distort the shape of certain areas in the north and south, for example, making Greenland look bigger than Australia.

Christians can have problems with distortions as well. When we try to understand spiritual truths within the limitations of our sinful world, we can end up exaggerating the minors while minimizing the majors. Not all spiritual teachings have equal importance. The liturgy of worship, for example, is not as important as Jesus whom we worship. How we pray is not as important as to Whom we pray.

Distortion can also happen in what we consider to be sin. When confronted with what science says about certain actions, we may be tempted to believe some wrongs are no longer wrong. What we've always believed to be right can be distorted by popular notions claiming them now to be wrong. It's confusing, isn't it?

The New Testament addresses distortions that come when the teachings of popular teachers become more important than the teachings of Jesus Christ. Sound and true biblical teaching does not distort the basics found in the Bible, nor does it divide the Church. Rather, it unites believers and builds up the Body. "New" teachings are often old sins in a new disguise.

Attempts to explain God and His will completely are always inadequate. Those who think they can explain all the mysteries of God usually end up distorting things. They confuse our thinking and over-simplify what it means to be a child of God. Sin demeans God's Word. What's most important is that we believe in Jesus and what He says.

Apostle Paul had this in mind when he wrote, **"When I came to you, brothers, I did not come with eloquence or superior wisdom as I proclaimed to you the testimony about God. For I resolved to know nothing while I was with you except Jesus Christ and Him crucified." (1 Corinthians 5:1-3)**

Relying on Jesus Christ can keep us from distorting the truth.

OCTOBER 14

Do you ever wonder how you appear to others? We all have a certain view of ourselves, such as how we look or act or talk. We all have a certain view of who it is that lives in this body of ours, and it's usually a much younger person than others might see. But is our view accurate?

One day I was walking outside a nursing home and glanced at the person walking beside me whose reflection I could see in the large windows on either side of the sidewalk. When I saw a gray-haired fellow walking with a slouch and a bulging tummy, I was suddenly shocked to realize that reflection was me!

What made it all the more amazing was that for some reason I'd just been thinking just then of a new outfit I'd worn as a sophomore in high school. It was a new white shirt with button down collar, dark trousers and new black loafers, a very trendy style for 1961. And I remembered how a cute junior girl named Judy had smiled sweetly at me and said, *"You look sharp today, Bob."* I wonder what she'd say if she saw me today. I doubt either of us would recognize each other now. Very few of us now look like that person we visualize in our minds. That's why we need a mirror!

Personal appearance may not seem important, but to a Christian it can be quite important. How others see us can help shape their view of God. If we are pleasant or joyful, they will use that attitude to make a judgment about our Christian faith. If we are fussy or cynical, or stern or cranky, those attitudes, too, will determine their view of God through us.

Traditional writings of the early church tell us that pagans and other unbelievers often remarked of Christians, *"See how they love each other."* They didn't say, *"See how big their church is,"* or, *"See how much they own,"* or even, *"See how well they follow the Bible."* They said, *"See how they love one another."* Wouldn't it be great if people said that about your church?

"Dear friends, let us love one another, for love comes from God." (1 John 4:7)

Be a loveable person today!

294

OCTOBER 15

Fear abounds in many parts of the world today. Fear can even drive a person to despair, yet fear will always be with us. A Bible teacher once said, *"God doesn't let us dance through life without our doing the 'mambo of fear' at some time."* Fear is as much a part of our daily life as joy, confusion, or contentment.

Five year-old Johnny was in the kitchen as his mother made supper. She asked him to go into the pantry and get a can of tomato soup, but he didn't want to go. *"It's dark in there and I'm scared."* She said it was safe, and he still didn't want go in. Finally she said, *"It's okay, Johnny. Jesus will be in there with you."* Johnny walked hesitantly to the door and opened it. He peeked inside, saw it was dark, and said, *"Jesus, if you're in there, would you hand me that can of tomato soup?"*

Some people understand fear and are able to deal with it better than others. We call them courageous. They know fear is part of the substance of life, the part that can motivate us to do things that are right and necessary.

For others, fear is a four-letter word. We cringe at our fears and let them drive us this way and that, forgetting that God gives us power to overcome them. For some of us, fear can be useful, but for others, it's toxic. It poisons relationships, wrecks families, shakes governments and even ruins churches that do not seek God's courage.

It's that kind of fear God says we must avoid. He has not called us to run and hide from those with whom we disagree. He has not told us to deny the obvious. Rather, He has given us a spirit of power and love and He's given us all a sound mind. We will always have fears with us. But will we give our fears to God or only try to deal with them ourselves?

Today if you must confront something difficult, look at it with the knowledge Jesus can help you though it. Look at it, pray about it, and then face it with Christ by your side.

"God has not called us to a spirit of fear, but of power and of love and of a sound mind." (2 Timothy 1:7)

With faith in Jesus, be a fearless person today!

OCTOBER 16

There is a little children's chant we all have heard:

> *"Ring around the rosies,*
> *Pocket full of posies;*
> *Ashes, ashes,*
> *We all fall down."*

To most people, this little chant envisions cheerful children playing a harmless game, but actually it was born out of a world of disease and death. Three and a half centuries ago, during the 1600's, the "Black Plague" was sweeping through England and other parts of Europe, killing hundreds of thousands.

Because they thought the disease was caused by polluted air, London's people took plague victims to flower gardens where they breathed in the fragrant scent of flowers to replace bad air with good. Those too sick to go outside were taken flower petals, and some even were brought burnt petals to flush out the bad air. Yet most always the victims died.

What we often hear our children sing came from the chant of men given the gruesome task of hauling out bodies for burial. *"Ring around the rosies, pocket full of posies; ashes, ashes, we all fall down."*

Though the plagues of years ago do not threaten us as much today, we all still face a form of black death. Because of the plague of our sin, it's still true, *"We all fall down."* But in Jesus Christ we won't stay down. His promise is that all who have faith in Him will be raised again.

Newton's Law of Gravity says, *"What goes up must come down."* Jesus' Law of Resurrection is, *"What goes down will come up."* That's a good thought to keep in mind when we consider our mortality.

Jesus said, "I am the resurrection and the life. All who believe in Me will live, even though they die." (John 11:25)

Be comforted today, knowing you're governed by Jesus' Law of Resurrection.

296

OCTOBER 17

The many storms and hurricanes that occur in the Atlantic ocean each year should make us realize we all need a strong anchor. Ships need an anchor to keep them from drifting, buildings need a strong foundation so they will be stand, and trees need a deep root system if they are going to remain upright and not be blown over in high winds. In each case, their very survival in the storm depends on being attached to something solid which cannot be moved.

Life has its share of stormy times, times of impending damage and destruction. Are we attached to the immovable, unchanging power of God, or to something else? Despite all our preparations, human anchors can give way, roots can pull up and foundations can crumble.

God provides us a faith that will endure. It is faith in Jesus Christ that holds us fast in life's stormy times. God the Holy Spirit provides us this faith. Jesus reassures us, saying, **"Lo, I am with you always." (Matthew 28:20)** It is His strength that surrounds and protects us from the buffeting of life's torrents and calamities.

"Built on the Rock, the Church shall stand," we sing in that wonderful hymn. We, too, shall stand if our lives are built on the Rock, Jesus Christ. If we are personally attached by faith to the Rock of our Salvation, we may still stumble and fall down, but we will not stay down. We may be badly hurt, but we will not be destroyed.

God loves us with an everlasting love that does not fade. Knowing and trusting His love, we can have a faith that will withstand the storms of life, no matter where they come from, or how hard they hit.

"Jesus is the Rock of my salvation,
And His banner over me is love."
(from the youth song)

Have you stumbled recently? What caused it to happen? How did you get up again?

Ravi Zacharias, well-known Christian author, once gave a lecture at Ohio State University. As he was being driven to the lecture, his car passed the new Wexner Art Center, and the driver said, *"That is our new art building. It's designed in the post-modernist view of reality. The building has no pattern, the staircases go nowhere, and the pillars support nothing. The architect designed it to reflect modern life, which to him goes nowhere and makes no sense."* Zacharias asked the driver, *"What about the foundation?"* He said, *"Well,"* said the driver, *"the building still needs a good foundation!"*

That building represents life without Jesus Christ. It goes nowhere and makes no sense, yet it still has a foundation. All people base their lives on something. If we build our lives on the sands of the latest trends and changing morals, our lives will be shallow and empty, and will blow down in the wind.

But if we build our lives on the rock-solid foundation of Jesus Christ, we will have strength enough for difficult times. A life built on anything other than the Rock of Christ is in danger of being empty, going nowhere and making no sense. But a life with a foundation in Christ will stand firm no matter how hard the winds blow.

Those who build their lives on secular humanism, or on a view of science that denies God, or on a worldview that has no moral sense of right or wrong, are standing on shaky, unstable ground. Without the truth of God in the Bible, they will fall and break. Only Jesus Christ can give us the strength to withstand the destructive winds of life.

"We are built on the foundation of the apostles and prophets, with Christ Jesus Himself as the chief cornerstone." (Ephesians 2:20)

That's all you really need to know about engineering!

OCTOBER 19

Is war worth it? Is America hurting itself with its periodic wars and conflicts fought overseas in other nations? A navy veteran I know has a lot of uncommonly common sense. Here is what he once wrote me:

> *"Last Tuesday I had a long discussion with a colleague who was making the all too familiar 'Is it all worth it?' argument (i.e., Is it worth it for our troops to die over there?). All I could say was, 'Is it worth it for a fireman with a wife and young children to risk his life saving an elderly woman from a burning retirement home? If he dies, think of the loss to society, but if she dies what is the loss?' Of course his answer was not about 'worth' at all, but that the fireman risks his life to help the helpless simply because he is the one most able to do so. That's his job!"*
>
> *"I told him that in the same way, America is the world's sole superpower, and we are the most capable and have the most means to change the face of the Middle East for the better. Every soldier and Marine I've spoken to have no doubt when asked about why they are there. Yes, they want to go home, but it only takes one look at some Iraqi kids playing freely or an Afghan school being re-opened or a busy market place or an empty prison to understand that the sacrifice they've made is not about political vanity but about commitment to helping people become free."*

Jesus of Nazareth lived and taught at a time when people yearned to be free. He preached Good News that the Truth would set people free, and His Word was truth in human form. He came as God's servant to bring hope to the nations, to all people who would believe in Him. He is the Son of God who brings hope to us today.

"If the Son sets you free, you will be free indeed." (John 8:36)

Thank You, Lord, for our troops and the sacrifices they make.

OCTOBER 20

A man wrote a letter to the editor of a small-town newspaper and complained that it made no sense to go to church every Sunday. *"I've gone to church for 30 years now,"* he wrote, *"and in that time I have heard something like three thousand sermons. But for the life of me I can't remember a single one of them. So I'm wasting my time listening, and pastors are wasting theirs by preaching all those sermons."*

This letter started a real controversy in the "Letters to the Editor" column of that newspaper, much to the delight of the editor. It went on for several days until someone wrote this short note:

"I've been married for thirty years now. In that time my wife has cooked me some thirty-two thousand meals. But for the life of me, I cannot recall what the menu was for a single one of those meals. But I do know this: they all nourished me and gave me the strength I needed to do my work. If my wife had not given me those meals, I would not be alive today."

That letter pretty well ended letters to the editor on that topic!

It's tempting to miss church, to act as if we don't need it, or to substitute church attendance with watching a television preacher or reading the Bible at home. Some of us will rationalize we just don't need it.

But we don't usually skip our meals, do we? At least not for long. May God grant us grace to include Him in our busy schedules at least once a week.

Our Lord Jesus feeds us the Bread of Life, His Holy Word that nourishes our faith and life. Without Holy Communion, His eternal and life-giving meal, our faith and life would suffer. But with His spiritual nourishment, we will grow strong for all times of life.

"I bowed down and worshiped the Lord, and I praised the Lord." (Genesis 24:48)

I'm looking forward to my next meal, too.

OCTOBER 21

Autumn is my favorite time of year. I'm not quite sure why, since it means the loss of summer, many bags of leaves to rake, and unpredictable weather. I guess it's because I love the crisp days with their blue skies, the smell of leaves and flocks of birds stopping in the trees on their flight south. I even look forward to the first snowfall, though I hope it won't last long. I don't really like change as much as I used to, but the change to the autumn season always feels good for awhile.

I once helped relocate a large refugee family from Laos to North Dakota and will always remember the father's question, *"Why so cold outside?"* I tried explaining the change of seasons due to the tilt of the sun in the northern hemisphere, but he finally said, *"Maybe it's time for earth to sleep here."* He thought the snow looked like a blanket, and I believe he had it right.

Life never stays the same. It's always changing, bringing something new or something surprising. We get older and our bodies change. The only thing that doesn't change is the grace of God. He never stops caring for His people, even when change uproots and unsettles them.

A continuous and unchanging aspect of the Christian life is our Lord and Savior Jesus. You and I have changed and so has the world around us, but He has not. I find comfort in that knowledge.

Perhaps you are familiar with the verse from the hymn, "Abide With Me" that says, *"Change and decay in all around I see, Oh, Thou who changest not, abide with me."* If your world is changing, I pray the Good Lord will be your unchangeable and unshakeable One, whether in the rapid changes of autumn or in any season of life.

"At that time His voice shook the earth, but now He has promised, "Once more I will shake not only the earth but also the heavens." The words "once more" indicate the removing of what can be shaken--that is, created things--so that what cannot be shaken may remain." (Hebrews 12:26-27)

How have you been shaken up recently?

OCTOBER 22

Yesterday morning our cul-de-sac got a cleaning. Five of our six homes bagged their leaves the same weekend and left over one hundred bags of leaves plus trash bags for the garbage men. I went out and helped the two fellows load everything from my lot. As they left, I thanked them and gave them each a bottle of water. It seemed the least I could do for what they had taken away.

I have always liked the garbage man. Every week he takes away the stuff I never have to see again, and I always feel fresh and cleansed when the truck drives away. All the unwanted stuff from the kitchen and garage, the sawdust, food scraps, waste paper and packaging materials, all are gone forever to a landfill.

No matter how much we recycle (and we faithfully do recycle as much as we can) there's always some garbage to remove. So I like my garbage man and even remember him kindly at Christmas.

The garbage man reminds me of Jesus. Every time we confess our sins to Him, He removes them as far as the east is from the west. The scraps of our sins, the waste of our iniquities and the garbage of our transgressions through rebellion and laziness, greed and stupidity, are all gone forever.

Jesus, the Divine Garbage Man, takes them to that spiritual landfill called Calvary and seals them forever in the tomb. You and I are forgiven, freshly cleansed by our faithful Garbage Man Jesus who has taken it all away. He does this again and again because He loves us.

What if the garage man didn't come? What would you do with all those bags and full trash cans? Where would you put everything? How would you deal with the smell and ugliness? In the same way, think of what it would be like if Jesus no longer forgave our sins. I don't even want to consider it!

"Grow in the grace and knowledge of our Lord and Savior Jesus Christ." (2 Peter 3:18)

All thanks to my Garbage Man and yours, Jesus Christ.

302

OCTOBER 23

Mom wondered why she sat in the stands so much, especially when he so rarely played, and especially on cold mornings like this. But one morning that all changed. *"Ma'am,"* said the coach through the fence, *"Joey will start in right field today."* Finally, she thought, his hard work will pay off. It would mean so much for Joey to finally start a game. But then she was nervous, so she went for a cup of coffee.

But when the team took the field, Joey wasn't in right field. Instead, Eddie was there, Eddie, the most inexperienced player, clumsy Eddie who always dropped the ball. She wanted to ask the coach why, but instead just sat there and hugged her cup and felt the disappointment only an expectant parent can feel. *"Atta boy, Eddie,"* his Dad yelled from the stands. At least he was feeling good about it.

Eddie didn't drop any balls because none came to him, but he never got on base either. Joey was finally subbed for Eddie, and he struck out on three pitches. At least, she thought, he got to play his position and get up to bat.

Mom again wondered what she was doing there. For four years she'd been sitting on uncomfortable benches, drinking terrible coffee, eating watery hotdogs and salty popcorn. Joey had little talent, but he loved to play, and that's why she came.

When the game was over Mom went to meet Joey. She hugged him, gave him money for a hotdog and he went away smiling. Then his coach came over. *"That's a fine young man you have there, Ma'am."* *"Why?"* she asked, waiting for him to explain why Joey hadn't started. *"When I told him he could start, he thanked me and then turned me down. He said I should let Eddie start, because it meant more to him. He's a good kid, Ma'am."*

Mom turned to see her boy stuffing a hotdog in his mouth and just then realized why she sat in the stands. Where else could she see him growing into a man? When God sees us doing good to others because we love Him, He, too, knows why He goes to all the trouble.

"Speaking the truth in love, we will grow to become the mature body of him who is the head, Christ." (Eph. 4:15)

I think that's why most parents sit in the stands.

OCTOBER 24

A University professor once challenged his students with a question. *"Did God create everything that exists?"* One student bravely replied, *"Yes he did!"* *"Everything?"* The professor asked. *"Yes sir,"* the student replied boldly. The professor continued, *"If God created everything; then God created evil. And, since evil exists, then we can assume God is evil."* The professor then boldly declared to all that he had proven once more the Christian faith was only a myth.

The student raised his hand and asked, *"Professor, does cold exist?"* *"Of course it exists."* he said. The student replied, *"Actually, sir, cold does not exist. According to the laws of physics, cold is the absence of heat. So cold itself does not really exist. Professor, does darkness exist?"* The professor responded, *"Of course."* The student replied, *"I'm sorry sir, but darkness is the absence of light."* The young man continued, *"Sir, does evil exist?"* The professor hesitated, but the student continued, *"Sir, evil is the absence of God. It is the result of what happens when people do not have God present in their life. It's like cold that comes when there is no heat, or darkness when there is no light."*

Jesus said, **"I am the way, the truth and the life."** (John **14:6)** He also said, **"The truth shall set you free."** (John 8:32) Jesus is the truth of God on earth. His words, His heart and His mission are what really count.

Whether you believe evil is just a term or a distinct entity, Christ has overcome it. Trust in Him, my friends. Let His Holy Word guide you, and then know and believe that you are forgiven and restored to God by what He has done. That's what the Bible says, regardless of what secular authorities may say.

"Deliver us from the Evil One." (Matthew 6:13)

Christ said it, I believe it, and that settles it.

OCTOBER 25

The Kennedy Space Center in Florida houses the Saturn V, the mightiest rocket ever built. How massive and impressive it is, nearly four hundred feet long and able to lift cargos weighing tons. It's twice the size of the Space Shuttle, but if one small thing goes wrong, it can disintegrate in flight.

All the key elements to the Saturn V rocket must be in place and working right. No matter how big or strong the other parts are, if one of the small parts malfunctions, the whole rocket will be lost. Thus, it is the small things that control the big rocket.

That's how it is in our lives, too. Unless the seemingly small elements of faith and hope and love in Jesus are at center of our lives, our whole life can go out of control.

Autumn in America usually means elections and decisions the voters must make that affect our future. National and international events in recent years should make us realize that even an entire world can get out of control. Now is the time for Christians to pray and trust in God for all things, including the leaders they elect. Regular voting helps!

Unless you and I keep our life centered on Jesus Christ, we also may find ourselves out of control. Trust Jesus and stick to His plan. Worship Him regularly, even when you would rather not. Pray to the Lord, even when it doesn't seem to work. Don't give up on the church, even with its faults. It is imperfect, but it's still the best and most lasting organization God has given us. Jesus is the Light for a world in darkness. May He bring light into the dark days of your own life, as well as to the nations of our world.

"I am the light of the world. Whoever follows Me will never walk in darkness, but will have the light of life." (John 8:12)

When the going gets tough, trust in the Lord. Trust Him when the way is smooth, also.

OCTOBER 26

Did you know that if you put a buzzard in a six by eight foot pen only two feet high and open at the top, the bird will be unable to leave it? In spite of its ability to fly, it will not escape. The reason is that a buzzard always begins its flight from a branch or else from the ground with a required run of ten to twelve feet. Without that space to run, it will not even attempt to fly, but will remain a prisoner in its pen.

The ordinary bat that flies around at night cannot take off from a level place. Though very nimble, if it is placed on the floor or flat ground, all it can do is shuffle about helplessly until it crawls up to reach a high enough elevation from which it can throw itself into the air. Then it will be able to take off like a flash.

A bumblebee, if dropped into an open tumbler, will remain there until it dies. Unless it is taken out, it never sees the top as a means of escape, but persists in trying to find some way out through the glass sides in front of it. It will keep seeking a way out where none exists.

In many ways, people are like the buzzard, the bat, and the bumblebee. We struggle every day with all our problems and frustrations, never realizing that all we have to do is to seek what is above us. We get angry at what happens and let our anger blind us. Sorrow looks back, worry looks around, and anger blinds us.

The person with faith in Christ looks up, sees God, and knows he will live. Faith in Jesus helps us get a running start on solving the problems we face. It helps us launch into each day, knowing we will have power from God to fly above our petty troubles. Faith in Jesus is the key to eternal life.

"When these things begin to take place, stand up and lift up your heads, because your redemption is drawing near." (Luke 21:28)

What we have is far greater than what we don't have.

Although a college and seminary graduate, my ignorance of biology was embarrassing, so I began reading some books on the subject. In one volume, <u>Fearfully and Wonderfully Made</u>, by Philip Yancey and Dr. Paul Brand, the authors not only explain the human body, they compare it to the Body of Christ in fascinating ways.

Dr. Brand describes the problem of rheumatoid arthritis. While the cause of this disease is unknown, doctors recognize it by what it does. Rheumatoid arthritis produces a hypersensitivity within the cells of joints. A joint becomes flooded with enzymes that normally occur when bacteria or abnormal cells are present and call into action the body's defensive mechanisms. But in this disease, there is no apparent "enemy" present, only the body's perception of one.

In rheumatoid arthritis, a healthy joint becomes a cannibal, destroying parts of itself. Yet when the joint is opened for examination, no "enemies" are found, only the body's defensive cells attacking healthy cartilage and ligaments. It's like a civil war has broken out in there, and the defensive mechanism itself has become the disease.

This pathology is similar to some activities in the Christian Church. Members become hypersensitive, taking offense at criticism, and their dignity or position becomes more important than the harmony of the group. An individual or a small group may grab a minor doctrinal or practical issue and make agreement on it the essential factor for unity - or else!

Is there friction and tension in your congregation or church body? Could it be from righteous indignation against perceived wrongs? Could "righteous" anger be causing more damage than the "wrongs" which anger some people?

Just as the human body goes to incredible lengths to prevent friction, so the Body of Christ should be as careful to lubricate itself against possible conflicts.

"Now you are the body of Christ and individually members of it." (1 Corinthians 12:27)

Are you contributing to tension or working to overcome it?

307

OCTOBER 28

It's quite a mixed-up world we live in. Sometimes it's all enough to make a person really angry. One Sunday in the children's message, an empty jar was placed before the little ones and filled with golf balls. But it wasn't really full yet, so marbles were added to it. But there was still lots of space in it so shelled peanuts were added and then it was shaken. Even then it wasn't completely full because there was still enough room for a cup of sugar to be added.

The pastor said the golf balls were the big things in life: God, life, family, church. The marbles were important things such as job, education, friends and health. The peanuts represented the small things in life, like clothing, money and entertainment. But the sugar represented the love of God which fills in all the cracks and binds all things together with sweetness.

The secret of a good life is to get the things of life in the right order. If we fill our life with little things first, there will be no room for the important things. Stuffing golf balls and marbles into peanuts and sugar can be done, but it's not easy, because we're doing things backwards.

It's better to take care of the big things first. When God, life, family and church come first in life, all the rest will fit. When first things come first, life is best.

Much of what happens in the world today is little more than peanuts. Fun can take away some of our sadness, but not for long. Money can help take away hunger, but not for long. Dwelling on the small things can block us from the bigger and more important things.

But if we make sure the really important things of life are given first priority, we can also enjoy or endure the smaller things that will also come later.

"Seek first His kingdom and His righteousness, and all these things will be given to you as well." (Matthew 6:33)

When Jesus is first, the rest falls into place.

308

OCTOBER 29

In his book, <u>Travels With Charlie</u>, John Steinbeck wrote, *"You don't take the trip, the trip takes you."* I thought of those words one vacation day in July when the temperature reached one hundred ten degrees in the South Dakota badlands, and the air conditioner couldn't cool our travel trailer.

I didn't consider going home right then, but I wished we were in a cooler place, such as Colorado. Yet a good thing occurred. That night the water in our trailer freshwater tank was warm enough to take a bath without heating it!

The day before we had driven through DeSmet, South Dakota, site of five of Laura Ingalls Wilder's "Little House" books. I had been thinking how the pioneers handled the heat, humidity and bugs. They had no propane, electricity, nor any of the conveniences we have. There must have been times when they felt they could go no farther, handle no more heat, or work no more. Still they continued on and lived through it and eventually made their lives better.

There are times when events seems more than we can handle. A situation gets out of control, a responsibility seems too great, or a challenge saps our strength. At such times we would like to quit, or at least let someone else take over. At such times we may not know to whom we can turn.

This is when we should give our troubles to someone who can handle them. Our Lord Jesus is willing to share our struggles. He will help us handle difficulties, or give us the strength we need. He may not take our troubles away, but He will help us deal with them. He won't remove our loads, but He will give us stronger backs. Sometimes He just gives us a needed hand or an encouraging word that helps.

It's like trying to carry a load that's too large. If someone helps you, the heavy burden can be carried. A shared load is always lighter. When the heat is too great, God is always there. When the load is too heavy, He'll help us carry it.

"Ask and it will be given to you; seek and you will find; knock and the door will be opened unto you." (Matthew 7:7)

Thank God He always comes with us on our trips through life.

309

OCTOBER 30

My elementary education was in a one-room rural school and I had the same teacher for nearly five years. Our teacher, Mrs. Sylvester, taught two dozen or more students in all six grades. We learned our lessons and had many privileges today's students might not have.

Mrs. Sylvester read to us every day. For all of the six years I was there, every day after eating our lunch brought from home, she would pick up one of Laura Ingalls Wilder's books and we'd retreat into the latest chapter of the Ingalls family life. We came to know them well, and some of us are still quite good at "Little House" trivia. Another privilege was having the older children teaching the younger. For two years I taught the younger ones various subjects, and in doing so, learned my own lessons as well.

In winter we square danced in the school basement or played in the snow. In the fall and spring we fought imaginary battles in the trees and around the school yard. Crossing the road was forbidden except to get drinking water from a neighbor farm. In 1971 Mrs. Sylvester came to my ordination as a pastor, and I still have a photo of us together.

The last time I saw her was in the local nursing home, sitting in the hallway across from my parents' room. She was strapped in a wheelchair and for the first time did not recognize me. I helped her eat a dish of food and said to her, *"You were my teacher."* She seemed surprised, *"I was a teacher?"* And then, after a pause, she looked straight at me and asked, *"Was I a good teacher?"* *"The best teacher there ever was,"* I said. I thanked her, although she was quickly distracted.

She died at age ninety-nine, a true pioneer who touched the lives of hundreds. Her brief obituary mentioned nothing about her country school teaching or her half-Indian husband Bob, nor about having met Laura Ingalls Wilder in person. Her work still lives on in her students. Good teachers will always live on through their students.

"Teach me your ways, O Lord." (Exodus 33:13)

Thanks, Mrs. Sylvester. You were a great teacher.

OCTOBER 31

October 31 is Reformation Day, and it's Halloween, too. I wonder what this day means to today's Christians. It was formerly a time to sing great hymns and recall the Reformation, an important historic event. But the impact of the protestant Reformation has all but disappeared.

Think for a moment what it must have been like as a humble parish priest and peasant scholar who stood up for his principles against the world's mightiest powers. In 1521, Martin Luther stood before the Imperial Conference at Worms, Germany, with Emperor Charles V and the Pope's lawyer. Think what courage it took for him to stand up for what he believed was true. How would we have reacted if powerful people condemned us and declared us an outlaw?

Suppose we were required to stand before a Pope, a President or some other powerful person, and told to retract what we had written. How would we answer? Could we be as courageous? How would we measure up?

Some people can still put the fear of God into us, such as a policeman writing us a citation, an IRS agent questioning our deductions, or a masked man robbing us with a gun. But these people are weak compared to those Luther faced.

We Americans can't be imprisoned for speaking against government or be condemned or burned at the stake for our religious beliefs, at least not at this time or in this place. We come and go with ease, living mostly as we choose.

But Christians in Saudi Arabia, Sudan, Indonesia and other Islamic nations are persecuted for their faith and even die for what they believe. Would we be willing to do that?

I'd like to think I could, but some days I'm not so sure. May God spare us from such circumstances. There may come a day when we are called upon to stand for our beliefs. If such a day comes, may we have courage to speak up for the true God.

"Therefore put on the full armor of God, so that when the day of evil comes, you may be able to stand your ground." (Ephesians 6:13)

Today God's people still need to be willing witnesses for Him.

311

DAILY WALK WITH JESUS in...
NOVEMBER

+ + +

NOVEMBER 1

A recent cartoon coined the phrase *"Happy New ThanksChristoween!"* It referred to the period of holidays from October 31 through January 1. October 31, Halloween, is the first of these festivals, one running into the next, each with its festivities. There is a holiday during that time that I doubt will ever make it into the stores, November First, "All Saints Day."

As the Church developed its calendar, some days were set aside to remember the men and women who had made great contributions to God's work. The earliest mention of a day to commemorate the work of all the saints was in the Fourth Century after Christ. In the Eighth Century, Pope Gregory established November First as the official "All Saints Day."

But the church kept adding so many individual saint's days, that by the time of Martin Luther in the Sixteenth Century there were over four hundred saint's days. Most were chosen due to some good work by that person, but some days were purchased to commemorate a departed loved one. Lutheran reformers decided to set aside only seventeen days, those which would remember saints whose work could be affirmed in the Holy Bible.

On October 31, 1517, the Eve of All Saints, Martin Luther posted his Ninety-five Theses at Wittenberg, Germany. One hundred fifty years later, November First was appointed the day to remember those faithful Christians who had died.

November First gives us a moment to give thanks to God for the life of a departed loved one. We can all give thanks we are still here, for God is the giver of life and all good things.

"Blessed are the dead who die in the Lord." (Rev. 14:13)

What or who will you give thanks for today?

It is a basic human need to want to be loved, respected and appreciated by others. One Sunday night I watched a few minutes of the Academy Awards, the annual extravaganza for the movie industry to congratulate itself. There seems to be an ever-growing number of such annual award programs. Entertainers make their living pleasing the crowds, and how well they do it is important to them.

I've always been a bit harsh in judging entertainers and politicians (who also make their living acting in front of crowds). St. Paul discourages us from passing judgment on people, that is, deciding on the appropriateness of someone's actions without having all the facts. He says in Romans 14 that we should do what leads to peace and to mutual edification. He also says that anyone who serves Christ in this way is pleasing to God and may receive human approval.

The sacred and secular are not completely separate. We live with feet in both kingdoms, and Christians seek to please both our Lord and appropriate people. There is a place for gentle judgment, however, when we see what is wrong and inappropriate. Then it is important to **"speak the truth in a spirit of love."** (Ephesians 4:15)

Being able to judge right and wrong is part of what makes us human. Secularists would have us believe that all morals are relative, made up by society, and that there are no absolute truths. To a secularist, the only "absolute truth" is never to be judgmental. But to declare something right or wrong is not the same as being judgmental.

Calling attention to the rightness or wrongness of an action can be necessary. To fail to acknowledge wrong and not to try to change it can have serious consequences. Parents find this out quickly as they teach their children. We all need boundaries just to get along in the world. But still I enjoy being entertained, so long as it's done appropriately and wrong actions are not glorified.

"If anyone is in Christ, he is a new creation, the old has gone, the new has come." (2 Corinthians 5:17)

And the Oscar this year goes to....

314

NOVEMBER 3

Regardless of one's political leanings, no one can deny that it is difficult serving in elected office, especially the Office of President. Things are said and done in our Capital, as well as in all phases of state and federal government, that can show human sinfulness. An elected official may try to do his best but still fail to help the voters who elected him.

During November each year, we hold elections in which the American people choose leaders. In my personal Bible reading, I found these words which I believe speak volumes for our mutual sentiments at this time.

"Some day there will be a king who rules with integrity, and national leaders who govern with justice. Each of them will be like a shelter from the wind and a place to hide from storms. They will be like streams flowing in a desert, like the shadow of a giant rock in a barren land. Their eyes and ears will be open to the needs of the people. They will not be impatient any longer, but they will act with understanding and will say what they mean. No one will think that a fool is honorable or say that a scoundrel is honest." (Isaiah 32:1-5)

A sad commentary on our society is not that we should have faulty leaders, but that citizens so often find sin and deceit acceptable. Some even believe them to be preferable! It is not only leaders who may fail and fall, we the people often do, too. We not only deserve the leaders we elect, we are the mirror which reflects their faces and morals.

It is my prayer that we elect at least a few good men and women who will reflect the truth, morality and justice of God's Word. When we cast our ballot, we should consider what choices our Lord might make if He were to vote. It is as if we let God's will be our Voter's Guide.

"Let every person be subject to the governing authorities. For there is no authority except from God, and those that exist have been instituted by God." (Romans 13:1)

Pray for all voters to use common sense!

NOVEMBER 4

There once was a little boy who had a terrible temper. It became so bad that his Father gave him a hammer and nails and told him that every time he lost his temper, he must hammer a nail into their wooden fence.

After the first day the boy had driven seventeen nails, and he was tired! Over the next days as he learned to control his anger better, the number of nails he drove into the fence dwindled. He discovered it was easier to control his temper than to pound nails. Being angry can be hard work.

Finally after much work controlling his temper, the day came when the boy didn't lose his temper at all. He told his father of this and both were pleased. Then his father suggested the boy now pull out one nail for each day that he was able to hold his temper.

Weeks passed and finally the young boy was able to tell his father that all the nails were gone. The father hugged his son and they both went to look at the fence. He cautioned him, *"You've done well, son, but look at all the holes. This fence will never be the same. When you say things in anger, small scars are left. You can put a knife into a man and draw it out, but no matter how many times you say 'I'm sorry,' the wound will still be there."*

There is a lot of anger going around now about the condition of our country, and I pray we will all understand that anger will not help as much as prayer. God uses all sorts of events to get us to pray, and our political situation should cause us all to turn to the Lord, fervently and often.

Anger and frustration only give us high blood pressure. Giving it all to the Lord in prayer is good for both body and soul. God has ordained government, and, as the hymn says, *"What God ordains is always good."* If we lived in any other country than America, we would not have the freedoms we enjoy. Don't just be angry and frustrated with your country. Work to make it better.

"Blessed is the nation whose God is the Lord." (Psalm 33:12)

America – It's God's gift to us!

316

NOVEMBER 5

The doorbell rang at my house, and it was the little neighbor girl selling pies so she could attend camp. I ordered a blueberry pie to match the peach pie Carol ordered last night from her brother! Both pies will be arriving this Friday, and which pie will we eat first?

As the holidays approach, some of us are already anticipating the wonderful food associated with Thanksgiving and Christmas. The turkey and dressing, home-made candy and holiday pastries are so good! We should have started our diet long before now.

But did you know that there is time when **FAT** can be good? (With sensitivity to others, I hope I can use that word publicly.) Now before you start shouting, *"I'm all for that!"* or else you begin throwing rocks at me for being wrong, consider the meaning of **FAT**.

FAT in this instance means FAITHFUL, AVAILABLE, and TEACHABLE. God wants Christians who are Faithful - full of faith, filled with a yearning for God. He also wants Christians who are Available. We all know how unavailable our busy schedules can make us, so we must decide now to make time for God, perhaps by removing some of the questionable events the holidays will throw at us so that we can be Available for God.

God also wants Christians who are Teachable - people who listen to Him and each other, Teachable as they study and grow in His Holy Word. Are you willing to learn and grow and be taught? Are you a **FAT** Christian? Are you Faithful, Available, and Teachable?

Jesus will teach people who are Available. He will help them be faithful to show love and mercy in their service to others. FAITHFUL, AVAILABLE, and TEACHABLE - that's the best way to be a **FAT** Christian.

"But grow in the grace and knowledge of our Lord and Savior Jesus Christ." (2 Peter 3:18)

*Some day I wish I were more **FAT** in this way and less fat in another way.*

NOVEMBER 6

How do you deal with disappointment? How do you work through your feelings of disappointment when things do not turn out the way you expect?

Elijah knew all about disappointment. In 1 Kings 17, God called him to speak God's Word to King Ahab. Ever since the days of the good kings, David and Solomon, every new king for Israel or Judah was worse then the last one. Then along came King Ahab who **"did evil in the sight of the Lord more than all who were before Him."** **(1 Kings 16:30)** He married Jezebel and worshipped her gods, even participating in the horrible practice of infant sacrifice.

Ahab's behavior so angered God that He sent Elijah to speak His Word to him. Through Elijah, God showed His power, raising the widow's son from the dead, withholding rain over three years, and sending fire from heaven to consume the sacrifice on the altar as thousands of people watched.

Elijah then killed the prophets of Baal and ran ahead of Ahab's chariot when the rains returned. But Elijah was no match for Queen Jezebel. When she threatened his life, the mighty prophet ran and hid in a cave. In 1 Kings 19:9, God said, **"What are you doing in there, Elijah?"** The disappointed prophet answered, **"Your people have deserted You, O Lord. I am the only one left, and they seek my life."**

But God told Elijah instead of concentrating on his disappointment, he should remember what God had already done through him. The dead had been raised, fire rained from heaven and all the people had shouted, **"Jehovah is God!"**

When you and I are disappointed in people or events, we must not hide in fear or sadness, but remember that God is still in charge. He has done great things for us, and if we will trust Him rather than the world's leaders, our disappointment will fade. Trusting our God who provides forgiveness in Jesus, we, too, can speak with faith and confidence, **"Jehovah is God!"**

"It is better to take refuge in the Lord than to trust in princes." (Psalm 118:9)

May the Lord help you overcome your disappointments.

NOVEMBER 7

I play the piano a little. I took lessons for two years in junior high because Mom wanted me to and one year in college because the school required it. For several years I didn't play at all until I met my father-in-law Ed who played for the old folks at the Veterans Hospital in Ft. Wayne, Indiana. Ed wasn't that good, but he played with flair, and the old folks who heard him enjoyed his music.

One day he couldn't go and he asked if I'd sub for him. I told him I could barely play, but he insisted I was good enough. *"I've heard you play. Just keep playing and don't stop,"* he said. *"People won't mind your mistakes as long as you don't stop."*

I played for the chapel that day and was I terrible! Those old fellows winced as I pounded away at the keys, and I could almost hear them wishing aloud that chapel would end. But a few years later I tried it again at another retirement home, slowly got better and ended up playing for weekly devotional services at various nursing homes for more than fifteen years. I remembered Ed's advice, so no matter how many mistakes I make, I try to keep on playing.

Over the years I've played for old folks, children's choirs, retreats, and sometimes even for small weekend worship services when there was no one else to play. I just make sure I'm not asked to play a hymn I don't know.

Never underestimate the effect of your encouragement on others. Ed probably never knew what his encouragement meant to me about the piano. The Bible says, **"Encourage one another and build each other up, just as in fact you are doing." (1 Thessalonians 5:17)**

So keep on serving, no matter how many mistakes you make. To stop serving or to never try because you think you might not do it well enough is to forfeit your chance to help. God doesn't look for our perfection, just our willingness.

"I will sing of steadfast love and justice; to You, O Lord, I will make music." (Psalm 101:1)

Today be grateful for any encouragement you receive, and encourage someone else who needs it.

319

NOVEMBER 8

Today we'll consider the word "guidance." Do you see "dance" at the end of that word? Doing God's will is a lot like dancing. When two people both try to lead in a dance, it doesn't feel right. The movement doesn't flow with the music, and our feet get jerky and clumsy. But when one person lets the other lead, both bodies begin to flow with the music.

My wife loves to dance, and has danced since she was a small girl. She has danced in competition individually and in a team with her brother. It's been enjoyable, as well as giving good exercise and helping with coordination.

A good dancer gives gentle cues to the other, with a slight nudge to the back or by pressing lightly in one direction or another. When one lets the other lead, it's as if two become one body, moving together well. To dance together requires surrender and willingness from one person, as well as gentle guidance from the other.

Then look at the rest of the letters in "guidance." First comes a "G," then "U" then "I," then "dance." Those letters could mean God - You – I, and those letters lead us to "dance." The word "Guidance" can remind us of our relationship with God and each other!

If we are willing to trust God to lead in our life, and then put Him and others ahead of ourselves, then life can become a dance, a new and better one for all of us.

My prayer for you today is that God's blessings and mercies be upon you and/or your family in every way. May you let God guide you this day. Dance together with Him, trusting Him to lead and to guide you through each season of your life.

"To everything there is a season and a time for every purpose under heaven... a time to mourn and a time to dance." (Ecclesiastes 3:4)

Dance with the Lord! He will love being with you.

NOVEMBER 9

Can a clock experience a nervous breakdown? There is a story told that this happened once. A little clock in a big house ticked itself into a frenzy thinking about how often it would have to tick each day. *"I am required to tick two times per second,"* he muttered in fear. *"Oh my! That means one hundred twenty ticks a minute, seventy-two hundred ticks each hour, one hundred seventy two thousand, eight hundred ticks a day. My gracious, how will I ever be able to do it?"*

Calculating his responsibilities, the little clock realized he would have to complete one million two hundred thousand ticks every week, and that came to nearly sixty three million ticks a year! How would that ever be possible? The more he thought about it the more worried he became, until one day his mainspring snapped and he stopped ticking all together.

An old grandfather clock nearby said to the little clock, *"What's wrong, son?"* *"I just don't have what it takes to tick that often,"* the little clock lamented. *"Well,"* the old one asked, *"how many ticks must we do at a time?"* *"Just one, I guess."* said the little one. *"Then just think about that one tick at a time and you'll be okay. I can't think about the millions of times I've already ticked in my many years, but so long as I get wound up, I still do only one tick at a time."* Later when his mainspring was replaced, the little clock concentrated on one tick at a time, and he kept time very well from then on.

Our lives come only one day at a time, only one hour at a time, or even one minute at a time. Yesterday is gone forever and tomorrow may never come. All we have is today. Though our challenges and burdens may often seem impossible, we'll find renewed strength by taking life one day at a time. The Master Clockmaker will make sure we have all the strength we need for that day.

"She is clothed with strength and dignity; she can laugh at the days to come." (Proverbs 31:25)

We may take a licking, but we keeping on ticking!

NOVEMBER 10

When I was a young father there came a day when my growing boy decided he wanted to be Superman. Maybe it was from watching a TV show or maybe he just wanted to "fly." He was about three years old and standing on the arm of the sofa. *"Catch me, Daddy!"* he said. I turned and saw him almost ready, but he didn't jump yet.

"Catch me, Daddy!" he said again and put his arms up to jump, but he still didn't jump. Then I realized he thought I was too far away, so I stepped just a little closer and held out my arms. Then he smiled a big smile and jumped into my arms. I wasn't more than a foot or two away, but it seemed to him like a big jump. It seemed that way to me, too. The important thing was that he knew I was ready to catch him and wouldn't let him fall.

Today is that son's birthday, and he's a fine man, a dedicated Christian school teacher, loving husband and fine father of three. You and I are often ready to take a "leap of faith" but we may not be sure we can do it until God seems closer and things are "just right."

At those times we must rely on faith in Jesus. Faith may seem harder when God seems farther away, but that is when we need faith most of all. Faith is needed for all times, not only when things are just right.

God is always there for us, ready to catch us, ready to see if we will have faith to jump to Him. Some days will come that will move us to take a flying leap into the arms of our loving God, for we know He will be there reaching out to us. His loving and strong arms will catch us.

Jesus has gone all the way to the cross for us, and He will never leave us. Rather, He will be there to keep us from falling. And if we happen to fall anyway, He will be there to pick us up again.

"How much more will your Father in heaven give good gifts to those who ask him!" (Matthew 7:11)

Catch me, Daddy!

NOVEMBER 11

Today is Armistice Day, and also the birthday of the birth mother of my sons. She passed away in 1984.

At 11:00 AM on November 11, 1918, the Armistice was signed ending World War One, which was labeled "the war to end all wars." It did not, of course, for there have been many terrible wars since then. As long as this world exists, we know wars will continue to be fought.

A historian has estimated that in the four thousand years of recorded human history, only two hundred fifty of those years held no armed conflict somewhere in the world. This is because humanity lives in a fallen state. The rebellion that began with Adam and Eve will always have an evil effect on us. Only after Judgment Day will the effects of sin finally end.

That means we will always need Jesus Christ and what He did for us on the cross. There will never be a time in our lives that we do not need Jesus, whether we are an infant or an aged person, whether waking or sleeping. Jesus is our lifeline in turbulent waters and our defense amid the forces of evil. He is our Savior who gives us eternal life.

It was not my privilege to serve in the Armed Forces, but many among my family and friends have done so. I give thanks for their courage, duty and safety. The war we are in today is against radical terrorists. Over a million servicemen and women are in uniform today, and they are the best trained and equipped soldiers our nation has ever had. But it is probable there will never be a time when our nation will not need strong and well-equipped Armed Forces.

Psalm 46 says God is our fortress and our strength, our present help in every trouble. Therefore we do not fear as those who have no hope. Rather, we trust Him and rejoice that He will be with us always, in every circumstance, unto the end of the age. But we all need to trust Jesus, and we all need His forgiveness, and we can always reach out to Him through prayer.

"God is our refuge and strength, an ever-present help in trouble. Therefore we will not fear." (Psalm 46:1-2)

Today let us give thanks most of all for Jesus!

NOVEMBER 12

This time of year it is good to think of the men and women who defend our freedom and help the people of other nations achieve theirs. America is one of the few nations in the world which has consistently sent its Armed Forces to help other nations in need.

The average American soldier is twenty years old. He or she is a short haired, tight-muscled kid barely dry behind the ears, not old enough to buy a beer, but still old enough to die for his country. He's a recent High School graduate and has probably never collected unemployment. He was an average student, pursued some form of sports, drove an old jalopy, and had a steady girlfriend that either broke up with him when he left, or said she would wait for him until he returns.

He listens to rock and roll, hip-hop, jazz or swing music and also to a 155mm howitzer. He is ten or fifteen pounds lighter now than when he left home, has trouble spelling, but he can operate a laptop computer, as well as field strip and reassemble a rifle in a minute. He can recite to you the parts of weapons, can dig a foxhole and apply first aid. He can march until he is told to stop, obey orders without hesitation, but he is not without spirit or individuality. He has two sets of fatigues, washing one while wearing the other. He may forget to clean his teeth, but never his rifle. He can cook his own meals, mend his own clothes, and maybe fix his own hurts.

If you need it, he'll share his water, food or ammunition with you. He has learned to use his hands like weapons and his weapons like they were his hands. He can save your life, or take it, because that is his job. He has probably seen more suffering and death then he should have in his short lifetime.

He has wept for friends who have fallen in combat and is unashamed. He feels every note of our National Anthem vibrate through his body while standing at attention and he asks nothing for his service in return, except our friendship and understanding.

"Join with me in suffering like a good soldier of Christ Jesus." (2 Timothy 2:3)

"Dear Lord, hold our troops in Your loving hands. amen."

324

NOVEMBER 13

Two land surveyors went to study the mountains of North Wales. They stayed two weeks at a shepherd's cottage who fed them and gave them a good place to sleep. During the day the surveyors climbed the slopes, checked landmarks and followed mountain streams to their sources. Each night they returned to the warm and snug cottage.

One night, the old shepherd suggested he accompany them the next day. *"There's no need for that,"* answered the men. *"We won't get lost. We have compasses, charts and maps." "Just the same, I'd better come with you,"* insisted the old man. *"No, no, don't trouble yourself!"* they insisted.

"But I know well the mountain trails. I know where the steep gullies are, and where the bogs run deep," the old man said. *"But that's all on the maps,"* they answered. *"Why would we need anything further?"* The old man paused and said, *"You will need me because the fog is coming in tomorrow, and the dense fog of this area is not on the map."*

Jesus, our Good Shepherd, knows the trails of our life, and He also knows how to deal with the fog. He can guide us through any trial or danger we will face in life. Although He gives us the Bible, He still wishes to walk beside us. He knows that fog will come into our lives, and when it does, we will need Him beside us.

Without a personal relationship with Jesus, we may lose our way, even while holding the Bible in our hands. We do not have a relationship with a book, but with a man, Jesus of Nazareth. He is the One who will show us the way.

"Even though I walk through the valley of the shadow of death, I will fear no evil, for You are with me." (Psalm 23:4)

For a safer journey, let Jesus accompany you wherever you go and whatever you do.

NOVEMBER 14

When an old reclusive man died in the mountains of Colorado, his relatives came from the city to collect any valuables at his house. All they saw inside the rundown shack were a few mining utensils and some worn out furniture. They picked up what seemed useable and started to leave when one of the man's old friends rode up on a horse and asked, *"Mind if I help myself to what's left?"* *"Go right ahead!"* they yelled as they drove away.

The old friend went inside and moved the old man's cracked table aside. He lifted the floor boards and proceeded to take out all the bags of gold his friend had mined and hidden there during the past fifty years, gold that was worth a fortune. Watching the dust of their car disappear, he said, *"They should have gotten to know him better."*

How well do we know our Heavenly Father? Our Almighty God has heavenly treasures stored up for each of us that are precious beyond our imagination. Yet they are only ours if we know Him well and take what He offers us by faith. If we don't know Him, we will miss out on His blessings.

Too many people do miss His heavenly treasures because they're so busy with life that they don't take time to get to know God better. That only happens through Bible study, prayer, and fellowship or worship with other Christians. If we take the time, we'll know the Lord better.

We don't know how often the old man and his friend visited, but they knew each other well enough to know what each one had and valued. It is important for us to get to know other Christians for what they have and value, not in material goods, but in spiritual ones. Meeting together with other Christians in worship and service projects will help us know what God has for us that will last forever.

"You have searched me, Lord, and You know me." **(Psalm 139:1)**

Don't miss the treasures God has stored up for you!

326

NOVEMBER 15

Today I am especially thankful for the valuable people God has placed into my life over the years. I'd like to share a story of someone who showed his thankfulness in life by living every day the principles his father gave him.

In 1924, a boy named Johnny who loved to play basketball completed the eighth grade in a small rural school. His father had little money for a gift, so he gave Johnny a card on which he had written his own seven-point creed. He urged his son to start following these seven points daily.

Here are the seven points his father gave him: (1) Be true to yourself, (2) Make each day your masterpiece, (3) Help others, (4) Drink deeply from good books, especially the Bible, (5) Make friendship a fine art, (6) Build a shelter against a rainy day, and (7) Pray for guidance and give thanks to God for your blessings every day.

Johnny attempted to follow these points during his life. He excelled in basketball and was an all-American athlete at Purdue University, helping his team win the national championship. He went on to become a college basketball coach, winning ten national championships in a twelve year period. He was named national "Coach of the Year" six times and is one of only three players in the Basketball Hall of Fame as both player and coach.

Like his father had given him, Johnny gave his players short, inspirational messages, including his "Pyramid of Success" which helped them achieve success in basketball and, more importantly, in life.

When he died at age ninety-nine, Coach John Wooden had been a devout Christian, husband of fifty-three years, loving father and grandfather, and an inspiration to countless men and women, athletes and non-athletes. He wanted his faith to be apparent to others. Our heavenly Father has given us His Word that comes to us in the form of His Son, Jesus. His Word is the source of life here and the best life yet to come.

"I am the Way, the Truth and the Life. No one comes to the Father but by Me." (John 14:6)

By God's grace, may we make each day a masterpiece for Him.

NOVEMBER 16

Back in the 1920s a large city newspaper fired an artist because they said he had *"no good ideas."* He went to Kansas City but still could not sell his drawings to a newspaper, and some even told him he had no talent. But this artist had a dream, so he set out to achieve it and also prove those people wrong.

He wanted to use what talent he had for the good of others. He found a minister who paid him a small amount to draw advertising pictures and bulletin covers for his church. The artist had no place to stay, so the minister let him sleep in a garage that also happened to have little rodents running around in it.

The artist nicknamed one of them, and later on drew him into a cartoon that was carried by newspapers and magazines and later was eventually made into a movie. How satisfying it must have been later in life for Walt Disney to remember the days of his hard struggles, sleeping in that garage, living with "Mickey Mouse" and remembering those people who'd said he had no talent. When he opened Disneyland, his world-famous theme park, he must have chuckled at the frustrating days he had endured not so long before.

God calls us to develop the gifts and talents He gives us, and to help others do the same. A part of our Christian walk through life involves caring for God's blessings. As the Master called his servants to account for the "talents" they were given in the Bible story, so God will one day ask us what we did with all we were given. May we all be able to say, *"I used what you gave me for the good of others."*

"Well done, good and faithful servant! You have been faithful with a few things; I will put you in charge of many things." (Matthew 25:21)

I can't draw, but I can write. What can you do for the Lord?

NOVEMBER 17

Are you getting what you want out of life? Do you feel that the government, or Wall Street, or the Church, or someone else should be doing more for you? Do you feel others are robbing you in life because they're not providing your needs?

A few years ago, a polling agency asked one thousand people what they most desired in their lives and how the Bible was important to them. Ninety percent identified themselves as Christians and most wanted these things: (1) a closer relationship with God, (2) a clearer purpose in life, and (3) a higher degree of integrity or deeper commitment to their Christian faith.

It's interesting that these heartfelt desires are all things people can do something about, without outside human help. There's no need for a government program or public assistance to achieve these goals. Difficult economic times need not take them away. These noble spiritual goals are achieved as we allow God's Word to rule in our hearts, and as we pray for and receive the strength of the Holy Spirit to build up our faith.

St. Paul wrote the people of Ephesus, **"I pray that out of His glorious riches He may strengthen you with power through His Spirit in your inner being so that Christ may dwell in your hearts through faith." (Ephesians 3:16-17)**

In our increasingly complex world, it is tempting to put the quest for what we desire into the hands of others. Many Americans and other people today have come to expect some outside human or government entity to fulfill their needs instead of seeking needs for themselves. This is counter-productive and wasteful of the talents God has given us.

At times we may need help, but outside human help will not provide our true happiness and contentment. That must come from God being in our hearts by faith in Christ.

"Seek the Lord while He may be found; call on Him while He is near. Let the wicked forsake their ways and the unrighteous their thoughts. Let them turn to the Lord, and He will have mercy on them." (Isaiah 55:6-7)

That's getting help we need from a source that will never fail!

329

NOVEMBER 18

In 1969 Hurricane Camille slammed into the town of Pass Christian, Mississippi, the worst on record to come ashore with its twenty-four foot storm surge. St. Paul Catholic church was destroyed, its structure and contents all scattered. Parishioners collected remnants of the interior as keepsakes, and Tim Taylor Sr. took home the only thing that still stood in its original place. It was the large crucifix that hung above the altar and had somehow survived undamaged amid the wreckage. When the church was rebuilt in 1972, Tim brought the crucifix back and it was put over the altar again.

The new building was built to be "hurricane proof" and remained so through every storm until Hurricane Katrina in 2005. Its brutal force laid St. Paul's in ruins once again. Holes were blown through the walls, pews floated away, and carpet was stripped from the floors. It was a horrific scene.

Tim Taylor, Jr. was one of the first inside. He had already lost his house, truck and most everything he owned. But inside the church he could hardly believe his eyes. There above where the altar used to be, on what was left of the ceiling, hung the figure of Christ, "Taylor's Crucifix," untouched and undamaged once again.

This story reminds me of a hymn Christians have sung for ages:

"In the cross of Christ I glory, towering o'er the wrecks of time;
All the light of sacred story, gathers 'round its head sublime."

Whatever storms of life we may encounter, we know God will be with us. His Son Jesus Christ will never leave us nor forsake us. Jesus will keep His church alive, for He is its Founder and its Head. Even when time seems to shake the "unshakeable," Christ remains our faithful Savior. His cross is our constant reminder of His presence in the world.

"May I never boast except in the cross of our Lord Jesus Christ." (Ephesians 6:14)

He is the only sure One we must trust.

NOVEMBER 19

Jeff was going through his neighbor's garage sale items. Hidden in the back under an old tarp was the unmistakable shape of a motorcycle. *"Is that a Bike for sale?"* he asked. *"Yup,"* his neighbor said, *"But the motor's seized up. It'd cost you a bundle to get it running."* *"How much do you want for it?"* Jeff asked. *"I was once offered $35 for its scrap metal."* Jeff looked at the rusty old heap and said, *"I'll give you $35 for it."* Soon a rusty old Harley Davidson sat in his own garage.

After a few weeks Jeff called a Harley shop to see what a few major parts would cost and was asked for the serial number. Jeff gave him the number and after a long few minutes the man said, *"Sir, I'm going to have to call you back. What's your name, address and phone number?"*

After he hung up, Jeff wondered why they wanted his address. Was the old bike stolen or involved in a crime? Days later a man called back who said he was a Harley executive.

"Would you look under the seat and tell me what you see?" Jeff did as he was told, and came back to the phone. *"It says 'THE KING'. Is there some trouble here?"* The man on the phone hesitated a moment and then said, *"Jeff, my boss has authorized me to offer you $300,000 for that bike, payable immediately, no questions asked. He really wants to buy it. Do we have a deal?"*

Jeff stammered and said he'd think about it. The next day's phone call really jolted him. It was Jay Leno the famous comedian, and Leno offered $500,000 for the old Harley. *"I have a thing about old Harleys,"* Leno told him. Jeff agreed and then did some research on his computer, discovering that old rusty bike had belonged to Elvis Presley, "the King of Rock and Roll." Jeff had bought a fortune for only $35.

Its value came from the one who had owned it. It's the same with you and me. Our value comes from our Lord to whom we belong. In our baptism, God adopts us into His family. We are now His children and have priceless worth.

Today is my sister Marian's birthday. She is one of those people in my life who are priceless to me.

"I have called you by name, you are Mine." (Is. 43:1)

We have been restored by forgiveness and faith in Jesus!

Ken, a former member now with the Lord, found his service to God in retirement by keeping our church's vehicles in good repair. He serviced the motors and tires and often even cleaned the inside. He made a small sign and attached it to the inside of each of the church vehicles. It said, "*God gave us this vehicle, so take good care of it!*"

That's what God does. He gives us life on earth, people to care for and things to use, including our planet earth, and He wants us to take care of them. But God does not tell us stop using them. He doesn't say, "*God gave you this world, so keep out of it!*" or, "*God gave you these things, so don't touch them!*" God gives us life and the whole earth, and He expects us to use them, but also to take good care of them as we do.

People today are being told that human beings are intruders on earth, that the earth is more important than they are and would get along better without them. But that's getting backwards.

The Bible says, **"The earth is the Lord's, and all that is within it."** (Psalm 24:1) It also says God gave the earth to the people He had created, and told people to multiply and have dominion over the earth. The Bible is clear that the earth is given to mankind, not the other way around.

This distinction is important. If the earth were the most important thing, then people should feel guilty every time they take away something from it or kill an animal for food, or cut down plants, or use trees for lumber.

But the earth was given to people, not people to the earth. We are the highest of His creation, not the dolphins, flowers or fish. God has given it to us to use and maintain. We are is caretakers.

"For we are His workmanship, created in Christ Jesus for good works which God prepared beforehand, that we should walk in them." (Ephesians 2:10)

Today, give thanks for the wonderful world God has given us, as well as the wonderful country you live in.

NOVEMBER 21

One day as I took out the garbage, I wondered how much of it my mother would have kept. I grew up in the 1950's with practical parents. My mother reused aluminum foil, washed plastic bags, and kept containers we routinely toss out today. She was the original "recycle queen," and my father was "the fixer." They valued their friends and were good neighbors. Mom usually preferred getting her old shoes fixed rather than buying new ones, and Dad did, too.

Their marriage was solid, their dreams were focused on farming, and their main job was raising us five kids. Their best friends lived less than a mile away. I can see them now, Dad in his farmer's shirt with sleeves rolled up, and Mom in a house dress, drying her fingers on her apron or dish towel.

They spent their time doing what was needed: fixing the kitchen door, hemming a dress, papering a room, greasing the combine, feeding livestock or going to church. All the fixing, cooking and worshipping was their way of life. They always felt there needed to be a reason for throwing things away.

My mother died at age ninety-four, and Dad followed her a year and a half later at ninety-seven. Sometimes what we care about dies, gets used up or goes away. So while we have them, let's love and care for them. Let's fix it if we can when it's broken, and love people while we still have them. Let's value our aging parents, struggling children, ailing marriages, and faltering church memberships, for they are important.

We keep them around because they are worth it, and because we are worth it. There's much that is precious about the church we belong to, or the friends who move away, or our family members who annoy us. Some people make life important, and we should work to keep them close.

Not everything is worth keeping. It's okay to toss out old and useless stuff, but maybe we should retrieve that old relationship. You and I won't be measured by the stuff we leave behind, but by the friends we've had.

"A friend loves at all times, and a brother is born for a time of adversity." (Proverbs 17:7)

I'm looking forward to God's grand reunion in heaven.

333

One autumn most of the entire civilized world watched the rescue of the thirty-three trapped Chilean miners who'd been underground over two months. It was moving to see them come to the surface and show their relief and gratitude.

Most of the world, however, missed the fact that each miner emerged wearing a shirt that said, *"Thank You Lord"* on the front, and on the back, *"To Him Be the Glory and Honor."* On the sleeve of each shirt was written, *"Jesus."*

It's obvious that all of these miners were grateful to God for saving them. One of them told a reporter, *"God and the devil were fighting over me and God won."* Another said, *"I always knew they would get me out. I always had faith in the professionals here in Chile and in the Great Creator."*

Another miner, when he came to the surface, knelt down to pray and pointed to heaven, giving thanks to God. The youngest miner, Jimmy Sanchez, wrote a letter he sent up to the surface before their rescue that said, *"There are actually 34 of us, because God has never left us down here."*

It doesn't matter that the press didn't report any of this, but we can be sure faith in Christ was the center of life for those thirty three men as they endured the sixty-eight days of being trapped a half mile underground. Being no fan of the deep underground, I can hardly imagine how they would have gotten through those days without trusting in Christ.

There are many times in life when we are faced with forces beyond our control. Whether it's waiting for the government to act, waiting for help to come, or waiting to find a solution that eludes us, we must rely on the One who has the whole world in His hands. Help may come quickly or take days, but however long it takes, we must wait and trust that God's solution is best and His time is right.

We give thanks when people are rescued from disaster. May we, like Jimmy Sanchez, realize there is another One with us when we feel trapped, One who never leaves us.

"My times are in Your Hands; deliver me from my enemies and from those who pursue me." (Psalm 31:15)

To Him be the glory and honor!

NOVEMBER 23

A woman was making a major change in her life. She was retiring after working for the same employer for over forty years. Some of her co-workers had been with her for much of that time, and as she hugged them, she said, *"Sorry about the tears."*

Why do we often feel the need to apologize for our weeping? It might be tears of happiness at a wedding *(I cried when our son was married)*, tears of farewell at a funeral, *(funerals of friends or family can bring them)* or even tears of relief at hearing long-awaited good news *("Congratulations, it's a girl!")* Whatever the case, we often feel apologetic for our tears.

There is a time and a place for tears, but not all agree when or where that is. I once said to a group of pastors that I was uncomfortable when pastors "break down" during a sermon, and several agreed with me. I was surprised, though, at how many fellows there thought I should let such emotions show, even during a sermon. I've always felt that people are uncomfortable seeing a leader weep while speaking.

God Himself grieves. Our positive emotions are God-given. In Genesis 6, God became sorrowful and angry about the sins of His people. Scriptures record Jesus weeping at least twice, at Lazarus' tomb **(John 11:35)** and as He entered the city of Jerusalem. **(Luke 19:41)** Jesus is God in the flesh, and He joined his friends in their tears of grief or joy. I can think of no greater example to follow than Jesus.

One day when we get to heaven there will be no more tears of sorrow or separation or pain. In the meantime, our tears may often flow, but we are confident that joy will come in the morning. **(Psalm 30:5)**

"God will wipe away every tear from their eyes." (Revelation 21:4)

And for our tears, no apologies are needed.

NOVEMBER 24

Do you ever get the feeling that you'd scream if you have to read another set of instructions? You can't buy anything without a warning to read the instructions. They even come now in several languages. You even need instructions to open can of beans or set your new clock.

A man sent his parents a new DVD player at Christmas. They were both excited because now they could be a part of the instant generation. Now they, too, could record movies and watch them later or even edit out all the commercials. But when they unpacked their new DVD player, the directions didn't make sense. It took them two hours just to connect it with their TV, but it didn't work as it should.

When they tried to have it record a movie, they were stumped. This wonderful new electronic DVD gadget had now turned expectant smiles into angry frowns! A whole afternoon was ruined by "time-saving" electronics. They called their son who lived too far away to come over, and he suggested they call the tech support number on the manual. *"If you call that number, they'll help you get it working."*

The mother called the number, and after being transferred several times and put on "hold" for a time, she was told difficult instructions that still didn't make it work. Finally she said in frustration, *"I don't need better directions from you; I need my son to come along with his gift!"*

When God gave us His gift of salvation, He didn't just send us a book of complicated instructions, He sent us His Son. Some think the Bible is too difficult, and that parts of it are just too confusing. Fortunately, the parts that tell us how to get connected with God are not. The story of how He has connected Himself with us, through a child born in a stable, is wonderfully simple.

"When the set time had fully come, God sent his Son, born of a woman." (Galatians 4:4)

God didn't send us theology to save us, He sent His only Son.

NOVEMBER 25
(Thanksgiving Day)

Every Friday night until he died in 1973, old Eddie walked to the pier with a large bucket of shrimp. There the sea gulls would flock to him, and he would feed them. Many years before, in October of 1942, this same man, then a much younger man known as Captain Eddie Rickenbacker, was on a mission in a B-17 to deliver an important message to General Douglas MacArthur in New Guinea.

Somewhere over the South Pacific, Eddie's Flying Fortress became lost beyond the reach of his radio. The fuel ran out, so Eddie and his men ditched their plane in the ocean. For nearly a month Captain Eddie and his companions fought the water, weather, and scorching sun. They spent many sleepless nights as sharks bumped their rafts. Their raft was nine by five feet, and the big sharks were ten feet.

But of all their enemies at sea, the worst one was starvation. After eight days out, their rations were gone, and Eddie knew it would take a miracle to sustain them. But then a miracle did occur. Captain Bill Cherry had just finished Bible reading and a prayer for deliverance, and they had sung a hymn of praise. With hats pulled down over their eyes to keep out some of the glare, the men tried to doze off.

Then something landed on Captain Eddie's head, and somehow he knew it was a sea gull. He and his men stared at the big bird, because it meant food. Captain Eddie reached up and caught the bird. Its flesh was eaten, its intestines were used for bait to catch fish, and the survivors were sustained. They were all rescued alive because one lone sea gull, hundreds of miles from land, offered itself as a sacrifice.

Captain Rickenbacker and his men made it back, but he never forgot. After he retired and until he died, every Friday at about sunset, he fed the sea gulls from his bucket in honor of that one bird which gave itself for them.

"Who provides food for the raven, when its young ones cry to God?" (Job 38:41)

Now that's something to remember on Thanksgiving Day!

NOVEMBER 26

A small congregation in the Smoky Mountains built a new church on a tiny piece of land willed to them by a church member. Ten days before the new church was to open, the town building inspector informed the pastor that their parking lot was inadequate for the size of the building. He told them until the church doubled the size of their parking lot, they wouldn't be able to use their new church.

Unfortunately, the church had used every inch of land on its tiny lot, except for the hill against which it had been built. In order to have more parking, they'd have to move a large part of that hill.

Undaunted, the pastor announced the problem the next Sunday morning and said he'd meet that evening with all members who had "mountain-moving faith." Twenty four of the congregation's three hundred members prayed that night that God would somehow remove the hill and provide funds to pave the parking lot before next Sunday's dedication. At ten o'clock the pastor said, *"Amen! We'll open next Sunday as scheduled. God has not let us down before, and I believe He will be faithful this time, too."*

On Monday morning there was a knock at the door. A rough looking construction foreman came in, *"Excuse me, Reverend. I'm from Acme Construction over in the next county. We're building a shopping mall over there and we need some fill dirt. Would you be willing to sell us a chunk of that hill behind your church? We'll pay you for the dirt and pave all the exposed area free of charge if we can have it right away. We can't do anything else until we get fill dirt."*

The little church with its enlarged and paved parking lot was dedicated the next Sunday as planned. Not surprisingly, there were more members with "mountain moving faith" on opening Sunday than there had been the previous week.

Would you have shown up for that prayer meeting? And if you did, would you have believed the pastor?

"Trust in the Lord with all your heart. Never rely only on what you think you know." (Proverbs 3:5)

It takes faith to trust God will provide.

338

NOVEMBER 27

A father was showing his son the stained glass windows in a nearby church. The father pointed out some of the brightly illuminated figures that were pieced together in the glass. *"Who's that?"* his boy asked. *"That's Saint Peter,"* the father replied. Pointing to another, the boy asked, *"Who is that?"* *"That's Saint John." "And that one?" "That's Saint Mark."* Then the boy made a innocent observation, *"I guess a saint is somebody that the light shines through."*

Perhaps you've been blessed enough to know someone through whom the light of God's grace has shined. It may be a teacher who treated you with special kindness or a good neighbor. It may be your faithful spouse, or a fellow worker who always manages to see the bright side of things. Whoever it is, you have met someone the light shines through.

The Bible speaks about many such individuals, people through whom the Light of Christ comes. Most importantly, the Bible speaks about the One who is Himself the Light of the world, Jesus Christ. Without Him, the world remains in darkness, but with Jesus there is hope, joy, peace, forgiveness, release from guilt, as well as a whole host of other good and lasting things. Best of all, with Jesus there is a life to come that promises the best of everything.

Give thanks for the Light, and then be one of those through whom that Light shines. After all, it was He who said, **"Let your light so shine that people will see your good works and glorify your Father who is in heaven." (Matthew 5:16)**

Jesus is our best example of God's love in action. He was God's love in action when He gave Himself as a sacrifice for our sins. Because of His suffering and death, you and I have the promise of life with Him forever.

"You are the light of the world. A city set on a hill cannot be hidden." (Matthew 5:14)

Keep letting the Light of your faith shine through you life.

NOVEMBER 28

A shopper at the local mall needed a break, so she bought herself a little bag of cookies, a cup of coffee, and sat at one of the crowded mall tables to rest and read a newspaper. A man also sat down at her table to read his newspaper. She reached out and took a cookie, and the man seated across from her reached out and took one, too. She was a bit startled at this but did not say anything. A few moments later she took another cookie, and once again the man took a cookie also. Though uneasy at him eating her cookies, she did not say anything.

After a sip of coffee she took another cookie. So did the man! Now this upset her, especially since there was only one cookie left. The man also saw the one cookie that was left and before she could say anything, broke it, gave half to her, and walked away, eating the other half. She glared at him. *"What a jerk!"* she thought, *"Some men think they're so smart!"*

Her coffee break was ruined and already she was thinking what she'd tell her husband about this thoughtless cookie thief! But when she picked up her purse, underneath it was another bag of cookies, unopened, the one she had bought. She had been eating his cookies the whole time!

This is like how we often treat God when He provides us with so much. We assume everything we've earned or bought to be ours. But Deuteronomy 8:11 says: **"When you have eaten and are satisfied, then praise the Lord your God for the good land He has given you."**

We often think that all we have is ours and comes only from our own efforts. The Bible tells us not to forget that all we have is from God, things we may work to get, but nonetheless still things from God. Every Thanksgiving Day should remind us it is God who gives us all we have.

A magazine asked the question: *"If you could be granted one wish that will come true right now, what would that be?"* The answer that impressed the editors was this: *"I wish I could have an even greater appreciation for what I already have."*

"Give thanks to the Lord, for He is Good!" (Ps. 106:1)

Today have a cup of coffee (or tea) and a cookie, too!

NOVEMBER 29

In Colorado, snow can come at unexpected times, especially since we live in a city that is six thousand feet above sea level. Snow often comes in May and sometimes even in early June! The morning after a winter blizzard or deep snowfall can be spectacular! The crisp clean air and beautiful white snow hides the ugly trash on the roads and in our yards. Awesome snowdrifts rest on the rooftops, created by swirling white stuff with a beauty in the bright sunlight that is breathtaking.

Those who live west of us in the nine or ten thousand foot mountains may have snow fall every month of the year. Snow is a fact of life, one that makes life in Colorado unpredictable and beautiful. Summer rains fall in the August monsoons and we often see "virga," sheets of rain you can see falling from the clouds, but evaporate before hitting the ground.

Every morning we have the opportunity to awaken to a spectacular day of God's love for us. No matter what the previous day's sin has been, no matter how guilty we might feel over past sinful acts, each day of grace shows us the newness of God's mercy. Even when we've foolishly let guilt torment us, a sunny new day reminds us of God's forgiveness in Jesus.

Each day God says to us: *"I know your record of sin, and your ugly rebellious nature. But I gave all that to My Son and He forgave it on the cross. Those things are gone from My sight, and I see only His perfect righteous covering that makes you pure before Me, like all that fresh-fallen snow."*

One Colorado November, we had four snowstorms on four successive weekends. That's when it seems like the snow of winter may never end, but every year it does.

But God's grace does not end. It is with us always. He gives us some danger with the snow, but it is relatively minor. Thanks be to God His grace is always with us. What a joy it is to know this as we live in God's beautiful world.

**"His mercies are new to us each morning."
(Lamentations 3:34)**

May God bless you this day and show you His mercies.
341

NOVEMBER 30

The Sunday after Thanksgiving is usually the last Sunday of the Church Year. The following Sunday is the beginning of the Church Season called "Advent."

Advent is a time of preparation for Christ's coming. We live between two advents. "Advent I" was His first coming to the world through human birth as Mary's Son. "Advent II" is Christ's second coming in judgment on the last day. Eighty per cent of the world's two and a quarter billion Christians observe the season of Advent in some way.

Advent has been around since 490 A.D. when Perpetuus, Bishop of Tours, urged fasting from St. Martin's day, November 11, until Christmas Eve. Sometime later, Advent began to be observed on the Sunday closest to St. Andrew's Day, November 30. The Advent season can last anywhere from 22 to 28 days and is usually observed with solemnity. St. Barbara's Day (December 4) signals the beginning of the Christmas season in the Middle East.

In Austria, Belgium, Czech Republic, Netherlands and Germany, St. Nicholas' Day, December 6, begins Christmas festivities when shoes or stockings are set out and filled with gifts for good children. Dutchmen watch St. Nick's ship land in Amsterdam and then see him ride off on a white horse. Our American Santa Claus arrives in the Macy's Thanksgiving Day Parade and delivers his gifts on December 24th.

Swedish Christians commence Christmas observance on St. Lucy's Day, December 13th. On that day a girl wearing a wreath of lingonberry leaves and lighted candles on her head descending the stairway as all those present watch her and sing. "Lucy" comes from the Latin word for "light" which is celebrated in the midst of the long dark winter.

Advent II is a time of waiting, not just a celebration of Advent I (Christmas) but waiting for Christ's Second Coming. Jesus came to be our Savior, and He will come again in glory to judge the living and the dead.

"Blessed is he who comes in the name of the Lord." (Matthew 23:39)

Happy Advent!

342

DAILY WALK WITH JESUS in...
DECEMBER

+ + +

DECEMBER 1

Where did we get the Christmas Tree? History tells us that in the Seventh Century, a monk from England went to Germany to teach the Word of God. He did many good works while living in Thuringia and his name was Boniface.

Legend says he used the triangular shape of the fir tree to describe the Holy Trinity: God the Father, the Son and the Holy Spirit. The converted people came to revere the fir tree as God's Tree, like they had revered the Oak as pagans. By the Twelfth Century in that area the fir tree was commonly hung upside-down from the ceiling at Christmas time as a symbol of God. The first decorated tree used by Christians in recorded history was in Latvia in 1510.

Dramas in the Middle Ages were designed to entertain the masses while teaching them Christian truths, so they often used decorated "paradise trees." Apples and other fruit decorated the first Paradise Trees, and soon ornaments made from marzipan, glass, and other materials were added. Communion wafers also appeared on some of these trees. Eventually paper roses and shiny metal shapes were added, as were nuts, cookies, and other sweets.

Martin Luther is said to have brought the first Christmas tree inside the home. While walking outside one night, he was so inspired by the stars twinkling through the trees that he cut down a fir tree, brought it inside and decorated it with candles to symbolize stars. Electric lights have taken the place of candles today. Only a few rare European homes will still have candles on their Christmas trees today.

"Hope deferred makes the heart sick, but a longing fulfilled is a tree of life." (Proverbs 13:12)

And that's why we have decorated Christmas trees today!
343

Perhaps you know someone who is thrilled when it snows, especially the first snow of the season. *"It's snowing!"* we exclaim. Snow! How appealing it is when we see the first snowfall that magically transforms the dead landscape with clean newness. We know our feelings will soon change after shoveling it, getting stuck in it, or driving in slush and ruts. The thrill of snow doesn't last very long.

The thrill of most things in life does not last long. Sooner or later even the most exciting events or people grow old. Why else do children and adults buy so many toys to play with? Why do we soon get angry with each other? Why does the honeymoon in marriage end so quickly?

We learn that all the things in life, our relationships, our accomplishments or our possessions, do not make up our life. They may make life enjoyable or help us forget our aches and pains or interest us for awhile. But they do not solve our problems or heal our wounds. Most especially they do not keep us from dying. The writer of Ecclesiastes knew this when he wrote these rather pathetic words, **"Pointless, absolutely everything is pointless!" (Ecclesiastes 1:2)**

This is true of all things in our passing world. All would be pointless without Jesus. God's Son is our loving Lord and Savior, and He alone gives our life lasting purpose and joy. He makes life worth living and death worth dying.

By Jesus' suffering and death, we have been rescued from our sins. By His glorious resurrection, we have hope for a new life. When we have faith in Him, life is not pointless. It is good and pleasing to us, to God and to all mankind.

Jesus gives us eternal life after this earthly life, but He also makes life on earth enjoyable. Not all the time, of course, but in Jesus, most of life can be very good. It is far more interesting and productive than merely being born, existing and then dying, like an old tree.

"The grass withers, the flower falls, but the Word of the Lord remains forever." (1 Peter 1:24)

May your day be filled with good things as you trust in Jesus.

DECEMBER 3

One of the joys of this time of year is that so many people are willing to help others in need. Whether it's the Salvation Army bell ringers, people gathering Christmas toys for needy children, those who assemble food baskets, or those who sort used clothing for non-profit groups, many thousands around our great country work to help others at this time of year.

The inspiration for this kindness is our heavenly Father who first gave us His best gift, His only Son born in Bethlehem. Helping at Thanksgiving or Christmas is part of what makes our nation and people strong and good.

Americans show their goodness in many ways. Sarah Tucholsky, softball player for Western Oregon University, hit her first college home run against Central Washington but nearly didn't get credit for it. As the ball sailed over the fence, Sarah rounded first base, and in her excitement, missed it the base. When she skidded to a stop to go back, she twisted her knee so badly, she couldn't even crawl back. Unless she touched each base, she could not get her home run.

The rules said she could not be assisted by her own teammates, so Mallory Holtman, first baseman for the opposing team asked, *"Would it be okay if we helped her touch the bases?"* After conferring, the umpires agreed. So long as her own teammates didn't help her, the opposing team could do so if they wished. So Mallory and another teammate interlocked their arms, picked up Sarah and carried her around the bases, helping her to touch each one. By the time they got her to home base, there were tears on both sides at this selfless act, and Sarah got her first college home run.

When people around us struggle and fall, we need to be like those ballplayers. We need to reach out, lift people up, and even carry them awhile. Christmas is a wonderful time to do this. Whenever we help someone at Christmas, we mirror the love of God for all people in Christ Jesus.

"Minister God's love to one another as good stewards of the manifold grace of God." (1 Peter 4:10)

Who can you hold up, even carry, at this time of year?

DECEMBER 4

Today is my father's birthday and I'd like to tell a story about him. It was Christmas Eve and I was ten years old. Our church's Christmas Eve children's program was over and Dad asked me to help carry a heavy box from our car to Uncle Paul's car. *"What's in it?"* I asked. *"Plowshares,"* he said quietly, *"for letting us use his tractor and plow."*

Uncle Paul, my mother's brother, was a gentle man, a quiet island of thought amid the roaring sounds of our family. He farmed with John Deere tractors and often loaned Dad a tractor and plow for fall plowing. Dad always enjoyed using his newer and more powerful tractor.

Uncle Paul was special to Dad and Mom because he'd lived with them the first years of their marriage as their hired man. They were married on a bone-chilling cold day in February, 1930, and when they came home from their wedding at the Lutheran parsonage, Uncle Paul had already finished the chores. Because he lived with them as part of the family for some years, Uncle Paul was special to my parents.

Dad and I lifted the heavy box into Uncle Paul's trunk, and we headed home for our family Christmas Eve. Our tree was decorated with an array of glass balls, bubble lights and tinsel. There were usually relatives at home, too.

On the way home we'd sing a Christmas song or two and I munched nuts or my favorite candy, chocolate drops, from the church candy bag. They were so good and I tried trading with others to get as many as I could. At home other treats awaited us like Christmas wine.

After gifts were opened, Mom would pass around a tray of small glasses filled with dark sweet wine. Gifts, songs, chocolate drops and wine – that's my Christmas memory. My stomach still aches thinking about it!

I miss those days and would like to experience them once more: Christmas Eve at church, a decorated tree, chocolate drops, wine, family love and the gift of plowshares.

"Come home with me for a meal, and I will give you a gift." (1 Kings 13:7)

What amazing gift can you remember receiving at Christmas?

346

DECEMBER 5

Many years ago, on the day after a snowstorm, a teacher was busy helping children put on their warm clothes for recess. She said, *"By the end of winter, you will all be able to put on your own clothing, even your boots."*

One little girl struggled into her coat but couldn't manage her boots. She handed them to her teacher and stuck out her feet. After much pushing, the teacher got the first boot on, and then the second one. *"They're on the wrong feet,"* the girl said. So teacher helped her put them on the right feet.

"These aren't my boots, you know," the girl said, so the teacher dutifully pulled the boots off her feet, still trying to look interested. The girl said, *"These are my brother's boots. My mother makes me wear them!"* So the teacher gritted her teeth and patiently smiled as she put the boots back on her again. With a great sigh of relief, she said, *"Now, where are your mittens?"* The girl said, *"I didn't want to lose them, so I stuffed them into the toes of my boots!"*

The coming Christmas holiday may have frustrating moments like this. People will try your patience and ask you again to do things the hard way. Life will have its struggles this time of year, and you will need all the gentle patience you can muster.

Whether it's part of our work or helping a friend or family member, what you're doing is part of life's purpose for you. People may frustrate you but you can take it. You and I need to try doing the helpful things, the right things each day.

If we're not sure what is helpful or right, we can ask the Lord to show us. God is patient and He will help us, we can be sure of that. As we ask Him, let's be hopeful. Maybe this year we'll solve that impossible problem, or find the right person for work or friendship, or put on those boots correctly the first time.

"Fear not for behold, I bring you good news of great joy. Unto you is born a Savior, Christ the Lord!" (Luke 2:10)

Now, where are those mittens?

347

DECEMBER 6

Santa Claus was a real person named Nicholas. He lived in a village called Myra in Asia during the Fourth Century, A.D. He was a godly priest and eventually became Bishop of Myra. He gave away his money, and one night even slipped a bag of gold through the window of a poor man who had three daughters so each one could have a dowry and be able to get married.

Years after his death, Bishop Nicholas was declared a saint by the Greek Orthodox Church, and the day he is remembered in both the Orthodox and Catholic Churches is December 6. It is the day he formerly distributed gifts to the good children of his village.

In the Sixteenth Century, St. Nicholas was renamed in Protestant Churches as the "Christmas Man" in England and "Pere Noel" in France, both of whom gave gifts to children. In Holland "Sinter Klaas" was played by the village fathers who dressed up and left goodies for Dutch children. His name came down to us as "Santa Claus."

Most of what children know about Santa Claus today came from the 1822 poem, "The Night Before Christmas," by Clement Moore. His jolly old man gave gifts at Christmas while flying through the air in a sleigh drawn by reindeer. Our image of Santa as a fat man in a red and white cotton suit is attributed to some magazine illustrations in the 1860's by cartoonist Thomas Nast.

Christian boys and girls need to know that the story of Santa Claus is based on the story of a Christian man who wanted to share what he had with others. St. Nicholas gave gifts to people because the Wise Men gave gifts to Jesus. And God gave Jesus to all the world as the best gift of all.

It's okay to think of a jolly bearded man giving gifts, but we also need to know that our loving Heavenly Father gave us His Only Son Jesus as the finest Christmas gift of all.

"Then the Magi opened their treasures and presented Him with gifts of gold, frankincense and myrrh." (Matthew 2:11)

And that's the true story of Santa Claus!

DECEMBER 7

December 7 is the anniversary of Japan's attack on Pearl Harbor in 1941. One year on December 7, I was thinking of the sacrifices of those brave men and women when a newspaper article caught my attention. It was about the discovery that an additional element, arsenic, is part of the formula for human life. This new information produced media stories, including several which speculated about the possibility of intelligent life on other planets.

I believe there truly has been life on other planets, and so do you. On Sunday, July 20, 1969, at 3:17 PM Eastern Time astronauts Neil Armstrong and Buzz Aldrin landed on the moon. The moon is a minor planet, so on that day and other days during the next three years, a total of twelve astronauts spent time on the moon. During those days we can say without doubt there was intelligent life on another planet.

The Apollo Eleven moon landing has been celebrated and examined in detail, but one aspect overlooked is that Aldrin and Armstrong had Holy Communion on the moon. Aldrin's church had given him packets of consecrated bread and wine, and during the radio blackout when the Eagle was out of contact with earth, the two men gave each other Holy Communion two hundred thirty-five thousand miles away from the nearest church. As they did, Aldrin read John 15:5, **"I am the vine, you are the branches. Whoever abides in me and I in Him will bring forth much fruit, for apart from me you can do nothing."**

NASA kept this act secret for two decades because it was already embroiled in a legal battle with atheists over the Apollo Eight crew's reading from the Bible while orbiting the moon. Aldrin said he prayed aloud after communion that day, giving thanks for the intelligence and spirit that had brought two young pilots to the moon's Sea of Tranquility. It is heartening to know that the first food and drink consumed on the moon were the Body and Blood of Jesus.

"He will cover you with His feathers, and under His wings you will find refuge." (Psalm 91:4)

Isn't it good to know some astronauts were Christians?

349

DECEMBER 8

In the late 1980's as baseball fans all over the world watched the first baseball game of the World Series, there was a sudden interruption of the opening interview, and TV screens went blank. When the program resumed, there was a "Special News Bulletin." The San Francisco Bay area had experienced a major earthquake. Viewers watched live pictures of the destruction and fires in that area, as well as how the heroic emergency squads rescued people.

A few remote camera crews were there immediately and recorded what was said. One memorable scene involved a group of people standing around, gazing at the destruction when suddenly a police officer yelled, *"What are you people doing standing there? Go home! Fill your bathtubs with water while it's still light. Get ready to live without city services for days. The sun will set and time is running out, so go home and get ready!"*

That officer's message sounds a lot like John the Baptist calling Christians to be ready in Advent. A long time ago John was out in the wilderness, and his message of getting ready for the Kingdom of God was told with an urgent shout. *"Why are you just standing there? Why are you people not getting ready? Don't you see time is running out? The Lord is coming. You need to prepare the way for the Lord, making His path straight. Now go! Get ready for the Messiah!"*

Are you ready to meet Jesus? If He came tonight, would He find you ready with faith in Him? Or would He find you doing foolish things, gawking at the world, wasting precious time while the world is falling apart?

What does God want you to do to be ready for Jesus? He wants us to be faithful in your service to others, loving in your fellowship with others, joyful in our worship of Him, growing in your faith and reaching out to others with the message of Jesus your forgiving Lord.

"John the Baptist appeared in the wilderness, preaching a baptism of repentance for the forgiveness of sins." (Mark 1:4)

It's time for us all to be sure we're ready for Jesus!

350

DECEMBER 9

There are so many wonderful traditions that make Christmas a special time, and the Candy Cane is one of them. Its European origins go back several hundred years to "sugar sticks" given out to Christian children symbolizing a shepherd's staff of Jesus, the Good Shepherd.

In America many years ago, a candy maker from Indiana wanted to make a special candy cane that would be a witness to his faith. He tried several kinds of candy until he came up with the American Christmas Candy Cane.

He began with a stick of pure white, hard candy. White was to symbolize the pure, sinless nature of Jesus, and the candy was to be very hard to symbolize Jesus, the solid rock, the foundation of the church, and the firmness of the promises God has made to us.

The candy maker shaped it in the form of a "J" to represent the name of Jesus, who came to earth as our Savior. Turned upside down, he said it could also represent the cane or staff of Jesus, the "Good Shepherd," with which He reaches down into our world every day to lift up and rescue us like lambs who have gone astray.

Since the white cane was very plain, the candy maker interlaced the white with red stripes, and later with green stripes as well. He said the red stripe would symbolize the stripes of the punishment Jesus received by which we are healed. The green colored stripes would symbolize our eternal life that never dies.

Unfortunately, the candy maker's gift is now known only as the "Candy Cane," and its Christian meaning has faded, now just another ornament on the tree. But the meaning is still there for those who have **"eyes to see and ears to hear"** the message of a Christian candy maker.

"With His stripes we are healed." (Isaiah 53:5)

I hope you enjoy the sweetness of a candy cane this Christmas.

351

DECEMBER 10

In 1995, baseball great Brett Butler was diagnosed with an aggressive and rapidly debilitating cancer that is usually fatal. After recovering from the initial shock of the diagnosis, Butler became angry with God. He later said it seemed like God had turned his back on him. Yet, as a Christian, Butler also believed God was testing him and telling him to trust that this situation was part of His greater plan.

If Butler even survived this cancer, his doctors predicted he would never play baseball again, because the treatments would leave him too weak to get into good enough condition to play professional baseball again. It looked as if this was the end of his career, if not also his life.

But Butler survived the treatments, and in 1996 he was well enough to return to baseball for part of that season. In 1997, he played a full season before retiring from the Los Angeles Dodgers after sixteen years in professional baseball.

After his cancer was in remission, he said, *"God has been glorified through it all, and He has never given me more than I could handle. I learned firsthand that God's mercy is new every morning."* It was an amazing Christian witness by a man who used his time in the limelight to share his faith in Jesus.

We never know what miracles God can do for us until He gives us a problem so big only He can handle it. It takes little or no faith to ask God to do something simple, but it takes great faith to ask Him to do what only He is able to do.

Don't be afraid to ask God to do the impossible in your own life. He can help you handle your problems because He's done it a million times before. Whether it's during the holidays, the winter or summer, give God your troubles. Let Him show you how He can take care of you in the midst of the worst of situations.

"Lord my God, give attention to Your servant's prayer and his plea for mercy." (2 Chronicles 6:19)

Give thanks for such a faith witness as this, and ask for the faith to make a witness of your own.

DECEMBER 11

It was three weeks before Christmas, but Sam just couldn't get into the spirit of the season. Cars packed parking lots and the store aisles were crowded as carts and shoppers rushed to get things. Sam's list had several people on it who said they wanted nothing, but he was buying them something anyway. But he was in no mood for Christmas, especially since the checkout lines made him wait so long.

In front of him were two small children. The boy wore a tattered coat, old tennis shoes and raggedy jeans. The girl had a mass of matted curly hair. She had a few crumpled dollars in one hand and a pair of golden slippers in the other.

When they finally got to the register, she carefully placed the shoes on the counter. The cashier rang up the shoes and said, *"That'll be $6.21,"* and it was evident the two kids didn't have enough. *"I guess we'll have to put them back,"* the boy said. *"We'll come back tomorrow."* The girl sniffed, *"But she would love these shoes."* *"Now don't cry,"* said the boy.

Sam handed a five dollar bill to the cashier. After all, those kids waited in line a long time, and it was Christmas. A pair of grimy little arms hugged him and a small voice said, *"Thank you, Mister."* As they walked to the door, Sam asked, *"These for your Mom?"* The boy answered. *"Yeah, Mom is really sick. Daddy said she might go be with Jesus soon."*

The girl spoke, *"My Sunday school teacher said the streets of heaven are shiny gold, like these shoes. Won't Mommy be beautiful walking those streets in these shoes?"* Sam felt a lump rise in his throat. *"I'm sure she will,"* he answered as they parted. As he got in his car, he realized those little kids had just reminded him why he gave anyone Christmas gifts.

Christmas is not about how many gifts you get or what they cost. It's about God's love that He shared with us, love we can now share with each other. It's about hope from the birth of a baby. Even though Sa,e gave them money, the kids shared that love and hope and didn't even know they did it.

"Glory to God in the highest, and peace on earth, good will towards all people." (Luke 2:14)

What a gift those children gave that man!

353

DECEMBER 12

A mother was attending her son's Kindergarten Christmas program. She was very busy, barely having time to attend the event, and she wasn't looking forward to the same old school "Winter Pageant," blandly named by the school officials this year to avoid giving offense. The children filed in and sat down by classes, ready to get up and do their section of the program when called upon.

She had come not expecting more than commercial entertainment with songs about reindeer, Santa, snowflakes and things like that. But she was taken aback when her son's class stood to sing a song called, "Christmas Love."

"How about that," she thought. *"They mentioned Christmas! Somebody in the office must have forgotten to check the program."* One by one, the children in the front row held up large letters to spell out the title of the song. As they did, the class sang, *"C is for Christmas,"* and a child would hold up the letter "C." Then *"H is for happy,"* and so on until they had spelled the words, *"Christmas Love."*

All went smoothly until the final verse when everyone held up their letter and a small girl held her "M" upside down. Her letter was now a "W" and it drew snickers from a few adults and children watching. The little girl, of course, had no idea they were giggling at her. She just stood up proudly holding her letter "W."

Teachers tried to hush the children, but their snickers grew into laughter, loud enough to distract those singing the song till all the letters were held up. Then a hush came over all as they realized and understood what they saw. For now the words spelled, *"CHRISTWAS LOVE."*

Despite what the world does to cover it up, the message of Jesus can even come through by mistake. God's great gift to people will always be there, blessing us in each generation.

"The virgin will conceive and give birth to a son, and they will call Him Immanuel," which means 'God with us'." (Matthew 1:23)

Isn't God's sense of humor great?

354

DECEMBER 13

One of my grandchildren is an adopted baby girl from the Democratic Republic of the Congo. In preparation for her coming, my wife and I watched a news clip about the plight of the women and orphans in that once-great nation. Afterwards we wondered aloud how can we not give thanks that we live here in America, a great and free nation? We have life so much better here than the millions of oppressed people around the world have it. We really need often to say, *"Thank You, O God, for giving us life here in America!"*

This time of year many of us will see a children's Christmas pageant with its unexpected and charming moments. We may recall some childish surprises, such as the time Mary tossed a Baby Jesus doll into the manger as she went up to sing in the children's choir. Or when Mary and the shepherd, brother and sister, got into a shoving match because she corrected what he'd said. Or when a young Wise Man knelt at the manger and said, *"We brought gifts of gold, common sense and fur."* Or when the three-year-old followed his big sister and brother to the front and recited a little poem about rabbits.

The first Christmas must have had its memorable moments as well. A nervous Joseph may have struggled to know what do, and Mary may not have spoken so politely and sweetly while she was giving birth. The newborn baby Jesus surely cried a little in that drafty stable. After such a long journey and the difficulty in finding a place to stay, the young couple may have given thanks they'd made it there unharmed. Surely they marveled when they heard about the angels from the shepherds.

Our world has problems, many of them severe, but it also has God watching over His people, offering them hope for eternal life. If your life is relatively good right now, give thanks that God offers you hope for eternal joy with Him.

"It is good to give thanks to the Lord, and to sing praises to Your name, O Most High." (Psalm 92:1)

Thank you, O God, for eternal life through Your Son, Jesus!

355

DECEMBER 14

This time of year is "Messiah Time," when people of many communities join in singing Handel's "Messiah." Few people, however, know the circumstances under which George Friedrich Handel wrote his master work,.

The famous composer had been out for a long walk on a Sunday afternoon in August, 1741, and he was feeling depressed. Although he'd had a successful career writing operas, things were not going well. At age forty-one he'd had a serious stroke and though he was now recovered, people had stopped buying his works.

As he returned home he found a manuscript on his doorstep, left there by a friend, Charles Jennens. It was a possible "libretto" (musical story) about Jesus, starting with His birth, then His ministry, crucifixion and resurrection. And it all started with prophetic passages from Isaiah.

When Handel read Isaiah 40:1, **"Comfort, comfort ye my people, says your God,"** he said the clouds of gloom began to lift, and he started that day composing an Oratorio on the life of Christ. Amazingly, in just three weeks he finished it all. The entire "Messiah," two hundred fifty pages of original musical composition, was all written in just three weeks!

Christmas is not just about Handel's musical work, "The Messiah," but about Jesus, the true and living Messiah. Without Him, there is no meaningful winter festival. Hanukkah is about the rededication of the Temple in Jerusalem, and Kwanzaa was invented in the 1960's by an activist to honor African American heritage. Only Christmas is about forgiveness and peace on earth. Only Christmas gives us joy in the gift of God's Son.

We all need God's comfort for these unsettling days. We need His peace to lift us from the doldrums of winter storms, human problems and bad news. We need God's power to change for the better. We need Jesus, born of the Virgin Mary, who gave His life for us. We really need the Messiah.

"The glory of the Lord shall be revealed, and all flesh shall see it together." (Isaiah 40:5)

May each of us experience God's hope and joy this Christmas,

DECEMBER 15

Elie Wiesel, in his little book called, <u>Night</u>, describes an incident in Auschwitz, the place of terrible suffering, death and horrible human darkness during World War Two. In one chapter he described the execution of three people by hanging, one of them a small boy. Everyone in that part of the camp was forced to watch, so that they might learn the punishment for any infraction of the camp rules.

When the chairs holding them up were kicked aside, the two adults died quickly, but the young boy, being light in weight, took longer, struggling nearly a half an hour before dying. The whole camp was forced to march past him even as his body struggled in death.

Wiesel recalls someone, probably a camp guard, who said out loud, *"Where is your God now?"* Everyone was quiet, until someone, evidently a Christian amid the Jews, muttered, *"He's there on the gallows, dying for the sins of the world."*

God is with us still today. He's helping us get through the latest terrorist's act, or giving us strength in the cancer ward, or encouraging us to overcome an addiction, or calming someone's frenzied nerves, or giving hope to a lonely heart. God is not only in churches, He is anywhere that His people need Him. God does not remain apart from us, but is with us in His Word, in Holy Communion and in Holy Baptism.

We need never ask, *"Where is our God?"* as if He has abandoned us. He will never do that, but will be with us and give us strength for our Daily Walk With Jesus. Look around you. God is there, and He is ready to give you joy and peace amid all the clamor of the holiday season.

As you rejoice again this Christmas season, remember that God is with us, in good times and in bad, giving us strength for each day and hope for tomorrow.

"Never will I leave you, never will I forsake you, says the Lord." (Hebrews 13:4)

This is another blessed lesson of Advent.

357

DECEMBER 16

A little boy was helping his father move books out of a bedroom into his father's new office downstairs. It was important to this little fellow to help his Dad, because he would now have that bedroom as his own. The little fellow did his best, but often got in the way and slowed things down more than he helped. But his father encouraged him, knowing it was more important for them to work together than it was to move all the books efficiently.

Among this man's library were a few large reference books, each weighing several pounds, and it was quite a task for the little boy even to pick up more than one at a time. On one trip, the boy lifted a matched set of dictionaries, the largest of all the books. As he walked down the steps, he dropped them. He picked them up but dropped them again.

When he dropped them a third time, he sat down on the stairs and cried. He realized he wasn't doing any good at all because he wasn't strong enough. He felt badly that he couldn't do this work for his Dad.

With a gentle word, the father sat next to his son and hugged him. Then he picked up those big books, placed them in his son's arms, and then scooped up both the boy and his books and carried them both down the stairs. The next load of books he made a bit smaller for his son until all the books were in the new office. But every other trip Daddy carried the boy and his armful of books.

God carries us often, too. Sometimes we are able to hold everything and do the work, but more often God must help us with our loads. With all the busyness of this Christmas, let your Heavenly Father pick you up, hold you tight and keep you together as you juggle the burdens of work, family and friends, parties and concerts, church and shopping and all the rest. During these holidays, look for Jesus your Savior, and watch how He carries you through the days.

"Fathers, bring up your children in the training and instruction of the Lord." (Ephesians 6:4)

Give thanks that God has carried you so often.

DECEMBER 17

When you pray, be specific so God can answer your needs specifically. A woman had locked her keys in her car. Her child was home with a fever and she'd gone to get medicine for him. Someone passing by said, *"Get a coat hanger to open the car door."* The woman found some wire on the ground, but realized she didn't know how to use it, so she prayed and asked God to send her help.

She must have looked desperate because soon an old motorcycle pulled up, driven by a bearded man wearing a black cap. The woman thought, *"This is who you send to help me, Lord?"* The man asked if he could help, and she said, *"I locked my keys in my car and need to get medicine home to my child quickly. Can you help me unlock my car?"* *"Sure,"* he said. He walked over to the car, and in only a few seconds he had the door open.

She hugged him and said, *"Thank you so much! You are a very nice man."* The man replied, *"Lady, I am not a nice man. I just got out of prison for car theft."* The woman hugged him again and said, *"Praise the Lord. I asked God for help and He sent me a professional!"*

It's good to be specific in our prayers. A middle-aged widow, waiting in an airport, prayed that on this flight she might sit next to a fine single man, a Christian man her own age with whom she could perhaps become friends. Maybe God would hear her prayer this time.

After she was seated, a fine looking gentleman did indeed sit down next to her. He spoke very kindly and seemed to be about her age. As the plane took off, she noticed he was wearing a ring with a cross on it. *"Thank you, Lord, You answered my prayer!"* she said silently. The two of them had a nice conversation, and she was pleased with how God has answered her prayer. Until, that is, he told her he was a priest. God had answered the parts of her request – all except one she hadn't asked!

"Ask and it will be given to you; seek and you will find; knock and the door will be opened to you." (Matt. 7:7)

When you pray, be specific, and God will answer your needs.

359

DECEMBER 18

We Americans live in an age that prides itself in logical explanations for everything. We are materialistic people, and nowhere is this more apparent than in the days leading up to Christmas. Author C.S. Lewis wrote that our greatest human problem is not that we ask too much out of life but rather that we expect too little. *"We are far too easily pleased." Lewis* said. He meant that so many people, young or old, believe happiness will come if they just get, or give, the right gift, or attend the right party, or meet the right person.

Advent and Christmas are here to give people hope. William Willimon wrote, *"Hope tells us that there is more to life than meets the eye. Hope tells us that there is more to the past than history can tell us. There is more going on in the present moment than we know."* Our true hope is found in Jesus, the Son of God and son of Mary.

One December Sunday in Colorado, gunmen killed people in two Christian churches. They just walked in and started shooting. Their extreme actions showed they had lost hope in other means of dealing with life. Our sinful world can do that. It can rob us of joy and kill our hope.

Advent and Christmas give us new hope. If we look away from ourselves and see God who loves this world enough to forgive it, perhaps we can retrieve some of the hope we've lost.

Advent and Christmas are paradoxical. They are grounded in God's promises, yet often overshadowed by the glitter of Madison Avenue. Advent and Christmas are based on faith in the one true God, but our world seems interested only in what we purchase. This Advent and Christmas, God invites us to hold to a hope we can't find under a tree or at a party.

This year try to avoid the clamor of Santa and enter the world of God's promises. He invites us to hear Isaiah and Luke as they proclaim the mystery of the Word made flesh, the Son of God who came to lead His people through a sea of despair and into the Promised Land of grace and mercy.

"Nothing will be able to separate us from the love of God that is in Christ Jesus our Lord." (Romans 8:39)

Thank You, O God, for giving us our Savior Jesus.

DECEMBER 19

What is it that makes us truly human? Besides our eternal soul, what has God given people that He has not given the animals? The ability to reason? To laugh? To worship the Creator? To analyze life? To show gratitude?

This time of year is centered on gifts, those we give to each other and especially God's supreme gift to us in Jesus. I recall with tears some of the Christmas gifts my parents gave me and I've witnessed forgiveness that is given with tears. Sometimes a special gift comes when I have been thanked for doing something long forgotten.

A priceless gift is a second chance, the opportunity for a new life. When they were babies I baptized all three of my grand children and witnessed God's merciful gifts to them of faith and new life. Although all came from different backgrounds, each was given a new family life. By adoption, God gave them able and loving parents to raise them. God has an eternal plan for these children which only He knows, and it began with the baptismal gifts of faith and forgiveness given them in Jesus Christ.

Long ago a baby's cries were heard in a Bethlehem stable, and they signaled the coming of eternal salvation to the world. His cries frightened a king and frustrated Satan. Despite the message of angels, His mother did not fully understand what He would mean to this world of sin and separation from God until he grew up.

"Our life is a gift from God. What we do with life is our gift to Him." I wrote those words on the back of a book case I made for my son. I pray all the members of my family will take those words to heart.

As you count your blessings this Christmas, remember the gifts of being born where you are, into the family you have, with the gifts you can use, and at this time in history. We, among all people, are assuredly most blessed. What now will we do with the life He has given us?

**"For unto us a child is born, unto us a Son is given."
(Isaiah 9:6)**

This Christmas, consider who you are and also Whose you are.

DECEMBER 20

In 1861 an elderly American was filled with sorrow at the tragic death of his wife in a fire. The Civil War had begun that same year, and two years later this man would again be saddened when his own son would be seriously wounded as an officer in the Union Army. But on Christmas Day in 1863, upon hearing church bells pealing in the crisp winter air, the elderly American poet, Henry Wadsworth Longfellow, wrote the words to this fine Christmas song:

I heard the bells on Christmas Day,
Their old familiar carols play,
And wild and sweet the words repeat,
Of "Peace on earth, good will to men."

And in despair I bowed my head;
"There is no peace on earth," I said,
For hate is strong and mocks the song,
Of "Peace on earth, good will to men."

Then pealed the bells more loud and deep:
"God is not dead, nor doth He sleep."
The wrong shall fail, the right prevail,
With "Peace on earth, good will to men."

We recognize Longfellow as author of "Paul Revere's Ride," "The Song of Hiawatha" and other poems, but few of us know he penned these musical words of faith in the midst of a terrible Civil War. It was perhaps the lowest point in American history, and we still give God thanks that He spared our nation from division.

This Christmas time, whether you live in sorrow or in joy, know that God is not dead, nor is He asleep. He knows our needs and longs to comfort us and be our friend and Savior. Seek Him amid the glitz and glitter of the season, and He will give your life meaning and your heart peace.

"How beautiful on the mountains are the feet of those who bring good news, who proclaim peace." (Isaiah 52:7)

A peace-filled Christmas to you, now and always,

362

DECEMBER 21

What do you think of the Christmas music you hear? Do you like it? In the Bible, music is important. Whenever an evil mood came upon King Saul, David played his harp and the mood departed. When the prophet Elisha was about to inquire of God, he said, **"Bring me a minstrel," (2 Kings 3:15)** and when the minstrel played, the Word of the Lord was made known to him. During the reign of David, thousands of musicians sang in the tabernacle. Music has always been important to God and His people.

Most Christians love music and singing, even if he or she doesn't feel musically talented. God asks us to sing to Him and to love and treasure His psalms, hymns and spiritual songs.

However, there is also a destructive power in some of our secular music with its loud and screeching sounds and disrespectful lyrics. Many secular artists sing of hopelessness, anguish and hatred which can lead people to despair.

God created music and has enabled us to respond to it. Some sounds irritate us, others soothe us. There is music that makes us march and music that puts us to sleep. Harmonious music affects us positively and discordant music negatively.

The good music we utilize in worship brings Godly blessings. Today churches are trying to decide what kind of music is right for worship. Contemporary hymns can be a blessing, but they will be only a performance if no one can sing them. Liturgical music can be rich and joyful, but it can also be boring. Much of this depends on what we "put into" our worship, not just what we "get out" of it.

What role does music play in your life? Are you able to appreciate several kinds of music in worship, or are you locked into only one kind? Can you see the possible blessing of other Christian music for those who worship? Or do you believe anything written before 1975 is old?

"Be filled with the Spirit, speaking to one another in psalms and hymns and spiritual songs, singing and making melody in your heart to the Lord." (Ephesians 5:18)

Merry - - - - - mas! (Without Christ, it's just a mess!)

DECEMBER 22

This time of year may be frustrating because we don't know what Christmas gift to give certain persons in our life. We may solicit suggestions of what to get. I think the best gift is something we choose, making it a surprise to the recipient, something that shows we put thought into it.

Gifts need not be expensive. Cost should not determine whether it's good. Years ago I recall an old gentleman telling his family, *"If I can't eat it, drink it or spend it, I don't want it."* That's a bit harsh, but at least his family knew what he wanted.

There was a time when most Christmas gifts were hand-made. Today few people make their Christmas gifts. However, certain holiday foods, crafts, or pictures are always welcome. If we get something we don't particularly like, we should still be grateful, and we should show it.

If you're having trouble with your gift list, here are ten "home-made" gifts that only you can give. One of these might be just the thing for that special person in your life.

A HOMEMADE GIFT LIST

1. Mend a quarrel and apologize if you were wrong.
2. Be friendly towards someone you usually ignore.
3. Hand-write a letter and tell someone you love them.
4. Give something valuable to someone in need.
5. Forgive someone who has treated you wrongly.
6. Thank someone who has made a difference in your life.
7. For several days, thank all the store clerks who serve you.
8. Visit some residents in a nursing home.
9. Tell a child the story of the first Christmas.
10. Give Christmas cookies, especially ones you've made.

Christmas gift-giving began when God gave us His Son Jesus. We all need Him, and we know He is the perfect gift. Whatever your gift may be, give it as God has given to you in love, without obligation, reservation, or show.

"Give, and it will be given to you, good measure, pressed down, shaken together, running over." (Luke 6:38)

Regardless of that they are, give all your gifts with love.

DECEMBER 23

"Prepare the way of the Lord! Make a straight path for Him!" (Mark 1:3) This what John the Baptist shouted in the wilderness. There is so much noise in our world, especially in the days leading up to Christmas. Music in stores, children crying, loud voices, sirens and traffic congestion all make this noise unbearable. If we really want to be heard in the midst of this, we, too, may feel we need to shout.

During any typical weekday lunch hour at the University of California, Berkeley, spokespersons for a dozen different causes can be found on the plaza, each trying to speak louder than the others. One day a lone figure sat down in the middle of the crowd and held up a sign that said, *"SILENT PROTEST."* Someone tapped him on the shoulder and asked, *"What are you protesting?"* The sitting man held up another sign which said, *"NOISE."* His entire protest was held in silence.

That reminds me of a Salvation Army bell-ringer who was told by a policeman that a local ordinance prevented her from ringing her bell for contributions this year. But that ordinance did not stop the inventive bell ringer. The next day contributions were better than ever as she waved one sign and then another in the air. The signs said, *"DING"* and *"DONG."*

John the Baptizer had to contend with noise that all but drowned out his message to prepare the people for the coming Messiah. There has always been noise when God's people have tried to speak of God. Maybe that's why John shouted in the wilderness. He just wanted to be heard!

There is a time for shouting and a time for being still. During the coming days of this year, may you know the difference, especially in those times when you wait on the Lord to hear His still, small voice of divine guidance and love. The "Silent Night" of Christ's birth is most precious of all.

"Be still and know that I am God." (Psalm 46:10)

Can you hear the Lord speaking to you amid all the noise this year?

365

DECEMBER 24

Tonight let us think of Mary's love for her infant child Jesus, and how she typifies a mother's love that shows itself in so many ways. To illustrate this I'd like to share with you a story from my life about experiencing my mother's love.

Christmas, 1966, was approaching, and I was in my last year of pre-seminary studies. That year I was selected to be a soloist for Hugo Distler's "Christmas Story," a German cantata I'd helped translate into English. When I wrote my German immigrant mother of this, she wrote back wishing she could come out to hear it. In mid-November, she wrote that she and Dad would be coming for the concert and asked if I could pick them up from the train station. I was surprised, as my parents had little money to spare, and train tickets were costly.

Our parents raise the five of us children on one quarter section of Minnesota farmland, something impossible to do in today's farm economy. By today's standards we were poor, but we didn't know it, because we had enough.

When I picked them up at the station, Mom had to use the restroom and it gave Dad time to tell me her story. It seems the corn crop was huge that fall, but the wind and rain had laid many of the cornstalks on the ground. After harvest, Mom and my sister-in-law decided to glean some of the ears that would otherwise have been plowed under. For two cold weeks in November, they walked the fields until they had two wagonloads of corn, which they sold and divided. It was back-breaking work, but they had some extra money.

With her corn money Mom bought train tickets to come hear me sing. She was sixty-six years old that fall. As I write this, I am past that age, and I still get a lump in my throat when I think of the sacrificial love that made her walk those corn rows in November for my sake.

God's love is even greater. His only Son Jesus walked the bitter roads of life, sacrificing Himself so that you and I could sing with the angels. Remember that this Christmas.

"Honor your father and mother, and love your neighbor as yourself." (Matthew 19:19)

Someday I look forward to singing in that big choir in heaven!

DECEMBER 25

A very "Merry Christmas" to you! There were many miracles at Christmas: the miracle of the angels speaking to Mary and Joseph, the angels singing to the shepherds, the miracle of safety to mother and unborn child on the long trip, the miracle of coming to Bethlehem where the Scriptures had foretold the Messiah would be born, the miracle of the bright star and the Magi visitors, and the miracle of the incarnation, God becoming human, born of Mary His mother.

Perhaps the child's birth itself is the real flesh-and-blood miracle. By the power of the Holy Spirit, the child has grown in Mary's womb for months, slowly developing and becoming alive, growing until it could be born. Then birth takes place, the umbilical cord is cut, the baby's mouth cleared, and he lets out a cry so that the world knows he is alive. Then he is given to his mother, and even veteran doctors, experienced nurses, and old midwives will smile at the moment the baby first lies in the mother's arms. They think, *"What an amazing miracle is a birth, the beginning of a new human life!"*

The birth of a healthy baby boy born to an exhausted young mother and proud father is a gift only God can give. Complex human life is neither common nor simple. It is a mystery only God can grant to us from His power.

The day after the child's birth must have been a busy time. While Joseph went for supplies, people hearing of the stable birth may have visited Mary. Perhaps the innkeeper brought food, or his wife brought a blanket or more swaddling clothes. Someone must have offered them a better place to stay, and the young couple moved to a house. Christmas was not a quiet day, but busy with new life.

The birth of the Christ child was sweet, and it was also very real. The Magi's appearance came with word from the angel to leave for Egypt. There was little time of rest for the holy family. God was at work bringing the world salvation, and there was much to do!

"But Mary treasured up all these things, pondering them in her heart." (Luke 2:19)

May you have peace, knowing God did all this for you.

367

DECEMBER 26

One December night Carol and I entered our mini-float in the annual Christmas Parade of Lights around our retirement park. I constructed a large lighted nativity set and put it on a little yellow trailer that we pulled behind our golf cart. Of all the entries, ours was the only one about Jesus' birth. Every other one was secular. The parade was fun, but the many silly entries reminded me how far removed we've come from the true story of Christmas.

I also heard a fine story about singer Becky Kelley. While at the mall with her four year old nephew, Kelley, the boy and his mother were watching as children lined up to see Santa. Having been taught Christmas is the time to celebrate the birth of Jesus, the boy asked, *"Where's the line to see Jesus?"* The boy's innocent question gave birth to an idea for a song.

Their songwriter father heard of the boy's question, quickly jotted down some lines, wrote music to the words, and recorded the new song at his home studio. His friends loved it, so he sent the recording to Nashville where a Christian song writer suggested some changes.

Her father sent the new demo tape to Nashville, but there was no response. Two weeks before Christmas, Becky's cousins decided to do an internet video of the new song, and it became a huge success. Her song, *"Where's the line to see Jesus?"* is now popular each Christmas.

With all the crass commercialism at this time of year, *"Where's the line to see Jesus?"* is a question we all might ask. We can find the answer by worshipping at church during a special midweek service, a Sunday morning church service, or Christmas or New Year's worship service.

But you don't have to get in line to see Jesus the Savior. He's already waiting for you to welcome Him into your heart. He knows your needs and is ready to bless you with His holy presence all through the year.

"For to us a child is born, to us a Son is given." (Is. 9:6)

What do you enjoy most about this time of year?

DECEMBER 27

Have you ever had a "morning after" experience? Most of us have had one at some time, and it's usually not something we're proud of. The morning after a passionate love affair can bring guilt and regret. The morning after an auto accident can bring shock and sadness. The morning after a bad decision can change your life for days or even years.

When life has severely and suddenly changed, we need strength to go on living. In the days following the baby Jesus' birth, life was very different for Mary and Joseph. Their travels to Bethlehem and Egypt would have been enough to change any couple's lives. But the child Mary bore into the world changed them and the entire world. He wasn't just a wondrous arrival, He was the promised Savior. Nothing was the same after the Christ child came into the world.

The child Jesus is God's greatest gift to mankind. Because of Him, we have hope for life now, and hope for the future life God promises us. We have hope because Mary and Joseph believed God and obeyed the angel. We have hope because the baby grew up and atoned for the sins of the world, my sins and your sins. We have hope because on the morning after the baby's birth, God was there with them.

On our morning after, God is there with us also, showing His mercy and love, offering forgiveness to the repentant, and showing a new path of life for the foolhardy. He is there with strength for all travelers along the road of life.

Give thanks today that on the mornings after the birth of Jesus, Mary and Joseph followed God's directions and travelled where He directed them. Though it would mean more change and upset of their lives, God showed them the path that eventually led back to Nazareth where they would live and the Christ child would grow up.

"Show me Your ways, O Lord, and teach me Your paths." (Psalm 25:4)

May your "morning after" bring you something good!

369

DECEMBER 28

An old pioneer traveled westward across the great plains until he came to an abrupt halt at the edge of the Grand Canyon. In amazement he looked at the magnificent chasm one mile deep, eighteen miles across, and more than a hundred miles long, and he said with his crusty old voice, *"Wow – somethun' musta happened here!"*

In a similar way a visitor to our world today would see the lights, decorated trees, parties, festivities and religious services and would probably say, *"Something must have happened here!"* Indeed, something did happen. God came to our world as a human being to redeem its people from sin.

Christmas is past for another year, and perhaps you have wondered, *"Why all the fuss about Jesus?"* Why remember a baby born in an obscure Middle Eastern village, and why have a yearly festival to honor His birth? Do we need to do all this? *"Why all the fuss about Jesus?"*

But think of it! The Son of the eternal God came to earth. God came to live with His people! Don't you think that's amazing? Jesus of Nazareth is the Son of God born into the world. He came to save the human race. Environmentalism won't save us, and neither will politics or science or economics or morality. Only Jesus can save us. He alone is, **"the Way, the Truth and the Life." (John 14:6)**

Advent is done for another year, too. Advent usually refers to the weeks before Christmas. Yet there will be another Advent, a Second Coming when He will *"come again in glory to judge both the living and the dead,"* as we say in the Apostle's Creed. Advent is a time for Christians to celebrate His first coming, so we need to observe it at least once a year. But it also helps prepare us for His Second Coming. If we're not ready for His Second Coming, Christmas won't matter!

Christians of the world observe Christmas in many ways, but all of them know Jesus came into the world, born of the Virgin Mary. "All the fuss" we go through helps us remember.

"She gave birth to her firstborn son and wrapped Him in swaddling cloths and laid Him in a manger." (Luke 2:7)

"Wow - somethun' musta happened here!"

370

In the second year of my ministry in North Dakota, I was asked to perform a wedding for a very young couple a few days after Christmas. It was at a town forty miles west of my church during a very snowy time of year. The bride was only sixteen years old and she wanted to get away from her parents. Her groom was twenty and seemed somewhat mature, although I prayed hard that they might be able to make their marriage work despite their youth.

Winter weddings are always unpredictable in North Dakota due to the weather, and sure enough, it snowed and stormed the night before their Wedding Day. It was scheduled on a Saturday afternoon, so I took a friend along in case I got stuck. I still had a Sunday service the next morning.

Sadly, due to the snowfall, few came except the bride and groom, her parents, a few giggling high school girl friends, myself and the man who rode with me. There were just ten of us all together. None of the wedding party or Groom's family came, so her parents were their witnesses.

During the reception the bride cried sad tears because her brightly decorated church basement was nearly empty. Her new husband tried to calm her, and I offered what comfort I could to both of them. Due to the short hours of daylight in December, I excused myself and we drove home. I often wondered what became of that couple.

I found out. Six years later I received a card. It was a happy note from the wife telling me they had two little boys and were doing well, and he had a well-paying job. She knew I'd wondered about them and wanted to assure me that they were okay. She'd married a good man, and they were happy.

I wonder if Mary's or Joseph's families had doubts about their marriage. Surely her announcement of early pregnancy caused talk. But Joseph was a good man and God was present with them. They trusted God and He blessed them.

"And Joseph arose and took the child and His mother and went to the land of Israel." (Matthew 2:21)

If you are married, do you recall your wedding day?

DECEMBER 30

A woman once asked me, *"Where do you come up with all your stories?"* I told her I look for things to write about. Sometimes I can't find something new, so I repeat an old story of years ago. Sometimes my stories are just rambling thoughts which may be the most profound things I think of all week.

Christmas is past for another year now, but it's still time to get ready for Christ's coming. Jesus came the first Advent at Christmas, and He will come again in the second Advent on Judgment Day. Living between the Advents may seem to be getting more complex for us, but life is not any more complex than it's ever been. We live, love, work, play and trust in God, much as we always have. We all hope to experience good things in this crazy, wonderful life God gives us.

There was once a game show with an interesting title, "Truth or Consequences." Today we tend to avoid them both. Truth is what we try to create, and consequences are what we try to avoid. Yet there is an absolute truth, not made by public opinion a truth that has its consequences.

Truth is greater than opinion, and the consequences of facing the truth can be difficult and scary. Jesus will one day come in judgment. That truth bothers some people so much they try to deny it. But truth is still truth, even if it seems out-of-date.

A few years ago Carol gave me a box with an amaryllis bulb in it. It was a dry, hollow, crusty bulb, ready for the trash and she'd forgotten she had it. I found a container, followed the instructions, added soil and poured on water. Two weeks later it sprouted leaves. The dead had come to life! By Christmas we had a lovely flower two feet tall.

Do you ever feel like a "dead" bulb? Do you feel empty and ready for the trash? I hope not. God is not done with you yet, and He'll give you a new start. Christmas is about Christ coming to take our sins upon Himself. Christmas is about new growth and a new start in Jesus.

"When the time was right, God sent His Son." (Galatians 4:4)

There was a time they thought He was dead, too!

372

On Christmas Eve in 1881, Matthew Miles was fifteen years old and felt like his world had caved in. He was sure he would not be getting what he so badly wanted for Christmas, a new hunting rifle. His Pa came in and said, *"Bundle up, Matt, it's cold out tonight."* That wasn't good news, because it meant extra work. He saw their team of work horses hitched to the big sled, and when he came out Pa sat up on the seat in the biting cold. Matt sat next to him, hating the thought of working on such a miserable night.

"Pa, what are we doing?" Matt asked. *"You know the Widow Jensen?"* his Pa said, *"I rode by today and it appears they're out of wood."* Matt loaded firewood high on the sled while Pa got some ham and bacon and put them next to a cloth sack under the seat. *"What's in that sack?"* Matt asked. *"Shoes."* Pa said. *"Her little ones don't have any. There's some candy, too. Every child should have some candy at Christmas."* Well now, Matt couldn't ever remember getting candy at Christmas. How come they were getting some?

As they rode to Widow Jensen's, Matt was deep in thought. They didn't have much themselves and Widow Jensen had closer neighbors than they. And shoes? Dad only had one pair himself. At the Jensens they unloaded the wood as quietly as possible. Dad took the sack and knocked on the door. *"It's Lucas and Matt Miles, Ma'am, could we come in?"*

Widow Jensen let them in, and their house was freezing cold. *"We brought you a few things,"* Pa said, *"shoes for the children, and something for you, too."* Tears came to the mother's eyes as she saw what he was giving them. *"There's a load of wood, too. Matt, go bring some in to warm this place up."*

When Matt came back inside, he wasn't quite the same person. He was cold, but soon the fire he started felt good. He'd gotten and given gifts at Christmas before, but never had he seen gifts make so much difference for people in need. He could see they were literally saving the lives of that woman and her children. *"God bless you, Mr. Miles,"* she said as they got up to leave.

Pa invited them to their home for dinner the next day, and then he did something Matt never forgot. He gave each of those little ones a big hug. Matt could see they missed their own Pa, and right now he was sure glad he still had his.

On the way home Pa said, *"Son, I hate to say this, but you're not going to get what you wanted this year. Your ma and me had been tucking a little money away all year for that rifle. But on the way to town this morning I saw that little boy scratching to get some wood. And when I saw his feet wrapped in gunny sacks, well, I spent your rifle money on them kids. I hope you understand."*

Matt put his arm around his Dad. That rifle could wait. His Pa had given him the best Christmas memory he'd ever have. And after that day and for years to come, when Matthew Miles grew up and had a family of his own, every Christmas he would tell to his children and grand children this true story of real generosity at Christmas, a story from his own father that would be passed down to many generations of people.

"Give, and it shall be given unto you." (Luke 6:38)

And now this true story has been passed down to you!

MERRY CHRISTMAS AND HAPPY NEW YEAR!

- The End -

AUTHOR'S NOTES

Rev. Robert L. Tasler is a native of Windom, Minnesota, and a career pastor in the Lutheran Church-Missouri Synod, a conservative Lutheran body in fellowship with dozens of similar churches around the world. A 1971 ordained graduate of Concordia Seminary, St. Louis, Missouri, Bob has served parishes in North Dakota, California, Utah and Colorado. Currently retired, he and his wife Carol divide their time between Castle Rock, Colorado, and Casa Grande, Arizona. They are parents of Brian, a Denver business executive in a non-profit organization, and Chuck and his wife Debbie, Christian Day School Teachers in Phoenix, and proud grandparents of three.

Author's other works include: E-Books DAILY WORD FROM JESUS, COUNTRY PREACHER, SMALL TOWN PREACHER, BOBBY WAS A FARMER BOY, IMMIGRANT SON and MURDER AT PALM PARK (now also in paperback). His daily devotional, "WEEKLY MESSAGE," is available without cost by contacting him at <pbt45@ecentral.com>. Those who do will receive it for as long as they wish and he continues to write them.
http://pbtsplace.blogspot.com/

Made in the USA
San Bernardino, CA
02 December 2013